Alpe d'Huez

Alpe d'Huez

Cycling's Greatest Climb

Peter Cossins

Aurum
Press

Quarto is the authority on a wide range of topics.

Quarto educates, entertains and enriches the lives of
our readers—enthusiasts and lovers of hands-on living.
www.QuartoKnows.com

First published in Great Britain
2015 by Aurum Press Ltd
74—77 White Lion Street
Islington
London N1 9PF
www.aurumpress.co.uk

p1 *all images* Offside/L'Equipe; p2 *all images* Offside/L'Equipe; p3 *top left* and
top right Offside/L'Equipe, *bottom* Photosport Int/Rex; p4 *all images* www.
alpedhuez.com; p5 *all images* Offside/L'Equipe; p6 *top* Photosport Int/Rex,
middle and *bottom* Offside/L'Equipe; p7, *top* Bernard Papon-Pool/Getty Images,
middle and *bottom* Offside/L'Equipe; p8 *top* Simon Wilkinson/SWpix.com,
bottom Offside/L'Equipe

A catalogue record for this book is available from the British Library.

ISBN 978 1 78131 449 4
EBOOK ISBN 978 1 78131 477 7

1 3 5 7 9 10 8 6 4 2
2016 2018 2020 2019 2017

Typeset in Electra LT Std by SX Composing DTP, Rayleigh, Essex
Printed and bound by CPI Group (UK) Ltd, Croydon, CR0 4YY

For Mum, Dad, Viv and Geoff

The Queen of the Mountains

The beauty of the bicycle is the unparalleled perspective it gives the rider onto their surroundings. Cars travel too fast, levelling out the landscape and neutralising the elements. Walking is better, but such slow progress limits the scope for exploration. Bikes are the ideal in-between, offering unrivalled efficiency as a mode of transport and unmatchable understanding of the terrain passing beneath its wheels.

Reflecting on more than thirty years of cycling, I can still summon up images of the countryside on many of the days I've spent in the saddle with particular clarity and in a particular way. Mexico's Yucatán, for instance, evokes days dodging rattlesnakes sunning themselves on arrow-straight roads cut through a tunnel of green scrub, while on Scotland's Isle of Mull sea eagles and golden eagles soar above one of the most stunning coastal rides anywhere on the planet. But the most indelible memories are of days spent in the mountains.

Seen initially from a distance, mountain ranges appear eminently conquerable. Move closer and it becomes apparent that this first impression is completely skewed. Foothills emerge, peaks begin to tower, the landscape starts to rise and surround you. Eventually, in the highest ranges, the peaks seem inaccessible. 'You see them and admire them,' said Sir Edmund Hillary. 'In a sense, they give you a challenge, and you try to express that challenge by climbing them.'

My own mountain challenges have never taken me to the heights or extremes experienced by one of Everest's conquerors. Yet they are still unforgettable. My first attempt to 'express that challenge' was on the Port de Larrau pass in the Pyrenees. On the early ramps, I recall looking up and seeing a group of bearded vultures, the region's famous *quebrantahuesos*, circling on thermals hundreds of metres above me. Half an hour later, I was looking down on them, marvelling at their size and agility. When I arrived sweating and breathless at the chilly summit, a Dutch tourist wandered over to me. 'You'll find it much easier in one of those,' he said, pointing to his car. Easier, yes: but not as rewarding, or as inspiring. Like Hillary, I was hooked.

When writing about cycling became my career, climbs took on even greater significance. Starting with the Poggio and Cipressa in March, continuing with the Muur de

Geraardsbergen, Mur de Huy and La Redoute in April, races and my reporting of them would reach the high mountains at the Giro d'Italia in May. However, as for most fans of the sport, it was the renowned passes of July's Tour de France that stood out, and none more so than Alpe d'Huez.

At that time I knew little of the climb's history, but was well aware of its huge significance to the Tour and its riders, and especially the Dutch, for whom it is an arena to compare with Feyenoord's De Kuip or Ajax's Amsterdam Arena. A win on Alpe d'Huez guaranteed legendary status, and a string of Dutch riders achieved exactly that in front of orange-clad, sun-baked and beer-addled hordes of fans.

On the Alpe, more than anywhere else in cycle sport, the spectators were part of the action, a fact I became more fully aware of when I first covered a Tour stage to Alpe d'Huez during the 2003 race. Approaching it from Bourg d'Oisans, the road was easy to pick out, with its thousands of camper vans, their windows glinting like supercharged cat's eyes, highlighting the climb's switches back and forth. Moving closer still, the route seethed with the movement of tens of thousands of fans, creating an ever-moving trail up an enormous anthill. Once onto the initial ramps, the steepest on the climb, the sheer number of bodies, banners, flags and colours resembled Wembley Way on Cup Final day, and progress was just as pedestrian.

Temperatures had risen to 40°C in the ongoing heatwave that had gripped France but, as my good friend and then *Procycling* editor Jeremy Whittle drove us towards Dutch corner, the most infamous of the climb's twenty-one hairpins, he insisted on all the windows being closed and doors locked. 'You'll never have seen anything like this,' he told me. 'It's amazing for the riders when they come through here, but the press don't get quite the same welcome.' After a brief halt among the frenzied throng, a few waved fists and curses as our tyres lifted newly painted names and slogans off the road, and a few choruses of, 'Boogie is de best, is de best, Michael Boogerd beter dan de rest,' in praise of that era's leading Dutch rider, we were through, having repelled all attempts to soak us with super-sized squirters filled with water and, as some journalists later revealed, rather more unsavoury liquids.

Just above the mayhem, there was madness. Approaching bend six, the next one on from Dutch corner, we were confronted by two dozen Elvis impersonators performing 'Hound Dog' on the back of a flatbed trailer. Techno music competed with the fifties classic, and fans danced in the road, unconcerned by the frantic hooting of press cars whose occupants were desperate to reach sanctuary and what was left of the buffet in the press room at the summit. Every metre of road was coated in emulsion, undercoat and gloss, these daubs encouraging even the most obscure members of the peloton. It was jaw-droppingly barmy and totally captivating. Thinking back, I remember more about the fans that day than the action the riders served up a couple of hours later.

Over the subsequent dozen years, I've returned to Alpe d'Huez many times, often staying in the kind of ludicrously overpriced and decidedly downmarket dorm-type room typical of so many ski resorts, and the atmosphere and race action on the mountain have never disappointed. More recently, I've gone there with the aim of getting a different perspective on the climb, one stripped of all the hullaballoo that the Tour brings. Climbing it by car, on foot and, inevitably, by bike, I've gained a better insight into a climb that is too often dismissed as an unremarkable road leading to a distinctly unattractive resort.

It lies in the heart of the French Alps, in the Oisans region of the *département* of Isère. Approaching it via the Romanche valley, having left behind first Grenoble and then Vizille, the main D1091 road emerges from a deep gorge carved by the river and turns south into a wide and flat-bottomed valley along which the wind often barrels, draining the resources of any solo escapee from the peloton, even before they have reached the mythic test that lies ahead. The road arrows into Bourg d'Oisans, a small town of tightly packed, steeply roofed houses that's home to just 3,000 inhabitants, but is the largest on the road between Vizille, 35km to the west, and Briançon, 70km to the east.

Looming over the town, the immense Signal de Prégentil rock face, its striations meandering in mesmeric, paisley-like fashion, indicate the uphill finale is imminent. After weaving through Bourg d'Oisans, crossing the

Romanche and then leaving the D1091 for the D211, the road makes a beeline for the rock face opposite the Prégentil. On Tour days, the fans and vans reveal the way ahead, but on any other day the sign indicating 'Alpe d'Huez 14' provides the only confirmation that there is any way out of what seems to be the most final of cul-de-sacs. But, just when it seems the only way out is to emulate Edmund Hillary rather than Bernard Hinault, the road angles left and up – very sharply up, towards the first of those fabled twenty-one hairpins.

When I first became aware of this mountain in the mid-1980s, avidly following Phil Liggett's commentary on Channel 4, my heroes were Scotland's King of the Mountains Robert Millar and Ireland's Tour-winner Stephen Roche. Both men generally climbed with the best, but both struggled every time they tackled Alpe d'Huez. 'I'd say for a non-climber the Alpe is the worst climb they are going to do in a race. This is the only hill I hated. I never got up here in a decent state, not once,' said Millar.

Roche was no fan either. 'Of all the climbs in the Alps, Alpe d'Huez is the one I fear the most,' he confessed, before going on to describe the devilish trap it sets those who take it on. 'What has always worked against me on Alpe d'Huez is the severity of the early slopes. There is no way you can maintain a rhythm on those slopes; instead you are changing gear, getting out of the saddle, sitting down. All the different motions. For a pure climber these things come naturally and such gradients provide an opportunity to distance rivals. For somebody like me who is not a natural climber, those early slopes are a nightmare. Try to go with the best guys and you may blow up further on in the climb. But if you let them go, you will never see them again.'

Thankfully, I've never had to race up Alpe d'Huez. Even so, as a non-climber who does love riding in the mountains, I can appreciate what Millar and Roche were describing. The initial three kilometres are excruciating; the change in tempo from the big-ring riding in the Romanche valley is so extreme that I soon found myself grovelling in my smallest gear. There was some relief when I reached the huddle of houses and the squat church that comprise the hamlet of La Garde en Oisans, but the sign-post indicating 'Alpe d'Huez 10' quickly extinguished that.

Although the gradient is rarely as abrupt above La Garde, it changes regularly, upsetting your pedalling rhythm, sapping reserves. At Huez, the village just beyond Dutch corner from which the resort derives its name, the effects of altitude tug on those resources a little more. It sits just below 1,500 metres, high enough to leave this flatlander gasping, my oxygen-depleted brain unable to compute how this terrain could have become so closely associated with riders from the Low Countries.

At Huez, after sixteen hairpins piled almost one on top of the other, the climb opens out into lush meadows. The jarring but also welcoming vision of the resort one journalist described as 'Pineworld meets *Star Wars*' – and which is branded 'The Island in the Sun', thanks to its three-hundred clear days a year – suggests the end is close. But the Alpe has another barb on which to snare the unwary or gung-ho. Taking wide sweeps, the road ramps up again until it finally reaches a platform on Alpe d'Huez's main street. However, the Tour peloton and the tens of thousands who imitate them every year still face one final obstacle in the shape of an unnumbered hairpin that carries them towards the upper part of Alpe d'Huez and – yes, at last! – up to the finish line at 1,860 metres on the Avenue du Rif Nel, which encapsulates the essence of this fabled ascent. Oversized wooden hotels and residences – chalets on steroids – line one flank, while on the other ski fields and pistes soar up to the crest of the majestic Grandes Rousses massif, its peaks touching almost 12,000 feet.

The Tour had tackled other famous passes and summits before Alpe d'Huez began to appear regularly on its menu in the mid-seventies. Many, such as the Galibier, were much higher and tougher than 'the great wall of Oisans'; while others, like the Croix de Fer, were much more visually arresting. But neither of these two near neighbours, nor any other climb, can now match the celebrity of the Alpe, the mountain that Tour historian Jacques Augendre famously dubbed 'the Hollywood climb'.

Although the Tour had visited the mountain for the race's first-ever summit finish in 1952, when Fausto Coppi was in his pomp and romped away with the stage and the yellow jersey, it wasn't love at first sight. Indeed, many race followers and even Tour director Jacques Goddet couldn't see the need for high-rise finales that induced day-long torpor in the peloton until the foot of the decisive test. Consequently, it was almost a quarter of a century before the race returned to the climb.

By that point, the look of the Tour had changed. Up to 1971 the race featured just ten road stages to high-altitude summits – with Mont Ventoux, Superbagnères and, most frequently, the Puy de Dôme among those that followed the Tour's first encounter with the Alpe. By the time Alpe d'Huez returned to the Tour's *parcours* in the sweltering summer of 1976, there had been almost twice as many again. The driver behind this change was television, which demanded spectacle within a precise timeframe. The Tour's organisers were quick to realise that summit finishes were the ideal way to guarantee this, the action conveniently condensed into the final hour of a stage when viewing figures were at their highest.

But why Alpe d'Huez and not Avoriaz, Orcières Merlette, Pla d'Adet, the Puy de Dôme or the Ventoux? The simple answer is that the resort high above the Romanche valley kept paying for the Tour to come back. The more esoteric explanation is that the race and the resort fell in love with each other, and that relationship began with Joop Zoetemelk's victory on the Alpe in 1976.

From a sporting perspective, the 1976 Tour doesn't

stand out as one of the most memorable, primarily because five-time champion Eddy Merckx failed to start due to injury. However, like many Tours that take place during an interregnum period – new pro Bernard Hinault still being two years away from the Tour-winning debut that set him on the path towards emulating Merckx's haul in *La Grande Boucle* – it started with a host of potential contenders and was fascinatingly unpredictable because of that. Especially so after the completion of an opening week dominated by the sprinters, particularly Tour debutant Freddy Maertens.

It would be unthinkable in the modern era where pure sprinters are little more than that, but such was Maertens' dominance and the extent of his lead that, on the first rest day, which came before the race's encounter with the Alpe, the strapping Belgian was being hailed by some as a likely winner in Paris. Although the stage to Alpe d'Huez immediately changed that, handing out a brutal mauling to Maertens and almost every other member of the peloton, the unpredictability continued as no single rider or team was able to control the race and the yellow jersey. It became a masterpiece of tactics and subterfuge, with teammates set against each other, team directors urging their leaders not to take the yellow jersey, and those leaders defying orders.

At the centre of it were three riders: Frenchman Bernard Thévenet, who had ended Merckx's Tour-winning streak in 1975; Belgium's Lucien Van Impe, who was strongly favoured on a mountain-heavy course; and Dutchman Zoetemelk, whom Merckx had picked out as the rider most likely to prevail. At the centre of their contest was the battle on Alpe d'Huez, towards which holidaying Dutch fans were already being drawn in their thousands.

The exploits of these riders, who would all ultimately end up as Tour winners, are too easily forgotten in the huge shadows cast by Merckx and Hinault, the two greatest racers the sport has ever seen. Having downed Merckx in 1975, Thévenet would, on Alpe d'Huez in 1977, put up arguably the gutsiest defence of the yellow jersey ever seen. It was, he still acknowledges, the most demanding day he has ever had on the bike. He ended it being picked up from his saddle and carried up the stairs to his hotel room, having hung on to the yellow jersey by a mere eight seconds. 'They say the Tour is won on the Alpe, and I guess I showed it that day,' he said at the presentation of the 2015 race in Paris. 'I knew that ending that stage in the yellow jersey was vital, that I would win the race if I had it.'

As for Zoetemelk and Van Impe, they are too often defined by descriptions that are misleading and even insulting in the Dutchman's case, and too one-dimensional in the Belgian's. Both the 'wheelsucker' and 'the king of the mountains' had previously finished on the Tour podium on two occasions and were guaranteed contenders for high honours, particularly in this interregnum period. Both had also had to battle back from the same appalling crash at the Grand Prix du Midi Libre stage race in 1974. The incident ended the most successful run of Zoetemelk's career and almost cost him his life. So strong early on in that season that even Merckx couldn't stay with him on the climbs, Zoetemelk never quite got back to that level.

Would he have been a multiple Tour winner without that setback? His long-time Gan teammate and friend Raymond Poulidor certainly felt that the Dutchman was on the verge of a major breakthrough.

Struck down in that same crash at Valras-Plage, Van Impe needed a year to get back to his best. In 1976, he had advanced again thanks to the influence of his team director at Gitane, Cyrille Guimard. New to the job having just retired from the peloton, Guimard knew Van Impe well, having raced with him for nine years. 'I had been warned that he was very stubborn. But the portrait that had been given was nowhere near the reality,' Guimard later recalled.

A bluff, gruff character who had the bloody-mindedness of a great champion, though unfortunately not the knees, Guimard, who would surely have been born a Yorkshireman if he were British, then explained in typically forthright fashion: 'Lucien Van Impe was the greatest climber of his generation – and one of the greatest of all time – but didn't have the character to match his qualities on the bike...However, you had to see him on a bike when the road started to rise. It was marvellous to see, he was royally efficient. He had everything: the physique, fluidity, an easy and powerful pedalling style. He could have won several Tours de France. Of course, he was up against Merckx, Ocaña and even Thévenet, and then Hinault as well. But the principal problem for Lucien wasn't his rivals, it was himself.'

The account of the battle on Alpe d'Huez in 1976 between these three too frequently underrated riders perfectly illustrates why the climb to that ski station, which is every Tour mountain in one mountain, has such huge resonance and significance today. It highlights the difficulty of the ascent, the splendour of an arena that has no rival in terms of its drawing power, its vital importance to any Tour that tackles it, the reasons why every professional wants to win there, why every amateur wants to climb it, and why it has become cycling's greatest climb.

1

It is only just after eight on this Sunday morning, but the Tour de France peloton is already heading away from its rest-day halt in Divonne les Bains on the 258-kilometre run to the Alpine ski resort of Alpe d'Huez. As the riders approach the border crossing between France and Switzerland on the edge of Divonne, the slight figure of Lucien Van Impe eases up alongside his hulking Belgian compatriot Freddy Maertens, whose capture of four stage wins during the race's opening week has not only put him into the yellow jersey, but has also established him as an unlikely candidate for the overall title.

Van Impe's next smile is never too far away. The one he offers his heavyweight rival is underpinned by mischief rather than encouragement or goodwill.

'I'm going to attack as soon as we reach the foot of Alpe d'Huez,' Van Impe warns the Tour leader.

Maertens grins back at him. 'I'm ready,' is all he says.

The Flemish rider, best known for the explosive burst of power that makes him so potent in sprints and short time trials, has indeed done everything possible to prepare himself for his Tour debut. Back in December, well before a string of hugely impressive performances during the first half of the 1976 season, including six stage wins at Paris–Nice and victories in the Amstel Gold Race and Gent–Wevelgem, Maertens travelled into the Alps with his best friend and Flandria teammate Michel Pollentier. The pair undertook a detailed reconnaissance of the Tour's new mountain, which is set to host the first critical summit finish of the 1976 race, scaling it at least twenty times before Maertens was sure he had cracked it.

Bolstered by the confidence instilled by this experience and a lead of more than three minutes on defending champion Bernard Thévenet, and almost four on three-time Tour mountains champion Van Impe, Maertens believes he can hold the yellow jersey as far as the Pyrenees. Some, including five-time Tour champion Jacques Anquetil, are even insisting he could emulate the great, but unfortunately absent Eddy Merckx and take the title on his Tour debut.

Writing in L'Équipe on the eve of the Alpe d'Huez stage, Pierre Chany, the doyen of cycling journalists, has backed this view. 'Those who aren't true climbers will never be a great threat to the specialists, but a champion who undertakes specific preparation on this terrain can improve,' Chany suggests. 'During the course of a stage race, when fatigue becomes a factor, a champion who has plenty of reserves can adapt if he doesn't commit the error of trying to respond to the accelerations made by the climbers and climbs at his own rhythm.'

Chany's assessment has been supported by Maertens' performance in the Vosges and Jura massifs, where he finished first and second on consecutive stages. Maertens can climb, but it is Alpe d'Huez, by far the highest and toughest test of the race so far, that will reveal how well. He will have close to eight hours to mull over what Van Impe has said and ready himself.

With the foot of Alpe d'Huez almost 250 kilometres away, the peloton is in a lazy mood as it heads through the western wing of Switzerland, where a quirk of summer time-zoning means that for a few minutes they lose an hour on this already warm Sunday morning. The return to French time after the brief Swiss sojourn brings no increase in tempo. In this most exceptional of summers, the drizzly run into Divonne two days earlier was the first time that any of them had ridden in the rain since the final week of May. While western Europe has luxuriated, the pro peloton has sweltered and suffered. During the opening ten days of the race, which took the peloton across northern France and into Belgium before veering south towards the Alps, the heat has been withering and unrelenting.

As the temperature steadily rises, building towards another day of la canicule, the torturous heat that most riders dread, the bunch is sauntering. Boredom begins to take over. TI-Raleigh's Gerben Karstens attempts to relieve *it by snatching a traffic cone and riding along with it on his head, before tossing it into the crowd at the roadside. The peloton shout their approval, but a race commissaire is less impressed and fines the Dutchman 175 francs for 'making ridiculous jokes'. This is the first of what will be a bumper return for the UCI's race officials, who will later hand out a record number of fines, chiefly for riders being towed or pushed on the fourteen-kilometre climb to the ski station finale.*

The peloton remains passive and intact until it reaches Uriage les Bains, where the sulphide and salt waters are used to treat eczema, psoriasis and osteoarthritis. It is, however, the prospect of a hot spot sprint that provides the peloton with a boost. Frenchman Jacques Esclassan, wearing the green points competition jersey that is rightfully the property of the yellow-clad Maertens, breezes through to take the points and cash prize, his classy riding style later earning him the award as the day's most elegant performer. Of more significance, though, is Maertens' decision not to defend his lead in the hot spot sprints competition. The king of the sprints has wisely chosen to preserve his resources for the mountains that now lie just ahead.

As the peloton passes Uriage golf club, the route flicks left onto the first-category climb of the Col du Luitel. Twelve kilometres long and topping out at 1,262 metres, this pass is not as lofty as the Grand Ballon which was no obstacle to Maertens winning the stage into Mulhouse three days earlier. However, with an average gradient of 7.8 per cent, it is a good deal steeper. Van Impe's Gitane teammates and the climbers from the Spanish Kas team lead onto it. Their pace is persistent, but far from full-on. Yet it is rapid enough to stretch the peloton. Riders regularly drop away from this large leading group as it zigzags towards the pass on the smooth, sizzling asphalt.

Nearing the crest of the Luitel, Gitane directeur sportif Cyrille Guimard is happy to see that his leader, Van Impe, is sticking to their pre-stage plan and allowing others to contest that prize. In previous Tours, the little Belgian would certainly have attacked, with his eye on the King of the Mountains competition. But he's holding back, his focus on the main prize so acute that for the past month he's been living with his watch set an hour ahead to French time to maintain the rhythm of his daily life. The main beneficiary of the Belgian's determination not to defend the red polka-dot jersey he won on its introduction twelve months earlier is Giancarlo Bellini. It is Brooklyn's Italian who leads over the Luitel, followed by Frenchman Raymond Martin, Van Impe and about forty other riders, including race leader Maertens.

While Guimard is content for now, his colleague in the Flandria-Velda team car, Lomme Driessens, is worried. Very much against selecting Maertens for the Tour, insisting he was too young and inexperienced, Driessens had to yield to the desires of Flandria boss Pol Claeys. Now Driessens senses that the 24-year-old sprinter has erred by staying on the heels of Van Impe, Joop Zoetemelk and defending champion Bernard Thévenet. He is concerned that the Tour leader is riding too hard too soon. Rather than sticking to his own pace and allowing teammates such as Pollentier to chaperone him up to the summit of the Luitel, Maertens is being tempted beyond his limits by the pull the yellow jersey exerts on its wearer. Instead of ceding a minute on the climb of the Luitel and then chasing back on its fast descent and the long faux plat of the Romanche valley that follows, he has opted to show his strength. Has he already forgotten what those twenty ascents of the Alpe told him?

On the twisting, testing, high-speed drop down into Vizille, once witness to a key moment in the French Revolution but now a small and rather grubby industrial town a few kilometres south-east of Grenoble, the front group splits. Van Impe isn't renowned for tactical sang-froid, and that trait emerges once again. Nervy and impetuous, he had earlier asked his roommate and road captain Robert Mintkewicz what his tactics should be on the stage. 'Sit tight until you reach the foot of Alpe d'Huez,' the Frenchman known universally as 'Bébert' had told him. But, when he joins Italian duo Fausto Bertoglio and Marcello Bergamo in an attack off the front of the lead group, it's evident that the Belgian's commitment to the instructions given by Guimard and his team captain is not complete.

The trio gain a dozen seconds on a group containing ten riders, including Zoetemelk and Thévenet, and the same again on a bigger group, where Flandria are leading the pursuit with Maertens tucked in behind them. Van Impe's foray with the two Italians from the Jolly team is brief, lasting only four kilometres. 'It was just to test the water,' he will later explain.

The attacks continue as the main D1091 road turns south into the Oisans valley at Rochetaillée. Each of these sorties is reeled in on the broad road that runs almost dead straight for eight kilometres towards Bourg d'Oisans. Weaving through Bourg's steeply roofed houses, which are already falling into the shadow cast by the immense rock face that dominates the little town, two groups come together to create a pack of fifty-odd riders, who sweep through and cross the bridge over the fast-moving Romanche.

Just fifteen kilometres remain. The first of them is covered in little more than a minute. It sends the group hurtling over the turbulent waters of the Sarenne, still frothing after tumbling down from the narrow gorge that provides the only opening in the steepling cliff face ahead. For a brief moment, as it dips slightly after crossing the Sarenne, it's not obvious where the road will send the riders next. There's no exit, only the wall ahead. At the very last instant, the road switches hard left and upwards. 'Sommet à 14km' announces a roadside sign...

THE ROAD TO ALPE D'HUEZ

The 2015 edition of the Tour de France marks two anniversaries, one sure to be very well commemorated and the other all but forgotten, but both extremely significant

to the event. Forty years have passed since the introduction of the iconic red polka-dot jersey worn by the
King of the Mountains in 1975. For an event that loves
an anniversary, this one will be celebrated with the most
mountainous route for years and the first-ever penulti-
mate-day finale at the summit of Alpe d'Huez, the Tour's
most renowned climb. In the midst of the frenzy this
innovation is sure to generate, a thought should also be
given to the engineers and construction workers who,
eighty years ago, completed the first sealed road up to
this Alpine ski resort.

Until the mid-1930s, nothing more than a gravelled
2.5-metre-wide track zigzagged up to the nascent resort,
which comprised just a few chalets and cabins.
Significantly, though, one of those chalets belonged to
Joseph Paganon, a representative for Isère in the National
Assembly, who held the post of French minister of public
works in 1933 and 1934. During this period Paganon
oversaw the final part of the construction of the Chambon
Dam, which is wedged into the steep-sided valley on the
main road up to the Lautaret pass which has so often been
the Tour's final stepping stone to Alpe d'Huez. Foreseeing
the likely boom in winter sports, Paganon also approved
funding for a new road up the Alpe.

The project was split between fourteen different construction companies, each tasked with completing a
kilometre-long section of a road that would be seven metres
wide. In complete contrast to the project to build the

N1091 linking Grenoble to the Oisans area via the treacherous and marshy Romanche valley, which required seventy-seven years to complete, the fourteen-kilometre ascent of the D211 from Bourg d'Oisans to Alpe d'Huez was wrapped up within a year, its conclusion almost coinciding with the opening of the resort's first mechanical lift at the end of 1935. On the outbreak of the Second World War in 1939, Alpe d'Huez was already prospering. There were five large hotels, as well as eleven smaller ones, and three lifts that took skiers up to 2,000 metres. One of the hotels, the Bel Alpe, was owned by Maurice Rajon, whose son Georges would play a fundamental role in attracting the Tour to the ski station and popularising the climb to it.

The resort flourished in the post-war years, its development encouraged by another very prominent and very regular visitor, Jean Monnet, one of the political and economic architects of modern Europe. Drawn up in 1945, the Monnet Plan made use of France's control of Germany's coal and steel industries in the Ruhr and Saar to reconstruct its own industries and develop new ones. In mountain areas, this meant funds became available for the construction of roads, pistes, ski lifts and other infrastructure. As the popularity of winter sports grew, Alpe d'Huez's profile rose, boosted by celebrities from the Côte d'Azur who quickly adopted it as a winter playground. Yet, in those pre-TV days, when radio and newspapers were the dominant media, there was no grand plan to build on this burgeoning popularity by showcasing the resort via the Tour de France. Instead, the encounter between race and resort came about almost by chance.

For the Tour's co-directors, Jacques Goddet and Félix Lévitan, Alpe d'Huez was the right place at the right time. After watching Hugo Koblet convincingly dominate the long time trials of the 1951 race, they set about preventing a repeat. In the expectation that the Swiss would be challenged by his compatriot and 1950 champion Ferdi Kübler, 1949 winner Fausto Coppi and France's fast-emerging star Louison Bobet, they pieced together what *L'Équipe* described as '*une épreuve pour champions d'élite*', a race designed to push this quartet to their absolute limit.

By a timely coincidence, artist and cycling fan Jean Barbaglia, who often gazed at the Alpe's hairpins from his home across the valley in Bourg d'Oisans, had realised the climb's potential as a huge sporting amphitheatre. He mentioned his idea to two Alpe d'Huez hoteliers, the aforementioned Rajon and André Quintin, and they set about trying to bring the idea to fruition. Rajon approached the Tour organisation, who dispatched Goddet's route-finder-general, Élie Wermelinger, to scout out the Alpe's possibilities.

A former athletics star, actor and Resistance hero who had had the code name Sirocco, in the post-war years Wermelinger had managed casinos in Hossegor and Biarritz, which was where Goddet came across him in 1948 when the Tour passed through. Taken with Wermelinger's enthusiasm and drive, Goddet made him responsible for looking over the proposed Tour route. In late 1951, with 1911 Tour participant André Renard as the driver of his snow-chained car, Wermelinger drove up to Alpe d'Huez to meet Rajon.

Impressed by the standard of the road, which was wider and better maintained than most of those that regularly featured in the race, Wermelinger gave a favourable report to Goddet, who decided the resort would be the ideal place for the Tour's first-ever summit finish. All that remained to be fixed was payment of the fee of two million French francs (approximately €40,000 or £32,000) which had to be paid to the Tour organisation by any town that wanted to host a stage finish. With a commitment from Goddet that the race would also spend a rest day in the resort after the summit finish, Rajon and Quintin rallied their fellow hoteliers, insisting this was an opportunity not to be missed, that Alpe d'Huez would become famous among the millions listening to the live broadcasts on Radio Française and Radio Luxembourg. That swung it. The Alpe had its stage and rest day; the Tour its inaugural summit finish.

Now largely remembered for Coppi's brilliance in winning it with an advantage of almost half an hour, the 1952 race failed to live up to expectations even before it started. Of the four *cadors* expected to start, Coppi was the only big-hitter to line up. Lying fourth going into the Alpe d'Huez, five minutes down on his loyal domestique Andrea Carrea, Coppi knew nothing about the new climb beyond the little he had gleaned from French rider Bernard Gauthier.

'The gear he advised me to use reassured me. If such a small gear was needed to reach Alpe d'Huez my chances were even greater,' Coppi told French magazine *But et Club* after wrapping up his overall victory. 'I impatiently awaited this first authentic challenge and the night before it at Lausanne was something of a vigil.'

While Coppi was reassured, his rivals were jittery. The stage ran 266 kilometres, which remains the longest ever to the Alpe, and the peloton's old guard weren't prepared to spend all day racing to the foot of this new giant. When riders attempted to break away in the opening kilometres, they were brought to heel by a gaggle of older pros brandishing their heavyweight pumps and threatening violence.

Although these antics led to a rest-day summons from the race referees to Luxembourgers Bim Diederich and Jean Goldschmit, and Frenchmen Raphaël Geminiani, Raoul Rémy and Lucien Lazaridès to explain their actions, the pump-wielding had its desired effect. It resulted in a lock-down. The peloton meandered for 250 kilometres through the mountain valleys to Bourg d'Oisans, where it arrived forty minutes behind schedule. At the foot of Alpe d'Huez, 1947 Tour winner Jean 'Leatherhead' Robic attacked and was joined by Geminiani. Lacking the distinctive headgear responsible for his nickname, because there was to be no descent off the final mountain, Robic pressed hard on the sharp rise to the first hairpin, by which point Geminiani was cooked.

Coppi, meanwhile, was sitting close to the front of the following pack and waiting. 'I had said to myself that I shouldn't deliver the first blow but wait to see who attacked,' he explained to *But et Club*. 'There was a three-fold benefit to that: I didn't break my rhythm, I could see who my rivals were that day and then I could deliver a morale-breaking blow by dropping them if possible.'

Having noted that Robic was the man to beat, Coppi stood on his pedals and accelerated away from the bunch. Just beyond La Garde en Oisans, he got across to the Frenchman. Rarely rising from the saddle as his long, sculpted legs eased the pedals around with no evident difficulty despite the gradient, the Italian took the lead. Robic, punchier and more energetic in his style, danced on his pedals when required to add a touch more speed in order to stay on Coppi's wheel.

They rode in this formation until, with six kilometres remaining, Coppi span his pedals a little faster coming out of a hairpin. Robic responded, but was right on his limit. When Coppi pressed hard again, Robic slowly slipped off his wheel. 'I knew he wasn't there any longer because I couldn't hear him breathing – nor could I hear his tyres crunching on the ground behind,' said Coppi, giving at the same time an impression of the road surface and the lack of fans, who were almost absent on all but the final section of the climb.

As his rivals had suspected would be the case, Coppi cruised to victory and into the yellow jersey, which, thanks to further summit wins at Sestrières and the Puy de Dôme, he would hold all the way to Paris. There was a success for the Dutch, too, as young Jan Nolten's brave ride to finish eighth earned him the sang-froid prize awarded by the makers of an artichoke-based aperitif.

On the rest day, while Coppi sought some peace in one of the bedrooms at the back of Rajon's Hôtel Christina at the top end of Alpe d'Huez, the first footage of a Tour stage in the Alps was broadcast on French TV with commentary by Georges de Caunes, father of *Eurotrash* presenter and huge bike fan Antoine. As only 5,000 French households had television sets, the audience was probably only in the hundreds, but the summit finish and its broadcast were undoubtedly hugely significant landmarks for television and the race, and indeed for Alpe d'Huez.

The written press's verdict on Coppi was euphoric. Writing in *Miroir-Sprint*, Charles Pélissier, winner of a record eight stages in the 1930 race, described how, 'Coppi didn't seem to produce any kind of excessive effort and had enough in reserve to be able to conduct the flow of traffic on the climb, signalling to cars when to pass and when to wait. This was really impressive to see.' In *But et Club*, two-time Tour winner André Leducq wrote, 'It must be a magnificent feeling to glide along like that, to have everyone at your mercy...'

In *L'Équipe-Elans* – the two titles having merged

– Claude Tillet declared that, 'Coppi is clearly in a class of his own, the best man in the race,' but was scathing about the stage as a whole. He described the first 250 kilometres as 'perfectly insipid' and concluded: 'This will be one of the big lessons of a day that we've already said resulted in just 15km of racing and therefore doesn't promote the value of "summit" finishes (although you can't make a proper judgement based on one isolated case).' *Le Méridional*'s Jean Denis was even less enamoured of the sojourn on the Alpe, insisting: 'It's an odd idea to stay up there, [the organisers] ought to be examined by a psychiatrist.'

Although Tillet was correct in pointing out it was unfair to judge the new climb on just a single viewing, Goddet and his organising team decided once was enough, guided by the fact that the peerless Coppi also went on to roast his rivals at Sestrières and on the Puy de Dôme in the days that followed. When the route of the 1953 race was unveiled, there were no summit finishes. It wasn't until 1958 that the Tour finished atop a peak comparable to the Alpe, when the race made its first stop on Mont Ventoux.

'After the exceptional number of difficulties in 1952, the course was more measured,' was Pierre Chany's take on the 1953 edition. 'The gains realised in the mountains by Coppi had made the organisers more prudent and hostile to courses that were too testing. The organising team in the suburb of Montmartre opted for an extreme solution: the dropping of summit finishes, the spreading out of the high mountain stages, the dropping of time bonuses at the top of passes, just one time trial, and the number of riders on a team cut to 10.'

Alpe d'Huez doesn't seem to have been captured by the Tour either. In her analysis of the 'Touristic Development of Alpe d'Huez', published in the *Revue de géographie alpine* in 1961, Marie Barussaud makes not a single mention of the Tour's passage through the resort. However, she explains how the ski station flourished in the mid and late 1950s, when a booming French economy boosted spending on leisure activities. Skiers began to flood in during the early 1950s, and this influx prompted the construction of a cable car in 1954. Previously, the highest piste had started at 2,114 metres, which was a mere 250 metres above the upper part of the resort. The cable car up to the ridge of the Petites-Rousses now carried skiers up to 2,616 metres, which not only extended the length of the main runs, but also guaranteed a longer skiing season. More visitors arrived, leading, in 1955, to a construction boom to increase hotel capacity.

This growth produced a knock-on problem, as skiers often found themselves queuing for long periods to get onto the few drag lifts that would return them to the upper slopes of the mountain. The solution? Investment on a communal basis via the Société du Téléphérique. Established in 1958, this company drew its funds from local hoteliers, restaurateurs and even ski guides, who were obliged to hand over a proportion of their income.

Not only did the Société du Téléphérique take over the running of the cable car and other lifts, but it also constructed new ones where they were most needed. This raised Alpe d'Huez to the very top level of French mountain resorts, which was officially recognised in 1959 with its elevation to join Megève, Chamonix and Val d'Isère as *les grandes stations de ski françaises*.

This promotion to elite status was undoubtedly much more significant than what then seemed to be the Tour's one-off call. Not only was it a PR coup, but it also made the resort eligible for funds designed to further boost tourism and enabled the commune to impose a *taxe de séjour* on all visitors. Almost immediately, construction began on a new cable car up to the summit of the Pic Blanc, standing at 3,327 metres on the southern end of the Grandes Rousses massif.

In the period before the impact of global warming was felt, this new lift provided access to a number of glaciers, which allowed skiing year-round, boosting visitor numbers in the previously out-of-season summer months. This was deemed a particular coup given the resort's south-facing aspect and much more southerly position compared to its three *grandes stations* peers. As the Tour has discovered to its advantage, the sun almost always shines on the Alpe, guaranteeing favourable conditions when activity at other resorts is hamstrung by the weather.

Barussaud concluded that the only thing that would hold Alpe d'Huez back was its position off the main N91 route between Grenoble and Briançon. This would, she said, militate against tourists heading up to the resort instead of sticking to the Romanche valley. Barussaud mentions plans for a road continuing over the Sarenne pass to the Chambon Dam, which would give access to the resort on two sides. Otherwise, she suggested, the resort would be constrained by 'its location very deep inside the Northern Alps' and, therefore, remain relatively unknown, especially among foreigners, who in 1960 made up a tiny percentage of the visitors to the resort's thirty-eight hotels.

Cyclists, either of the professional or the amateur variety, weren't regular visitors either. Over the course of almost a quarter of a century, between the Tour's first encounter with the Alpe and its second, the race only came within sight of its slopes on a single occasion. In 1966, the fifteenth stage from Privas hurtled into the Romanche valley via the lush greenery and slaloming turns of the Col d'Ornon before finishing in Bourg d'Oisans, where Spain's Luis Otaño claimed victory.

The members of the Tour peloton billeted in Alpe d'Huez that night must have noticed work being undertaken to widen and improve the surface of the road in preparation for the Olympic events scheduled to take place at the resort two years later. Some may have caught sight of the signs on the apex of each corner running in descending order from the bottom, which marked the twenty-one hairpins between the valley and the resort.

These had been put up at Georges Rajon's instigation. Each year, he travelled to what was then the northern part of Yugoslavia and is now Slovenia to hunt chamois, four-legged mountain goats. During his hunting trip in 1964, he went over the Vršič pass and noticed the numbered signs on its fifty bends – twenty-six on the southern flank and twenty-four on the northern. On his return home, he proposed that the Alpe be numbered in the same way. It's not known why he opted to number twenty-one bends but not the twenty-second hairpin in Alpe d'Huez itself. Perhaps blackjack was his other way of relaxing when he wasn't blasting wildlife.

Fabrice Hurth, the current director of tourism at Alpe d'Huez and effectively one of Rajon's successors as a pro-moter of the mountain, describes the relationship between the Tour and Alpe d'Huez over the past forty years as 'a love story, because we need each other'. He adds that, 'The climb has become a concept. It has its own person-ality, almost like a rider perhaps.' His description could be dismissed as no more than marketing speak, but the unparalleled popularity of the climb backs up his analysis. Unlike so many riders who have been elevated to hero status before being exposed as frauds, Alpe d'Huez's status has grown and continues to do so. After all, there is little that's more reliable than solid rock.

As a former tourism director in Briançon and Chamrousse, which hosted a Tour stage finish in 2014, Hurth is well placed to assess the greater reach and impact of the race's visits to Alpe d'Huez. 'When I got this job I went out and joined the crowds the first year and I can categorically say that this resort is a level above those. You could see that this year [2014] the crowds weren't as big at Chamrousse and Risoul as they are at Alpe d'Huez. Those resorts aren't as well known and there's no doubt fans are disappointed when Alpe d'Huez is not on the Tour route. They wait for it to return. It's good to have it every other year or so, because if it were to come every year it wouldn't be a surprise,' says Hurth.

What surprises him is the price that Alpe d'Huez has to pay Tour owners ASO for the right to host a stage finish. 'For us it's a little bit more than €300,000, which is not so much considering the resort as a whole will make perhaps €10 million or more from the event,' he confesses. 'Then you've got to take into account all of the live TV coverage and the 500 journalists. If we had to pay for that ourselves it would cost I don't know how many millions. We couldn't afford to pay for that amount of advertising. It goes all round the world. There are two aspects to it – the economic side and the marketing or branding side. We certainly couldn't buy a worldwide campaign with €300,000.'

The result, as Rajon and his hotelier friends had hoped back in the mid-1970s, has been Alpe d'Huez's steady development as a year-round holiday destination. Although the summer months are never as busy as the skiing season, many businesses in Alpe d'Huez and the towns and villages nearby are dependent on visitors in the warmer part of the year.

Intriguingly, the statistics on their make-up underlines the role cycling has had in boosting this summer trade. Fifty per cent of visitors to the resort are foreigners. In the winter, 50 per cent of those foreigners come from Great Britain, where Alpe d'Huez is still predominantly regarded as a ski resort, and only 10 per cent are Dutch. In the summer, 50 per cent of the foreign visitors are Dutch. Increasingly, though, the numbers coming from other countries are rising.

'It's like Mecca for people on two wheels,' says Hurth. 'If you ride a bike, you have to do it, and it doesn't matter whether it takes one hour or three. The important thing is that you make it. It's a challenge. It's not so hard when compared to some other mountains, but Alpe d'Huez has become mythical. It's the most famous climb in cycling.'

2

Perhaps it is because this is the first time any of these riders have raced up Alpe d'Huez, but for a few moments the sight of the D211 ramping up to 11 per cent takes the fight out of them. Those at the front of the fifty-strong group fan out across the road, waiting to see what happens next. Someone will attack, but who? The only certainty is that it won't be the man in the yellow jersey. Freddy Maertens thinks his twenty pre-Tour ascents of the mountain may give him the knowledge and ability to defend the lead, but heroic escapades are out of the question.

The pause before hostilities commence is fleeting. Raymond Delisle, a Peugeot teammate of defending champion Bernard Thévenet, ends it. Peugeot DS Maurice de Muer has ordered Delisle to 'open the road' for the defending champion. Either Thévenet's rivals will respond, enabling France's main hope to track them as they chase down his teammate, or Delisle will open a gap that could allow him to act as a springboard in the event of a late attack by his team leader. If no one responds quickly, Delisle, Thévenet's principal support rider in the mountains, could even win himself.

Within a few moments, the first of these three scenarios begins to unfold as Lucien Van Impe quickly realises he could be caught in a Peugeot pincer between Thévenet and Delisle. He implements the most fundamental of sporting strategies: to defend his interests, he attacks. Before Delisle has even reached the first rightward kink in the road leading up towards bend twenty-one, the first hairpin on the road to Alpe d'Huez, Van Impe accelerates at full throttle.

Like Bradley Wiggins in his time-trialling flow or Vincenzo Nibali plummeting down a mountain pass, Van Impe's style is majestic and effortless. Watching him, one can't help but think that riding up mountains is the easiest thing in the world. His initial acceleration comes as he stands on the pedals, en danseuse, dancing on them. His is no heavy-footed stomp, but an Astaire-like glide, the perfection of it so practised that it would be difficult to assess his power and speed without reference to the riders left in Van Impe's wake as he swishes away. His head and shoulders are almost unmoving as every little bit of power is funnelled through his lower back and his delicately muscled legs to the pedals, spinning his forty-four-tooth inner chainring briskly in combination with one of the larger sprockets on his six-speed 13-23 cluster on this severe opening pitch.

In this era before in-car televisions and earpieces, Guimard, driving the Gitane team car in among the cars *behind the yellow jersey group, can't see what is happening beyond that first rightward kink, where Van Impe is shooting across the gap to Delisle. All he knows from the Radio Tour channel transmitted to every vehicle on the race is that there is an* 'attaque de Lucien Van Impe'. *A few seconds pass before Radio Tour reveals that Joop Zoetemelk, Michel Pollentier and Thévenet have bridged across to Van Impe's wheel.*

When Van Impe accelerates a second time, the already fading Delisle is quickly distanced. Thévenet is the next to join his wingman in losing ground. Pollentier hangs on. Maertens, his best friend, in the yellow jersey of race leader, has conveniently been forgotten.

Van Impe glances back, realises that Thévenet is adrift and sends his pedals spinning for a third time. 'Thévenet I didn't see again, and Pollentier was dropped,' he will explain later. Realising his chance of personal glory has gone, Pollentier finally falls back to play the loyal lieutenant's role for Maertens, who has wisely stuck to his own pace but has already lost a good deal of ground. According to L'Équipe's Pierre Chany, he is 'a greyhound lost among the mountain goats…It's well known that it's rare to change from one to another at these heights.'

IT BEGINS WITH A KICK IN THE TEETH

Alpe d'Huez is, claims Jacky Durand, the easiest *haute-catégorie* climb on the Tour de France roster. The one-time king of *baroudeurs*, the term denoting those riders who like nothing more than a stage-long escapade off the front of the peloton in the company of a small band of adventurers, the Frenchman was, it should be said, more at home on the rolling terrain of northern France than in the high mountains. However, as a veteran of ten Tours, he raced up most of France's most famous passes and summits, and he felt that the many sweeping hairpins offered regular and very welcome opportunities for recovery. Durand did, though, qualify his description of the Alpe, confessing that the opening two kilometres of the climb made him 'want to hit my head against the rock walls at the side of the road'.

A glance at the mountain's profile reveals why Durand considered self-harm. Unlike most climbs, and especially lofty mountain passes such as the Galibier and Tourmalet, riders encounter the steepest sections of the climb up to Alpe d'Huez immediately rather than late on. The routes up to the majority of ski stations are built with access for tourist coaches and heavy trucks in mind, but the road up to Alpe d'Huez is necessarily more taxing. The geography and geology of the landscape demand it.

Once described as 'a staircase with no landing', the first section of the ascent is nothing less than a massive climbing wall on which the hairpins are effectively huge pitons cut out of the cliff face to provide the road with a foothold. Often wrongly described as granite, the surface rock between Bourg d'Oisans and Alpe d'Huez is not igneous (derived through the cooling and solidification of magma or lava), but sedimentary. That is to say, it has been formed by the deposition of material on the Earth's surface and within bodies of water. Indeed, evidence of the Romanche valley's ancient undersea past and subsequent geological mangling are clearly evident heading up to bend twenty-one, the first rung on the ladder towards cycling nirvana.

The rock face beyond this bend comprises many upward (anticline) and downward (syncline) folds, the swirls in these sedimentary layers resembling a gigantic paisley mural. These huge patterns are even more evident on the approach to bend twenty, when the view across the valley first opens up. At this point, riders can – although racers most certainly don't – glance across the bottom of the spectacular glacial valley to Bourg d'Oisans. Towering above it, and already overshadowing the town if it is late afternoon, the Signal de Prégentil is impossible to ignore thanks to the exaggerated ripples and curves on its face. This astounding natural artwork is evidence of the huge forces exerted on the landscape when a vast Alpine ocean began to disappear due to the convergence of two plates during the upper Cretaceous period, around eighty million years ago. This process of subduction resulted in the deformation of the original horizontality of the rock, producing folding, which was increased still further during the rising of the Alps, which continues in the current era.

The first 2.6 kilometres up to bend sixteen, adjacent to the church at La Garde en Oisans, average more than 10 per cent. Taking into account that the gradient even on the apex of each sweeping hairpin is much less than half of that, some of the ramps in those initial sections are more than 12 per cent. The consequence of this 'upside down' feature, where the steepest ramps are near the valley rather than the summit, is that riders have to start the ascent with their limitations as a climber very much in mind. Attack them too hastily and the risk is blowing further up the climb, which at fourteen kilometres in length is on the long side for a summit finish. However, tackle them too cautiously and there is a risk of dropping out of contention almost as soon as the climb has started. Getting the correct balance between the two ends of this narrow spectrum requires very careful judgement.

Two-time Alpe d'Huez winner Hennie Kuiper was happy to let other riders pull him along on these sections, thereby keeping a little bit of power under the pedal for the moment when he was ready to show his hand. 'How you get through the first five turns is very important. You should try to avoid pressing too hard as you need to make a lot of changes in tempo. You have to try to take the turns as widely as possible in order to maintain your rhythm as well as you can,' he said when assessing the problems set by the mountain.

While Kuiper was a *grimpeur-rouleur* who was a shade more the former, 1987 Tour champion Stephen Roche tended more towards the latter. Although certainly not in Robert Millar's category of 'non-climber', as his 1985 stage win atop the Aubisque testifies, the Irishman confesses he never got to grips with Alpe d'Huez, which was the climb he feared above all others. In 1983, he reached the bottom of it in the yellow jersey group alongside Laurent Fignon, Pedro Delgado and Lucien Van Impe and crawled in more than fourteen minutes behind them, his ascent almost completely blanked out by the effect of hunger knock and fatigue.

Four years on, his lead over Charly Mottet was forty-one seconds back riding towards Alpe d'Huez, but the real threat was third-placed Delgado, who was a minute and nineteen seconds back. 'I knew the key for him as a specialist climber on Alpe d'Huez were the first few kilometres because that is where the ramps are steepest and they offered his best chance of gaining time on me,' Roche recalls. 'There is no gentle build-up to Alpe d'Huez, no 6 per cent ramp to ease you in. Another oddity that certainly adds to its status is those initial corners. On the majority of climbs, the gradient tends to get steeper on the corners or, if not, only gets just a little bit shallower. On Alpe d'Huez, however, the corners flatten out a lot, which makes it hard to maintain your rhythm, or at least it does if you're not a pure climber.'

Roche describes himself as being 'a good climber, but a good, steady climber'. He explains the difficulty he faced when matched up against flyweights like Delgado and Colombia's Lucho Herrera. 'Those flat sections on the corners used to kill steady climbers like me. On those first few kilometres, when you're zigzagging straight up the mountain, you'd have thirty metres or so of flat between the start and the end of the bend, which would force a change in your rhythm. The specialists aren't bothered by those changes. They can deal with them no problem.'

A car fanatic who switched to rallying with some success after he ended his career on two wheels in 1993, Roche further explains his assessment by saying: 'Imagine you're in a car and approaching a corner on Alpe d'Huez in second gear. Normally, that would be the ideal gear in which to take a corner on a mountain, but because the road flattens out so much you get the urge to put it into third gear for a moment to avoid over-revving the engine, and you then change back down into second coming out of the corner as the road ramps up again. My physiology is the same as that car engine.

'I would be climbing in a 41x22 gear and doing, say, 100 revs a minute approaching the corner. Then, as I went round the corner, I'd go up to 160 revs for 100 metres, then drop back down again to 100 revs coming out of the corner. It was that change in rhythm that used to kill me. A pure climber, on the other hand, could change from 160 to 100 to 160 to 200, and keep making changes in pace like that time and time again.'

Roche lost 1-44 and the yellow jersey to Delgado that day, but believes it was the best ride he ever did on Alpe d'Huez. 'I lost most of that time in the first three k's. After that I was able to limit my losses and even claw a little bit back. But those first three or four kilometres are a non-climber's nightmare because of the differences in the gradient – steep then flat, steep then flat, steep then flat,' he says, before offering a comparison with the climb up to La Plagne, which followed the next day.

'That is a very steady climb, much more typical of a road up to a ski station. Although Delgado rode away from me at the bottom again, I knew the climb was much more gradual. My plan was that once the gap between us had settled, I would then ride hard and come back at him. I knew once I'd got a good pace going I could maintain it on that climb. But it was almost impossible to do that on Alpe d'Huez because even further up you have to deal with regular changes to your rhythm.'

There are plenty of examples of riders attacking Alpe d'Huez too hard and paying the price for their exuberance. One of the most notable episodes of this kind occurred in the centenary Tour of 2003. Frenchman Richard Virenque was wearing the yellow jersey on a 219-kilometre stage that featured four climbs before the Alpe, the last of them the immense Galibier. Defending champion Lance Armstrong's US Postal team led the charge into the final climb up to Alpe d'Huez. Their plan was to keep the pace high on the tough early ramps and to then continue slowing down and then speeding up the pace in order to prevent the American's principal rival, Jan Ullrich, getting into his metronomic rhythm.

Postal's newest climbing recruit, Manuel 'Triki' Beltrán,

was leading the line as the yellow jersey group swept over the River Sarenne and took off towards bend twenty-one. But in his determination to set a rapid pace, the Spaniard immediately put everyone behind him on the limit. 'There's no doubt that Triki went too hard at the base of the climb, but he's new to the team and I guess the system isn't clear enough yet. A fast tempo is a good thing but that tempo was supersonic and that's not a good thing,' Armstrong said after the finish, where he took the yellow jersey but lost two minutes on stage winner Ibán Mayo. 'We'll talk about that tonight and it won't happen again,' he added rather ominously. 'I can confirm if it looked fast, it was very fast!'

Bearing in mind Armstrong's subsequent admission of extensive use of performance-enhancing drugs, as well as the confession also made by Tyler Hamilton and Mayo's positive test for the blood-boosting product EPO at the 2007 Tour, it is still interesting to consider the times recorded for the 2003 ascent of Alpe d'Huez. At thirty-nine minutes and eight seconds, stage winner Mayo's is the seventeenth fastest of all time, but second-placed Alexandre Vinokourov's time of 40-54 only ranks ninetieth in the all-time list, while Armstrong's 41-21 only puts him one-hundred-and-eleventh.

This is more than three minutes slower than the time of 38-05 the American recorded when winning the Alpe d'Huez stage just two years earlier. Naturally, the extremely hot weather in 2003 and the difficulty of the preceding climbs would have had an effect on climbing speeds on the Alpe, but that stage in 2001 also featured the 2,000-metre Madeleine and Glandon passes over 209km, so was not an easy day either.

Consequently, the key factor in the performance in 2003 appeared to be Beltrán's sprint in the initial half-kilometre. Even Armstrong, who had boasted in 1999 that he could have won on the Alpe even if he'd been on a tricycle, was forced well into the red zone. One of the Texan's other teammates, Chechu Rubiera, who had led US Postal's charge onto the Alpe in 1999 and was due to take up the pace-making when Beltrán pulled aside, confirmed his compatriot had erred; that in his enthusiasm to carry out his orders and please Armstrong – with the aim also of securing a contract for the following season – he had simply gone off too fast.

'He did the first 500 metres, and even a bit more, in the big ring; he didn't come out of it. I was hanging on and hanging on, but I knew that when he finally moved aside I would also have to pull over,' Rubiera explained. 'You know what they say, "accelerate like a horse, stop like a donkey", and that's what happened to me. I came to a dead stop after covering 300 metres at a laughable speed.'

In 1976, with only the distant memory of Coppi's stage win to go on, the tactics adopted by the contenders for the yellow jersey covered all of these possibilities. Van Impe and Zoetemelk, the pick of the specialist climbers, revealed their colours almost from the very bottom of the

Alpe. Maertens was wise enough not to sprint after them, but to stick at his own pace, which was so comfortable that it quickly became apparent that his yellow jersey was up for grabs. In *L'Équipe* the next morning, Pierre Chany used that memorable description of 'a greyhound lost among the mountain goats'.

Bernard Thévenet, Michel Pollentier and Hennie Kuiper did try to react to these specialist climbers, but each of them failed to stay the pace. Thévenet, who admitted he was never at his best on the first big stage in the mountains, did at least sustain his pace and continue the chase behind the two leaders. Pollentier, quickly realising his hopes of a stage win were zero, fell back to help to ride point for Maertens. As for Kuiper, he confessed he'd felt so strong on the Luitel that he was overconfident when they reached Alpe d'Huez. 'I took too much out of myself on the opening kilometres of the climb. I should have stayed at my own pace and then counter-attacked, but the initial ramps completely broke me,' said the Dutchman. It was a lesson he remembered well the following year.

3

First thing that morning Cyrille Guimard had told Lucien Van Impe to attack at the foot of the Alpe and see what happened next, to establish who the race's strong men really were. The plan is working to perfection, but almost too well. Guimard had been expecting half a dozen riders or more to emerge and share the workload on these initial steep grades, where Van Impe is in his element, as ramps of 10, 11 and 12 per cent are interspersed with sweeping corners on which the gradient falls to just one or two. Whatever the grade, Van Impe reacts to it, his chain chattering as it moves up and down his rear cassette as the Alpe demands. Meanwhile, the bigger men, the rouleurs-grimpeurs *like Thévenet, Pollentier and especially Hennie Kuiper, are struggling to cope with the constant changes of rhythm.*

Like Van Impe, Zoetemelk, who has reduced his early season race calendar to focus on the Tour, can deliver an acceleration that few can quickly follow. Unlike his Belgian rival, though, the gangly Dutchman is no stylist. This assessment stems not so much from his pedalling tech-nique, which is very smooth and fluid, but from his expression, which is that of a man gripped by every kind of pain. His head and upper body bobbing much more than Van Impe's as he pedals, the Dutchman resembles nothing less than the two-wheeled version of Jack Nicholson's Joker, his wide rictus grin revealing his top row of teeth, his fur-rowed cheeks and brow testament to the physical brutality of his profession, his eyes slightly crazed, his hair wild.

Belittled by the Belgian press and fans, whose oft-told quip is that Zoetemelk is so pale because he has spent so much time in Eddy Merckx's shadow, he is derided as a 'wheelsucker', as a rider who piggybacks on the exploits of others. But staying on Merckx's wheel when he was at his close-to-unbeatable best was some feat. And now, riding against another, but a very different Belgian, Zoetemelk has the chance to demonstrate his class, for which he seldom receives credit outside his home nation or France, his adopted country.

Initially his goal is to prevent Van Impe opening a gap that can't be closed. Then, without any discussion, an agree-ment is made. Initially content to find his rhythm and follow his Belgian rival, just after the short run between bends twenty and nineteen Zoetemelk eases past Van Impe after he flicks out an elbow to encourage the Dutchman to come through and take up the pace-making. The little Belgian, easing off on the throttle a touch, glances back and thinks: 'There's only two of us in it now. It's in

Zoetemelk's interest to keep riding with me if he wants to win the Tour. The rest are going to end up many minutes behind us tonight.'

Zoetemelk maintains the pace heading into bend eighteen, beyond which there is a huge drop into the Sarenne gorge. Most days, the sound of the river cascading down towards the valley would be clear, but as the two riders sweep around the bend the noise is drowned out by the shouts from clusters of fans on either side of the road and by the race officials and photographers buzzing around them on motorbikes. With twelve kilometres to the summit, Pollentier is sixteen seconds behind and the group led by Thévenet is already thirty seconds in arrears. Race leader Maertens, who has been clinging onto the back of this group, is now sliding off the back of it, with no teammates around to help him.

For the fourth time, the road rears up steeply coming out of an almost flat corner. Bend seventeen is 300 metres away, and Van Impe is at the front again as the two leaders climb through woods thick with oak, hazel, elder, ash and silver birch. The next hairpin is another wide one, the last section of it cut out of the rock face with a stand of pines perched precariously atop it, the trees leaning over to get a better view of the riders passing below.

Coming out of this bend, the road rises again and then jags left. There are no real straights at all on this lower half, ensuring that the riders setting the pace are almost always invisible to the chasers behind, offering them a *psychological boost to cope with the pain that is increasingly racking them. The agonising burn of lactic acid filling their muscles is the brain's unignorable method for demanding that legs and lungs be given a rest. But, even as this pain builds, Van Impe and Zoetemelk persist with their effort, knowing that they must make the edge they have as specialist climbers count on these most demanding sections, experience telling them that everyone behind will be suffering more than they are.*

They are still sharing the pace-making approaching bend sixteen, where the gradient eases yet again. Taking the tightest line on the 'wrong' left-hand side of the road, the two Lowlanders are moving into slightly easier climbing terrain as they pass the Église Saint-Pierre in the tiny village of La Garde en Oisans. Rather than cutting 180 degrees back on itself, the road only turns half that distance and, for the first time, runs parallel to the gorge and straight into the mountain. A marker at the roadside next to the turn to Auris en Oisans, which can be reached by a jaw-dropping and knee-trembling 'balcony' road cut into the cliff hundreds of metres above the Romanche valley, indicates that Huez is six kilometres further up the D211 and Alpe d'Huez another four beyond that.

THE CLERIC AND THE COMMENTATOR

Arrival at La Garde en Oisans offers riders of every level the opportunity to catch their breath, although a quick glance up brings an immediate reminder that, even though some of the steepest ramps have been passed, there's still an awfully long way to go. On race days, the switchbacks are clearly evident thanks to the camper vans and fans lined out all the way up to the Église Saint-Ferréol at bend seven, or Dutch corner as it's usually known. This is a fitting final resting place for a Dutchman who added significantly to the myth of the mountain, although he never rode a bike.

Jaap Reuten, whose grave lies just over the cemetery wall from the road, was the pastor for Alpe d'Huez and the surrounding region for twenty-eight years. During that period, Reuten became almost inextricably linked with the Tour's encounters with the Alpe. Consequently, it is entirely fitting that his final resting place should be in the lee of the eleventh-century church that sits sentinel-like above the Sarenne gorge, which over the previous millennium had often been occupied by a fortified look-out point over the Romanche valley. Even today, no one rides the Alpe without passing Reuten.

Appointed by the Bishop of Grenoble in 1964 after spending eight years as a priest in that city, he arrived in the resort when skiing was becoming very well established as a holiday activity. He had five parishes to oversee, the furthest of them thirty-five serpentine kilometres from the Alpe. He was also made the local dean, his deanery, the largest in the Grenoble diocese, stretched even further afield, covering twenty-six surrounding parishes.

The life of a Roman Catholic priest in France is often

one of abject poverty. Supported financially neither by the state nor the local diocese, a priest has to earn every penny required for his own and his parish's survival. When Reuten arrived at Alpe d'Huez in the mid-1960s, just four years before the resort was set to host events for the 1968 Grenoble Winter Olympics, he found a decaying wooden church more suitable for demolition than restoration. The best that could be said about the existing church was that it had a central position in the resort. After lobbying the local *mairie* and the Touring Club de France, which had been inspired by Britain's Cyclists' Touring Club and was established in 1890 to encourage tourism throughout France, Reuten was granted extra land to accommodate a more substantial place of worship.

The Dutch priest's quest was assisted by a former Resistance member, Jean Le Boucher. In the summer of 1944, he had been part of an operation to move a clandestine hospital from the resort in order to prevent its discovery by the Germans. Temporarily established in the Chalet du Signal hotel, the hospital housed a number of Resistance and Allied fighters, including eleven members of an American B-24 Liberator bomber that had been shot down in the Alps after a bombing raid over Munich from its Italian base on 19 July 1944.

On 11 August, the staff and patients at the hospital moved higher into the mountains to avoid capture by German forces, and as they did so Le Boucher vowed to build a new church devoted to the Virgin Mary in Alpe d'Huez if they survived the operation. For eleven days, during the course of which the Germans came close to discovering them on a number of occasions, they stayed in barns and other animal shelters, some close to the Glandon pass, which is now another regular point of passage for the Tour. Relief came when American and Resistance forces took control of the Oisans region, enabling the injured to be moved down to Grenoble and Le Boucher to fulfil his commitment.

Having secured the land he needed, Reuten's next task was to find an architect whose vision for an eye-catching, multi-purpose building married with his own. He foresaw a building that was open to all, even those coming straight off the ski slopes. There would be, he insisted, an access ramp for skiers and changing rooms. The belfry, he decided, would be topped off by a wok-shaped cauldron where the Olympic flame would burn.

His search led to architects Louis and Jean Marol, a father and son partnership whose design combined a modernist look using basic construction materials, principally concrete, copper, glass and wood, with a good deal of religious symbolism. With a central white tower, which from up above the resort looks like the most misplaced of lighthouses or a windmill stripped of its sails, and a copper-covered wrap cascading down around it like an oversized helter-skelter, the Église Notre Dame des Neiges symbolises God pitching his tent in Alpe d'Huez just as Abraham planted his tent in the desert.

Industrial and even brutal from the outside, the interior of the church couldn't be any more different. Passing from a very functional but bright vestibule, where a skier could store their skis if arriving straight from the pistes, worshippers and curious passers-by have a choice of stairways that lead around the base of the 'spire' and into the darkness of the semi-circular chapel. Initially, the only evident light is that which filters in through a dozen stained-glass windows which were commissioned from local artist Jean-Marie Pirot-Arcabas by Reuten and Le Boucher and run around the outside wall – a thirteenth is located above the main door into the church. Completed in modernist style tending towards cubism in places, they depict stories from the Bible, including Jesus casting the moneylenders out of the temple, the Last Supper and the death of John the Baptist.

Moving a few steps further into the auditorium, it soon becomes apparent that the central tower is very much the lighthouse it could be taken for from the outside. Topped off with a glass dome, which allows light to plunge through into the focal point of the church, it illuminates the altar, pulpit and mesmerising 'Hand of God' organ below. Designed by organist and composer Jean Guillou and constructed in 1978 by Detlef Kleuker, it sits in full view of the congregation, its 'thumb' and 'fingers' pointing towards the heavens, while some of the other pipes curve towards the auditorium to ensure worshippers miss none of its rich sound.

The white inner walls of the tower bounce light out into the seats where the congregation gathers and reveal the size and beauty of the immense curved wooden beams that support the copper-clad roof. Fading black-and-white pictures in the entrance hall depict the tortuously slow journey that was required to transport each of these colossal beams up the twenty-one hairpins, each one of the bends negotiated at a snail's pace.

The impressive auditorium can accommodate several hundred worshippers during peak winter season, and has, as Reuten hoped, hosted plenty of other rather less godly events as well, although the Marols didn't, in the end, include the flame or ramp access for skiers in their design. With one eye always on fundraising and the other very much on serving the local community, Reuten, a boyhood friend in the Brabant town of Geldrop of future Dutch prime minister Dries van Agt, was happy to host films, concerts, fashion shows and sports contests, including boxing.

For some years, the Tour de France press corps was also billeted in the church on race days prior to the construction of the adjacent Palais des Sports. Was anything beyond the pale for Reuten when it came to profile-lifting and fundraising activities for his church? 'Fashion shows are OK, but I wouldn't allow one for swimwear. That would be a step too far,' he once said.

What was once a slate roof finally became copper in 1983 thanks to a donation from Matsushita, the parent company of Panasonic, which backed Dutch team manager Peter Post for so many years. Taking advantage of his double role as the local agent for Dutch beer Heineken, Reuten also persuaded the brewer to donate 10 centimes to the church for every one of its beers consumed in the resort. In line with Heineken's slogan that suggests it refreshes the parts that other beers don't reach, Reuten boosted his funds still further by inviting Dutch bike fans to drink it in the vestibule area, which inspired legendary *L'Équipe* writer Antoine Blondin to pen the wonderful line: 'You are beer and on this beer I will build my church.'

After some months when services took place in the midst of a building site, Reuten's church was consecrated in December 1969. When the Tour returned to the Alpe in 1976 and the press moved in for the day, the extraordinary hand-shaped organ was still on Guillou's drawing board, but the church bells were in place and they rang out a few minutes after Zoetemelk had outsprinted Van Impe for the stage win.

Legend has it that Reuten celebrated every Dutch win on the Alpe in this fashion, but that first time at least the bells were doing no more than sounding out the Angelus devotion, as they did every day at 6 p.m. 'A journalist asked why I had done that and I said jokingly: "Well, obviously because Joop won." That became the joke of the day,' Reuten said after his retirement in 1989. 'The next year they asked me if I would ring the bells again if a Dutchman won. "Why not," I said, and the first rider to come up was Hennie Kuiper. The joke has now become a legend.'

Joost de Waele, the Flemish priest who succeeded Reuten at Alpe d'Huez, took a less nationalistic approach with the bells, letting them ring out when the first rider got to bend one, a couple of kilometres out from the finish. '*Que le meilleur gagne*' – 'may the best man win' – was his non-partisan stance.

Reuten's final resting place next to the church in La Garde couldn't be any more suitable on this most cathedral-like of climbs. If it were possible to follow a straight line from his grave up the mountain to Notre Dame des Neiges, you would pass through the church of Saint-Ferréol on Dutch corner. Even in the afterlife, Reuten, who died in 1992, is not far from the centre of the action on Alpe d'Huez.

If Reuten's role in adding to the legend of Alpe d'Huez as 'Dutch mountain' is often overstated, the opposite can be said of another Dutchman. Theo Koomen, a radio commentator for the national broadcaster NOS, became an iconic figure for many Dutch sports fans between the 1960s and the mid-1980s, yet he is almost unknown outside the Netherlands. Especially towards the end of that period, Koomen's radio reports from the Tour were avidly followed by an audience that some estimated was close to a million listeners, and perhaps even exceeded that figure in a country where the population was then around fourteen million. Although he died in 1984,

Koomen is still widely and fondly remembered by Dutch sports fans today, despite – or perhaps because of – his unusual approach to journalism, which often stretched to making up facts rather than simply reporting them.

Born into a Catholic family, Koomen studied to become a priest but abandoned this career for journalism, initially working on newspapers before switching to radio in 1966. His unbridled enthusiasm and dramatic commentary on the events he covered quickly earned him a substantial following. His popularity continued to grow as he reported on a string of ground-breaking sporting successes by Dutch athletes and teams, including European Cup champions Ajax, Olympic skating champions Kees Verkerk and Ard Schenk, and cyclist Jan Janssen.

In 1968, when Janssen sobbed after claiming the Tour de France title on the very last day of the race, Koomen blubbed along with him, and in doing so set off hundreds of thousands of fans listening on the radio back home. This was exactly the kind of response that Koomen wanted to achieve with his broadcasts. Rather than reporting impassively and objectively on what was happening in front of him, Koomen aimed to give listeners the full atmosphere and flavour of whatever event he was report-ing on. He wanted them to feel that they were inside the stadium or on the Tour finish line, resulting in theatrical performances that often bore little relation to the action he was watching but which made for riveting listening.

'When Theo spoke, he inundated listeners with his

words and enthusiasm. His reports were outright declarations of love,' said Gerrie Knetemann, who was frequently the subject of Koomen's outpourings during his long spell as one of TI-Raleigh's biggest stars in the late 1970s and early 1980s. *De Volkskrant* journalist Han van der Meer described being at a Tour finish line and watching Koomen in full flow: 'Those standing around him were openmouthed with wonder at the waterfall of words pouring out of him.' Mart Smeets, one of the most renowned Dutch TV journalists of the late twentieth century, who worked on the Tour with Koomen for two years, described his former colleague as 'plaguing the radio in the 1970s with a long cascade of words that could only be ended with the closure of the radio station or the playing of the Dutch national anthem'.

Among Koomen's most famous broadcasts was his report on the finale of Peter Winnen's first victory on Alpe d'Huez in 1981. Subsequently produced on a CD with music added, it is an astounding listen even for those who don't have a word of Dutch. Two years before the first Colombian radio journalists arrived on the Tour with their non-stop machine-gun commentary, Koomen's delivery is equally and absolutely relentless. He employs almost every type of device to raise suspense, except the dramatic pause. He includes a description of his own attempts to escape from the clutches of Tour director Félix Lévitan, who is determined to prevent him from breaking through the press cordon to reach the exhausted Winnen as he approaches the line. The irrepressible Koomen, inevitably, evades capture and gets to his man.

'Lévitan has gone away. I don't care, let's take the risk,' Koomen tells his colleague Raymond Nackaerts and everyone listening in. 'Guys, guess what I'm going to predict – I'm going to predict that Peter Winnen will win this stage. He has a lead of at least 300 metres over the trio of Alban, Hinault and Lucien Van Impe. I'm very cheeky, aren't I, Raymond?...You see, he's winning the stage. He's winning the stage, guys, and I'm still broadcasting...'

The ten-year-old Servais Knaven was one of the hundreds of thousands of Dutch people listening in to Koomen's broadcast that day. More than three decades later, he can still remember it. 'He was like a fan doing the commentary, and he'd get even more carried away when there was a Dutch rider in contention. His commentary on the radio was ten times better than watching on TV. When Peter Winnen won that day on Alpe d'Huez he made me feel like I was there,' says Knaven, who would go on to win a Tour stage of his own as well as Paris–Roubaix before becoming a directeur sportif with Team Sky.

Even before TV coverage of the Tour became more widespread during the early 1980s, it was already abundantly clear to many that Koomen's theatrics regularly stretched into the make-believe. 'Most people soon realised that the riders weren't always racing at seventy kilometres an hour or attacking each other all the time, as he was describing it,' says Knaven.

Winnen reveals that the riders in the peloton also knew what Koomen was up to, but were happy to go along with it given the audience he had. 'He always made up funny stories. If he was not near the front of the race he would make something up. He had to say something as he was giving updates on the radio, but it wasn't really an issue in those days because there wasn't so much coverage on television, so no one could really see what was happening. He talked one day about there being two riders in the break. One was Duclos and the other was Lassalle,' Winnen recalls of a stage that featured an escape by Frenchman Gilbert Duclos-Lassalle.

'He even used to preach on occasions from the back of the bike as if he were a priest,' adds Winnen. In one excerpt from a commentary reproduced in Nico Scheepmaker's biography of Koomen, *Een Leven in Woord en Beeld* (A Life in Words and Images), Koomen fills a gap in the racing action during a stage through Provence with a musing on the beauty of the lavender fields, and how such splendour must certainly prove the existence of God.

For most Dutch fans, including those who knew what he was up to, Koomen added an essential ingredient to the Tour experience. Indeed, he drew in many listeners who usually had little interest in cycling at all. Newspaper reports during the Dutch reign on Alpe d'Huez describe

Koomen receiving a reception from fans almost as rapturous as the riders when he passed by on the back of the NOS radio bike, while photos from that era often feature his name painted alongside those of Kuiper, Zoetemelk and Winnen.

Leon de Kort, former cycling correspondent of *Algemeen Dagblad* and now editor of Dutch magazine *Procycling*, was also a Koomen fan and, like many, one happy to overlook his distortions of fact in exchange for a good listen. 'I can remember when I was a schoolboy working in the greenhouses where tomatoes were grown and every time there was an update from the Tour we'd all stop working and sit down to listen to what Theo had to say,' recalls de Kort. 'I think almost everyone was aware after a while that most of it was made up, because he was on a bike with a helmet on and there was no way that he could tell exactly what was going on in the race. But he came up with the most brilliant stories. He made the race come alive. He was an artist more than a radio commentator. It was quite incredible to listen to him.'

Speaking about the liberties Koomen took with the truth, his former colleague Smeets confirms, 'He made everything up, he was good at that. If it was a dull stage on the Tour de France, he would turn it into a tremendous stage: "There are seven riders in front, four riders have collapsed, wah, wah, wah…" – but nothing was happening. That was his forte. He made up stories and he did it in a great way. Sometimes I was doing the same broadcast as him, and I'd be wondering if I was watching the same race as him. How did I react? I ignored what he was saying.'

Although he didn't agree with Koomen's approach, Smeets acknowledges he could understand how he arrived at it. 'Radio is all about creating a world that nobody can see. I have to say that he did that in a tremendous way. He could build up stories beautifully. But television became his biggest enemy,' he explains.

Smeets, who has covered forty-two editions of the Tour and was the long-time presenter of Dutch TV's post-stage programme *De Avondetappe*, does not accept, however, that Koomen played any role in popularising the Tour or Alpe d'Huez in Holland. 'The riders did that and they always have done. We, as journalists, we write the stories. His stories, as has been proven, were not the truth,' declares Smeets. Indeed, he's dismissive of Koomen's style, describing him as being 'very loud-mouthed and very popular with certain kinds of people. Let me say that the common people liked him, but intellectuals laughed about it.'

Others, though, are more forgiving of Koomen's over-the-top commentaries, and mention of his name is almost certain to produce an anecdote or memory from every Dutch rider and fan. His commentary was as indivisible from cycling as Harry Carpenter's was from boxing, 'Whispering' Ted Lowe's was from snooker and Sid Waddell's was from darts. In Koomen's case, that celebrity is hardly fading. He has streets named after him in his hometown of Wervershoof, as well as Eindhoven and Amsterdam. Since 2013, the Theo Koomen Award has been presented to the winner of Holland's best sports commentary of the year.

Two-time Alpe d'Huez victor Winnen describes him as 'a legend in Holland', while Knaven supports the view that 'he played a key role in popularising the Tour and particularly Alpe d'Huez in Holland. You've got to remember that not everyone then had TV and even if they did there wasn't a huge amount of Tour coverage on it. So everyone had to listen to Theo Koomen. Even now, he's an icon in Holland. Everyone knows him.'

4

Unlike Van Impe and Zoetemelk, who have reached an understanding and are steadily increasing their advantage, Bernard Thévenet finds himself without any allies. And why would he? He's the rider who vanquished Eddy Merckx twelve months earlier, the defending champion and one of the outstanding favourites for the title. He is expected to lead the pursuit. Spaniard Francisco Galdós, Italians Gianbattista Baronchelli, Giancarlo Bellini and Fausto Bertoglio, and Frenchmen André Romero and Raymond Poulidor just have to sit on his wheel and wait. Tenacious Thévenet will either drag them all back up to the two pace-setters or fold in the attempt to do so, and they will benefit from either eventuality.

Wise enough to attempt just one response to Van Impe's multiple accelerations, the Frenchman has been hoping a collaborator will emerge, allowing him to gather himself and then contribute to the pursuit. But, ten minutes into the climb, no one has. Thévenet realises that if he doesn't react, the Tour will become a two-man race within half an hour.

He goes to the front of the second group, which, thanks to his pacesetting, can now properly be described as the chase group. After a couple of hundred metres on the front, Thévenet eases off slightly, endeavouring to encourage one of the riders behind to come off his wheel and maintain the momentum. Within a couple of seconds, though, he senses they have all let up too. He understands they will follow him, but will not permit him to follow them.

Well aware that some of those stuck to his back wheel will counter and attempt to drop him further up the climb, Thévenet can't afford to hesitate any longer. The gap between him and his two most dangerous rivals has now reached a minute. He has to maintain his effort. Hands clamped on his brake hoods, jutting chin just a few centimetres above his bars, streams of sweat running from his dark curls, Thévenet is effectively on his own.

With his shoulders bowed and rocking from side to side, he looks like he's fighting to maintain his rhythm even when he's not. But today he is straining. The tempo that put paid to Merckx is elusive, thanks to the effects of a crash earlier in the race. The gap continues to edge out, suggesting this particular chase has come too soon for Thévenet, who is renowned for struggling on the first day or two in the high mountains and for finding his rhythm on the climbs in the race's third week.

MORE FRENCH THAN DUTCH?

'This isn't just any old stage I've won, this is Alpe d'Huez!' exclaimed Pierre Rolland after he outwitted and outrode his far more illustrious Spanish rivals, Samuel Sánchez and Alberto Contador, in 2011. 'When I was told that the last Frenchman to have won there was Bernard Hinault, I was even prouder. It's the most beautiful victory of my career without any doubt; there is no comparison.'

Although Rolland's first French win on the Alpe in a quarter of a century was quickly followed by another home success in 2013, courtesy of Christophe Riblon's reeling in and casting away of American Tejay van Garderen, the home nation's haul of four wins in twenty-nine attempts is hardly glorious. To an extent, that tally mirrors France's relative paucity of general classification contenders, particularly since Hinault's retirement in 1986 soon after that last great win of his career on Alpe d'Huez, where he finished hand in hand with his tormented teammate Greg LeMond, as their La Vie Claire team boss Bernard Tapie wept like a baby in the car just behind them.

Yet that quartet of wins only tells part of the story. Stage wins on the Alpe may have been elusive for the home nation, but yellow jerseys haven't. France has celebrated no fewer than nine *maillots jaunes* at Alpe d'Huez, eight of them overseen by arguably the best directeur sportif the Tour has ever seen. Set against the Dutch record for yellow jerseys on the mountain, which totals just a single parading of the famous fleece by Joop Zoetemelk in 1978, the French could certainly claim to be the Alpe's high rollers, more focused on the main prize than the huge, but more fleeting exposure a stage win brings.

The Tour's first encounter with the Alpe was, as far as the French were concerned, typical of many that would follow. With the notable exception of second-placed Jean Robic, the home riders were outclimbed and outclassed by the outstanding Fausto Coppi. The result was the first of many post-Alpe maulings in the press. Twenty-year-old Jean Le Guilly did receive plaudits for having the bottle to attempt to chase behind Robic and Coppi at the foot of the mountain. However, after quickly opening a thirty-metre gap with an eyeballs-out counter-attack, he paid for it by becoming the first rider to blow up on the climb's steep opening section. Subsequently, many more riders, a lot of them far more experienced than young Le Guilly, have shared that fate.

The Tour's belated return to the Alpe in 1976 made a new generation of riders aware of the perils that lay in wait for the overeager over the opening three kilometres of the climb, but particularly on the first two or three ramps. When he rode onto the fourteen-kilometre ascent in the yellow jersey in 1977, Bernard Thévenet dosed his effort as he led the chase behind Lucien Van Impe, refusing to respond to Zoetemelk and Hennie Kuiper's accelerations. He found a rhythm on just the right side of obliteration and stuck to it. *L'Équipe*'s Pierre Chany described 'the fantastic tenacity of Thévenet, crouched over his bike as if attempting to tame it, saving his jersey and his hopes,' as Van Impe eventually yielded and Kuiper failed by a mere eight seconds to take the race lead.

Thévenet's exploit, which is analysed later in this book, opened a period when the Alpe was certainly as French as it was Dutch. Indeed, over the following dozen years, these two nations divided the spoils on the mountain between them. In doing so, they popularised Alpe d'Huez, turning it into the sport's Maracanã, into the consummate arena where passion for cycling quickly became unparalleled.

While the Dutch hogged the victory garlands, the French dominated the yellow jersey thanks to three men – Bernard Hinault, Laurent Fignon and, sitting behind them both in the team car, Cyrille Guimard, who had already witnessed the damage the climb up to Alpe d'Huez could wreak on both riders and strategy when in 1976 he watched his Gitane team leader Van Impe take the yellow jersey when his French DS didn't want him to have it.

Even as he was guiding Van Impe towards the goal of winning the yellow jersey that year and then keeping the Belgian set on that goal in spite of his determination to follow his own more erratic path, Guimard had been thinking of his team's future – with Hinault as leader. He was careful when blooding 'The Badger', deciding against offering the young Breton his Tour debut in 1977, opting instead to give Hinault his first experience of the particular demands of racing in a three-week grand tour at the Vuelta in the spring of 1978. Victory there, the first of an astounding eight consecutive successes in grand tours that he finished, led to a winning debut at the Tour, based primarily on his all-conquering superiority as a *rouleur*.

Michel Pollentier's ejection from the race for attempting to cheat the dope control following his 1978 victory on the Alpe scuppered valid assessment of the Frenchman's potential as, along with Kuiper, Zoetemelk and Guimard, Hinault insisted his tactics would have been very different if the Belgian hadn't been away on his own. However, 1979 provided a perfect insight into the often despotic grip Hinault and Guimard imposed. Sensing something special, thousands of holidaying Dutch filled every campsite in the Oisans, hoping to see their 'Jopie' trounce 'The Badger'. At the same time, tens of thousands of French fans streamed into the valley and onto the Alpe to urge on their new idol. The result was that a record number of fans, estimated at well in excess of 100,000, converged on the Alpe to savour a succulent double helping of Breton brilliance dished up by the Renault leader and his boss. Zoetemelk alone provided any resistance to Hinault's crushing hegemony.

Round one produced a hard-fought stalemate between Hinault and Zoetemelk, who, after Joaquim Agostinho had taken advantage of the impasse between the star performers to slip away for the best win of his distinguished career, stuck together in limpet-like fashion. The Frenchman, as race leader, didn't have to attack. The Dutchman, slaughtered yet again in the press for his passivity, explained that he had tried to attack three times at the foot of the climb, only to see Hinault respond on each occasion and then counter with an effort that almost finished the Dutchman off.

As thousands descended off the mountain, jamming the road to Grenoble until four in the morning, Tour director Jacques Goddet tapped out an exultant editorial in the press room inside Jaap Reuten's church. Describing Alpe d'Huez as 'the summit of summits', Goddet rejoiced. 'The turnout of the public between the Galibier and Alpe d'Huez consecrated the loving union that links our old but always revitalised event to the popular masses.' In full, flowery flow, the Tour boss explained that 'the bicycle is a magical machine that allows the athletes to challenge each other, a bike between their legs, to show the very best of themselves, to sublimate themselves, and when the competition set before them presents difficulties beyond human measure, then we can admire them, venerate them and love them.'

Drawing on great French literature, as he often did, Goddet went on to draw a comparison with Victor Hugo's depiction of 'ocean-men', saying, 'We think that our riders are summit-men.' He exhorted them, and Zoetemelk in particular, to live up to this billing on the following day's stage starting and finishing at Alpe d'Huez.

There was nothing stale about Monday's rematch. Extending to just 118.5 kilometres with only a single climb prior to the Alpe, the stage offered Zoetemelk a final chance to unseat Hinault. The Dutchman acknowledged that was never likely to happen, but his attack at the foot of the mountain brought the best out of both men. Zoetemelk made 'the peloton explode as if a grenade had gone off', said *L'Équipe*'s Jean-Marie Leblanc. He opened up a gap of forty seconds on the steep sections that suited him. Hinault responded when the gradient eased, cutting his deficit back to twenty seconds. High on the mountain, Zoetemelk pushed hard again to finish forty-seven seconds clear of Hinault as Jaap Reuten set the bells ringing to mark a third Dutch triumph at Alpe d'Huez. Future Tour director Leblanc described 'the unforgettable climb towards Alpe d'Huez' as one of the best he'd seen. 'To achieve this kind of exploit, you need talent and real racing ability. And despite what people say about you, you've got that,' he signed off.

Of Hinault's performance, Pierre Chany wrote: 'The heavier *rouleurs-grimpeurs* don't generally like these sudden changes of rhythm and Hinault dealt with this as Jacques Anquetil used to. He limited his losses as well as he could and started to accelerate progressively with the goal of rejoining his rival.'

Although Hinault's grip on the yellow jersey was never in doubt, Zoetemelk's second stage win on the Alpe did, finally, put an end to his reputation as a wheelsucker

– outside Belgium at least. According to Chany, the Dutchman had achieved the challenge that he had been set by a doubting public and demonstrated that he was not 'a rider who was too economic with his effort'.

Chany's assessment is fair, but it doesn't make clear the extent of the gulf between the Frenchman and the rest of the pack in the late 1970s and early 1980s. Although not as unrelenting as Merckx throughout the whole season, Hinault was just as voracious as 'The Cannibal' come the summer months. A supreme time triallist and *rouleur*, a capable sprinter, and rarely outshone in the mountains, Hinault's only weakness was his belief that he was capable of almost anything. But, with Guimard's astuteness to prompt him, he seldom succumbed to ridiculous temptation, although his team boss was all too aware of Hinault's internal battle to quell his desire to attack, to excite, to prevent boredom setting in.

'I would like him to be less aggressive...It's something I talk to him about quite a lot, but I'm afraid it's quite difficult to change things,' he told *L'Équipe*'s Noël Couëdel during the 1979 Tour. 'He realises there's an issue, tries to make an effort to control it for a few days, and then his temperament gets the better of him again...I have to explain to him that this aggressiveness is detrimental to his image when it goes beyond the bounds of competition. What also annoys me is that it also automatically creates lots of enemies and provokes a climate of hostility towards him.'

For those who have come to cycling in the twenty-first century, Guimard's honest assessment of his star rider will perhaps summon up a comparison with Lance Armstrong, but Hinault was a very different kind of *patron*. While the American was happy to let his team ride his rivals to their limits before he delivered the final thrust, Hinault wasn't so patient and clinical, not as one-dimensional. If he sensed an opportunity to gain time on a long, flat stage into a headwind, he'd join the break. It used to drive his teammates, Guimard and his rivals demented. But the unpredictability of his aggressiveness was a fundamental part of Hinault's make-up as a racer.

It showed clearly in 1981 on the huge 230.5-kilometre stage from Morzine to Alpe d'Huez, which crossed the lengthy Madeleine and Glandon passes. Leading by almost eight minutes going into it and with no obvious challenger apparent, Hinault went to the front on both of these climbs and rode almost the entire peloton off his wheel. 'Being on the front all day was his way of controlling the race,' explains Peter Winnen, one of the few who managed to cling on that day. 'He always did it all by himself. It was only later on, and it started with Miguel Indurain and later on Lance Armstrong, the tactic was to have the whole team leading all day. But Hinault used to do it all by himself. He was quite an animal. It was really impressive watching that man, watching his back all of the time.'

That aspect of his nature is still apparent now when he

talks about the modern-day sport. His strategy for every rider who isn't guaranteed the yellow jersey is to attack, anywhere and everywhere. This approach would never work now because the members of the peloton are too evenly matched. But Hinault still persists. The sport has advanced, but he's still in a bygone era, one where his way of racing was commonplace, because the quality of the roads and equipment, fitness levels, nutrition and tactics were inferior, and brute strength mattered as much as anything.

The Alpe d'Huez stages in 1981, 1984 and 1986 all demonstrate this tendency towards the ridiculous. Yet, on two of these occasions, Hinault carried the day. In 1981, Hinault whittled the lead group down to seventeen riders on the Madeleine, then to just eight on the Glandon. On the Alpe, he couldn't follow Peter Winnen's accelerations, the final and winning move coming just below Dutch corner. But on each occasion, he ground his way back up towards the ashen Dutchman, who finished just eight seconds clear at the line.

After Winnen had been helped away, held up beneath his shoulders 'like a half-dead bird', Hinault faced the press. Having come second on the stage and pushed his lead out to almost ten minutes, he was furious when the questions put to him implied he had been found wanting on the Alpe. Guimard was equally piqued, declaring, 'Anyone who thinks they saw that doesn't know anything about cycling. When you take into account the work he put in, all day, and that he finished eight seconds behind Winnen, whom he would have beaten if the race had lasted another 500 metres, you can see, on the contrary, the extent of his resources. Bernard didn't move off the front for 100 kilometres.'

Icily polite at the finish line, Hinault let rip once he was in his hotel room. Noël Couëdel reported that he raged at Maurice Le Guilloux as his roommate washed his feet in the bath. 'You know what they asked me, "Mau-Mau"? Well, they asked me why I faded, if I was on a "*jour sans*" like at Roubaix, and what effect it had to be dropped by Van Impe and Alban? It seems that I wasn't riding well today,' Hinault fumed. 'They're idiots,' Le Guilloux told him.

Hinault continued with his rant. 'If I wasn't riding well today then I've never ridden well in my life. On the front on the Madeleine and Glandon, like a motorbike, with all of the others on my wheel. That's not nothing, is it? But it seems that it created a shock in Alpe d'Huez to see me losing fifty metres on Alban and Van Impe. They said it was a real event to see me behind, committed to a pursuit. That really makes me laugh... What about those riders? They spent the whole day sitting behind me and I was just 300 metres short of winning the stage.'

Trying to placate his team leader, Guimard chipped in: 'But the Alps aren't finished and I have the impression that we're going to enjoy ourselves tomorrow.' Hinault did precisely that, taking arguably his most impressive mountain victory at Pleynet Les Sept Laux, which he departed with an advantage of more than twelve minutes over second-placed Van Impe. For the Belgian, who had won earlier in the race at Pla d'Adet, there was no question about the Frenchman's dominance in the mountains. 'Hinault uses his strength on climbs and he is perhaps better than me, but he's not a true climber. He's got phenomenal strength in his back and he pushes impressive gears,' he said, revealing how it was always possible for the pure climbers to get a gap on Hinault, but why they were rarely able to maintain it.

As well as press criticism, it had also been noticeable that the public's response to Hinault on Alpe d'Huez hadn't been fulsome either. While the Dutch were euphoric in their backing of Winnen and their other favourites, waving banners, daubing their names on the road, the French were not exactly indifferent towards Hinault, but not as effusive in their support. Le Guilloux put this down to the false impression his fellow Breton and close friend gave to the press, which led to him coming across as aloof. 'I do wonder if he's cut out for the glory that has come his way. You know, he comes from the same background as me: a hole deep in the countryside with a father on the minimum wage...he doesn't like his starring role. Interviews are a real chore for him,' he said.

Le Guilloux explained how Hinault was much happier talking about farming and tractors than cycling, and said that he wasn't even that popular in Brittany, where many viewed him as cold and having airs and graces as a result of winning too much money. He suggested there was something to this, explained how Hinault was unique, both as a rider and as a man, as he revealed, 'I started racing bikes to earn five francs so that I could go to the cinema on a Saturday evening. He did it with the goal of winning the Tour de France.' He recalled Hinault telling a mutual friend, 'The first Tour de France that I ride, I will win.' And that was before he had even turned pro.

Asked about the surprising lack of support for Hinault, Guimard put it down to one simple fact: 'To unleash passion and inflame the public there need to be duels … Hinault is too far out on his own to be popular and also he would need to be up against riders who have a different mentality.' But such a rider was about to surface and, just as Hinault had when Van Impe was Gitane's leader, he emerged from within Guimard's team.

Laurent Fignon was part of the Renault line-up that ensured Hinault managed to see off the massed Spanish ranks at the 1983 Vuelta. That victory came at considerable cost to Hinault, who was forced to miss the Tour due to persistent tendinitis in his right knee. In his absence, Fignon took on the leadership and started the critical Alpe d'Huez stage lying second behind stricken Peugeot team leader Pascal Simon, who had crashed and broken his shoulder blade the morning after taking the yellow jersey in the Pyrenees. Simon had spent six agonising days being pushed, pulled and coaxed by his teammates, while all the time Fignon had been desperate to attack. Guimard, though, had persuaded him to hold back, knowing an early move on the yellow jersey could prove fatal to the young Parisian's victory hopes, especially as he wasn't convinced by Fignon's qualities as a climber.

Yet, after Simon finally quit at the top of the Côte de la Chapelle-Blanche when already several minutes in arrears, Fignon showed he had all the qualities required to succeed Hinault. While Winnen and Jean-René Bernaudeau went head to head for the stage win, the Dutchman edging the under-geared Frenchman in a contest that was more of a flounder than a sprint, Fignon finished fifth to take the yellow jersey.

Resting at home, Hinault was already unhappy with Guimard's stewardship of the Renault team, believing the roster had split between him and the older riders and a new generation led by Fignon, Pascal Jules and Marc Madiot. Subsequently rebuffed by Renault's management when he asked them to choose between him and Guimard, Hinault departed to join La Vie Claire, setting the scene for what many informed observers insist is the stage on which Alpe d'Huez fully captured the public's imagination.

Although the same argument can be made for the stages on the Alpe in 1977 and 1979, for the French at least the 1984 stage was very special, even if the much-hyped duel on the Alpe was more rout than contest. Still not fully recovered from an operation on his damaged knee, Hinault began that day almost three minutes in arrears to second-placed Fignon, whose teammate Vincent Barteau was sure to cede the yellow jersey he had held for several days. As bullish as ever, Hinault 'conducted himself like a warrior drawn from cycling's legends', wrote Jacques Goddet. 'He attacked the road like someone going into the ring, with the aim of delivering a knock-out, bent on destruction.' He made his move on the climb of the Laffrey, only to see his rivals ease back up to him. Almost immediately, Fignon joined a counter-attack by Colombian Lucho Herrera.

Refusing to yield, Hinault managed to regain contact with the front group on the flat road leading into Bourg d'Oisans. Any other rider would at the very least have paused to catch their breath. But not Hinault. Instead, he bolted away, causing Fignon to laugh at his gall and lunacy. In his 2010 autobiography, We Were Young and Carefree, Fignon recalled: 'When I saw him get out of the saddle and ride away up that long straight bit of road, I started laughing. I honestly did. Not in my head, but for real, physically, there on my bike. It was too much for me. His attitude was totally nonsensical. When you get dropped the least you can do is to take advantage of any lull to get your breath back. Bernard was just too proud and wanted to do everything gallantly. But the battle was already lost.'

Hinault led onto the Alpe, but his bluff was quickly

called. Herrera darted past him, then Fignon, the manoeuvre apparently signalling a definitive handover of
power. In his report Chany concluded, 'In the career of a
champion, the most cruel moment is without doubt the
one when he suddenly discovers the extent of his weakness in the face of an assault by insolent youth, and it
seemed that the former world champion reached that
moment today.'

Yet Hinault wouldn't admit that. He was adamant he
would come back, even as he crawled in, three huge
minutes behind Fignon, who described him as being 'in
a state verging on distress'. He continued: 'And do you
know what he came out with, less than ten minutes after
he had crossed the line on his knees? "Today, it didn't
work out, but I won't stop attacking until we get to Paris."
Hinault was amazing.'

The following two Tours would highlight just how
incredible Hinault was, culminating in the 1986 stage to
Alpe d'Huez, which remains the best remembered on the
mountain, but more for its unprecedented denouement
than the action that took place on the climb, which was
a victory parade rather than a sporting contest.

At the end of the 1984 Tour, Hinault's reign appeared
over. Fignon's looked certain to continue. Staggeringly,
though, it was the older man who went on to win the Tour
again, a feat his younger rival put down to his own problems with illness and injury, and also to Hinault's ability,
which he confessed was without parallel.

'Hinault was a better all-rounder, a better time triallist, better at hurting himself, and less susceptible to getting ill at the start of the season,' Fignon admitted. 'I wasn't driven by the same forces. I didn't have pride like his, nor as uncompromising a personality. One thing must never be forgotten: I did not have the class that was Hinault's. To me, that was obvious, there was no question of it.'

Fignon took the yellow jersey that day, but seethed at missing out on the stage win. He blamed Guimard's 'excessive caution' for his loss to Herrera, saying it had deprived him of the most prestigious stage win in the Tour. 'That evening I pulled on the yellow jersey a happy man: that was my goal. But could I ever have imagined back then that I would never in my entire life manage to win at l'Alpe d'Huez?' he said later. Guimard recognised it, too, revealing the anger Fignon had directed at him that evening and acknowledging, 'He felt that setback for the rest of his life.'

Hinault and Fignon would both savour one further day of grace at Alpe d'Huez. On both occasions, a yellow-jer-seyed Greg LeMond was the other protagonist. In 1986, the American had joined Hinault at La Vie Claire, where DS Paul Koechli's philosophy fitted neatly with the Frenchman's. The bespectacled Swiss encouraged his riders to make the race, to put their rivals on the defensive whenever possible. He might as well have told Hinault to do whatever he wanted. Shackled under Guimard, Hinault was unleashed and the result was unmissable mayhem.

For the Breton, his final Tour outing was a romp. Rarely can an authentic contender for a grand tour title have enjoyed himself so much, to the extent that he was smiling as he rode up the Alpe d'Huez, the final big climb of his illustrious career. 'It was the smile of a kid who'd just been offered a toy he'd been dreaming of,' said *L'Équipe*'s Jean Amadou.

He seized the yellow jersey in the Pyrenees with a raid so audacious that his lead on LeMond stretched to almost five minutes. Ignoring any kind of strategic common sense, he attacked in the same way the following day, only to blow up on the final climb to Superbagnères, where LeMond slashed his advantage to just forty seconds. The American took the lead on the eve of the Alpe d'Huez stage on the Col du Granon, where Hinault fought back tears as he struggled with a calf injury and fell to third overall behind Swiss Urs Zimmermann.

Logic suggested that La Vie Claire's leaders would sit on Zimmermann's wheel until the Alpe, then take turns to attack and finish him off. Perhaps that was what LeMond was expecting when Hinault accelerated away on the descent off the Galibier. Even after the American had shown he was the Tour's strongest rider by dropping Zimmermann and bridging up to Hinault, the Frenchman kept pressing, descending like a loon off the Croix de Fer and pressing all the way to the foot of sun-baked Alpe d'Huez, where hundreds of thousands of fans had gathered to witness Hinault's final fling before retirement.

Long respected by his home fans but never loved, the Breton's fall and rise again had made him more popular than he'd ever been in his all-conquering prime. As the pair rode onto the Alpe, they sensed an atmosphere that had shifted from festive to threatening.

They were chanting Hinault's name, which he admitted made the hair on his arms stand on end. Seeing LeMond was edgy, he instructed his teammate to stay on his wheel. 'It will all be OK. I know how to deal with the crowd,' he told LeMond. They rode between two unbroken hedges of spectators, whose enthusiasm was so enormous that even Hinault later admitted that he had been concerned. 'I get the impression that they sometimes think of me as an animal and that they don't respect me sufficiently. And, you never know, a madman could always be hiding in the crowd,' he confessed. He may have felt threatened, but he received almost unanimous acclaim. 'By acting as the American's mentor, Hinault underlined his perfect understanding of what it takes to trigger the crowd's enthusiasm...if he wins the Tour he's a hero, if he loses he's an idol,' said Jean Amadou.

French writer Jean-Paul Vespini describes the pair's ascent to Alpe d'Huez as nothing less than 'high art'. LeMond wouldn't see it that way, but for Hinault and his fans it was precisely that. 'The Badger' asserted that, 'I am aware that Greg and me have just given the most incredible image of our sport that is possible.' The extraordinary mauling of their rivals, the triumphant ascent through an enraptured audience, the two men raising each other's hand as they cross the line at the top of cycling's most famous climb, the older champion savouring a final glory, his young cohort happy to play the supporting role in the knowledge that the bigger prize is his – all of these aspects combined. The Hollywood Climb had produced a spectacle that rolled *Red River*, *The Shootist* and *Butch Cassidy and the Sundance Kid* into one.

Of course, with Hinault in the starring role, there was always likely to be a final twist. As he described the day on French TV with LeMond sitting alongside him, Hinault affirmed the Tour was not over, that LeMond hadn't yet won it. 'The Tour is not finished,' he said with a shrug. 'There could be a crash, many things can still happen. But if we have a war, it will be a fair war and the stronger man will win.' As LeMond looked incredulous, Hinault is asked if he thinks he can still catch his teammate. 'I don't know. We'll see . . .'

Throughout the 1989 Tour, there was never more than a minute between the Frenchman and his former Renault team mate LeMond. The American took the yellow jersey in the long time trial during the first week, with Fignon a mere five seconds behind. The Frenchman relieved him of the jersey at Superbagnères and led the American by seven seconds for five days, before LeMond regained the lead in a mountain time trial to Orcières Merlette. He then boosted his advantage from forty seconds to fifty-three at Briançon, the location of the start of the subsequent stage to Alpe d'Huez over the Galibier and Croix de Fer.

Although analysis of where this Tour was won and lost tends to focus on the final twenty-four-kilometre time trial into Paris, where the race was decided in LeMond's favour by eight seconds, events on the Alpe were at least as important. Realising Fignon had to gain a substantial lead on the American before that final time trial, Guimard and his leader decided Fignon should attack hard at the first hairpin. 'That meant really attacking, as if the finish were only 100 metres away,' said the Frenchman, who stuck precisely to his orders, accelerating once, twice and then a third time. LeMond, though, clawed his way back on each occasion.

The pair remained locked together up to Huez. Watching from behind, Guimard began to notice one of LeMond's 'tells'. 'When he was on the verge of blowing up, he used to move about in an odd way in the saddle; he used to stand up a bit and then sit down again in a particular manner,' Guimard later explained. Noticing it, he managed to manoeuvre his car up alongside Fignon. 'Attack, he's cooked,' he told the ponytailed Super U team leader. 'Can't, I'm wasted,' Fignon mumbled.

As Abelardo Rondón set the pace for defending champion Pedro Delgado on the front of the four-man group, Fignon gathered himself as they climbed through Huez. Just above bend four, where the road straightens through the meadows beneath Alpe d'Huez, Fignon went hard again: 'One acceleration, and LeMond, flattened over his bike, couldn't come with me. In less than four kilometres I took one minute and nineteen seconds out of him, and that's bearing in mind that the last part of Alpe d'Huez is by far the least difficult part.'

Fignon now led by twenty-six seconds and he pushed that advantage out to fifty seconds the following day at Villard de Lans. Looking back, though, he admitted he had erred. 'Guimard had called a race right yet again, and it should be noted for posterity: if I'd gone for LeMond at the moment when he had told me to, the Tour would have been won. No question. Because LeMond was completely blasted. I was putting about twenty seconds per kilometre into him,' Fignon acknowledged. Guimard agrees, contending LeMond would have lost three minutes if the Frenchman had attacked six kilometres from the top of the Alpe. If he had, says Guimard, 'nobody would have been talking about Laurent's saddle sore and certainly not about those eight seconds…'

Fignon's capture of the yellow jersey that day remains the last occasion when a French rider rode onto the Alpe in contention for victory in Paris. The following year, Ronan 'Pinpin' Pensec made a courageous defence of the yellow jersey on the mountain, aided substantially by the pacesetting given by his Z teammate Robert Millar. But for two decades and more, the French have had little to celebrate on the mountain.

During the era defined as one of *cyclisme à deux vitesses*, there were near-misses, brave performances and lots of excuses, which have gained more substance given subsequent revelations, but only two instances when a home rider wore yellow on the Alpe. Richard Virenque was one, his day in yellow coming in 2003 after a typical long-range solo ride through the mountains to Morzine, a day that now has more significance as a result of the mid-stage collapse of Virenque's breakaway companion, Spanish rider Jesús Manzano, which set in motion events leading to the Operación Puerto doping investigation.

Two years earlier, François Simon offered up a more gladdening moment when he took the yellow jersey at Alpe d'Huez eighteen years after his injury-stricken elder brother, Pascal, had been forced to abandon it on the road to the Alpe. One of a group of riders who had gained more than half an hour on the peloton in a deluge on the stage to Pontarlier, Simon, the youngest of four cycling brothers and the only one who failed to win a Tour stage, went into the Alpe d'Huez stage four minutes behind Australia's Stuart O'Grady. That morning, Pascal called him to say: 'I left the yellow jersey in a corner somewhere. Pick it up as you go by.'

Having distanced O'Grady on the Madeleine, Simon stuck with the big guns until the foot of the final test, then kept to his own pace. 'I managed my effort rather than risk exploding,' he said. 'I've rarely had so much encouragement. Hundreds of times I heard: "Simon in yellow!"' The unheralded Frenchman, whose very modest upbringing meant that he wore hand-me-downs until he was fifteen, held the lead for another two stages before finishing sixth and leading Frenchman in Paris.

It would be twenty-five years before France had a second victory at Alpe d'Huez to celebrate. It came courtesy of Pierre Rolland and highlighted both a renaissance in the home nation's fortunes in the sport's biggest races and a significant switch in route-planning strategy by Tour director Christian Prudhomme and his team. Rolland, a super-lean beanpole of a climber, had spent ten days playing the main support role for his Europcar team leader Thomas Voeckler, who had taken the yellow jersey and, lifted by it just as he had been for ten days in 2004, had gone into the race's final three days with overall victory still a possibility.

Sadly for Voeckler and those who love an underdog and would relish another Tour being won à la Walko, harking back to Roger Walkowiak's shock success in 1956, there would be no fairy-tale finish for France's favourite rider. Voeckler came undone on the kind of short, high mountain stage that Prudhomme believes is the key to guaranteeing action from the instant the start flag is dropped.

Extending to just 109.5 kilometres, this nineteenth stage, just two days from Paris, took the race over the Télégraphe and Galibier before reaching the Alpe. Approaching the first of these tests, two-time Tour champion Alberto Contador, whose chances of overall victory had all but gone, attacked. Second-placed Andy Schleck joined him, prompting Voeckler to respond as well. Without Rolland or indeed any of his teammates to relay him, Voeckler, a *baroudeur* whose many faces of pain merit a César for showmanship, was out of his depth. As the two climbing aces breezed away from him, he thrashed away up the Galibier on his own rather than wait for his troops. When he finally sat up and waited for them, he couldn't manage to keep up and gave Rolland the freedom to ride his own race.

First onto the climb with Ryder Hesjedal, Rolland quickly escaped the Canadian but was himself caught and dropped by Contador. Aware that another Spaniard, Olympic champion Samuel Sánchez, was coming up to him, Rolland eased off, sat on Sánchez's wheel and gradually got pulled back up to Contador. But what chance did he have against two compatriots who were good friends? Little, it seemed, and Rolland cannily played on that, refusing to work, letting the Spaniards set the pace, before jumping them at the bottom edge of the resort. 'I know the Alpe extremely well. I climbed it ten times during a training camp,' Rolland revealed afterwards. 'When I got to bend number one I knew that I could put it in the big ring and ride *à bloc* to the finish.'

Realising that you can have too much of a good thing, Prudhomme has continued to include the Alpe in alternate years. But he's enhanced its special flavour by adding a twist to the stage. In 2011, it was by shortening it. In

2013, the hundredth Tour de France, he unveiled the first double ascent of the mountain, made possible by the inclusion of the tricky, but wonderfully wild and spectacular descent from the Col de Sarenne, which Prudhomme's route director, Thierry Gouvenou, says will be considered for inclusion in future editions, with Alpe d'Huez perhaps featuring as a mid-stage climb for the first time, with the finish in Briançon, or even going up onto the Galibier pass.

As was the case with Rolland's victory, this unprecedented stage resulted in the first and only French success in the race that year. Initially part of a nine-man group that went clear early in the stage, Christophe Riblon started the first ascent of Alpe d'Huez with American Tejay van Garderen and Italy's Moreno Moser. Despite a fall on the Sarenne, Riblon was still with his two companions for the exceptional second ascent. Yet, after Moser had yielded, the Frenchman found he couldn't keep pace with van Garderen, who opened up a lead of forty-five seconds.

'With five kilometres to go I thought I'd have to accept second place, but my directeur sportif told me to go for it, that van Garderen was going to crack. When I saw van Garderen, I thought: "It's Alpe d'Huez. I've been watching this climb at the Tour de France since I was six years old."' As the young American wilted, Riblon ate up the gap between them. No sooner had he reeled in van Garderen, than Riblon attacked.

'I've been riding a bike since I was six and I know that Alpe d'Huez is part of cycling history. During all that time only three French riders have won up there and I'm proud to say I'm one of them. In addition, it was during the hundredth edition of the Tour and the race went over the climb twice, and that remains an incredible moment, one that's gone down in history,' says Riblon.

'It was the most beautiful day of my career. I almost couldn't believe that I was going actually to win there. Of course, I could see that I was going to win, but it was so unbelievable. What followed was astounding too, with the fans, the media, the impact that it had. Even people who didn't really know much about cycling were coming up to me and saying they recognised me and wanted to speak to me. That was all part of it, of that win being the greatest moment of my career, and will ensure that it will remain with me for the rest of my days.'

In 2015, Prudhomme and Gouvenou came up with another innovation. The stage to Alpe d'Huez was intended to follow the same route as the thriller won by Rolland, but, for the first time in the race's history, the Tour's favourite mountain featured on the penultimate day of the race. 'Because it has all the fans and all that history, the Tour organisation always like to put on something special there,' says Gouvenou. 'This year's finish on Alpe d'Huez, the day before Paris, is the seal that Christian Prudhomme wanted to put on the 2015 Tour. We've got the final summit as close as possible to the Champs-Élysées and in addition it's the most mythical of all of the summits. We're in danger of having a really spectacular finish to the Tour this year.'

Like Gouvenou, Prudhomme evoked the mythical status of the Alpe and the fortieth anniversary of the red polka-dot jersey when he presented the particularly mountainous route of the 2015 Tour in Paris. But he also acknowledged a good dose of jingoism had flavoured his choice of terrain. Naturally, the route would favour the peloton's mountain goats. Far from coincidentally, the home nation had an impressively talented herd of them in the shape of Thibaut Pinot, Romain Bardet, Warren Barguil and Rolland.

Prudhomme's underlying message was clear: paying tribute to the race's history is important, but offering France's stars the best chance of success is fundamental. A fervent fan who was at the roadside in the Alps when Thévenet and Hinault claimed the yellow jersey in the 1970s, Prudhomme knows the significance of Alpe d'Huez. The Dutch may claim temporary ownership of it, but history suggests that it is France's lucky charm.

5

*Sitting in his team car behind the Thévenet group, Gan-
Mercier directeur sportif Louis Caput is another man whose
pre-stage plans aren't turning out the way he had hoped. The
first post-war French national champion and winner of two
stages in nine appearances at the Tour, 'P'tit Louis' was a
likeable and canny rider. According to* Sporting Cyclist's
*René De La Tour, 'He knew his job perfectly and I don't think
I have ever seen him make a serious mistake on the road.
Whenever he got into a break, he was the boss, the ruler of it.'*

*As Raymond Poulidor's DS for the past seven seasons,
Caput has seen 'The Eternal Second' suffer all manner of
disappointments, but had sensed that this stage would
produce something special. Riding his fourteenth and final
Tour, forty-year-old Poulidor started the day in fifth place
overall, 3-31 down on yellow jersey Freddy Maertens.
Crucially, though, with a twenty-three-second lead on
Lucien Van Impe, he was the best placed of the contenders
for the title. Yet that advantage has gone.*

Even so, Caput believes he can do something to retrieve it and bring about the result that all of France is desperate to see – Poulidor in the yellow jersey for the first time in his career, even if only for a single day.

Watching Poulidor playing the loyal teammate for his friend Joop Zoetemelk, Caput believes his leader is riding well within himself. Offered the opportunity, thinks Caput, Poulidor could jump bridge the gap to the two leaders, giving Gan two riders at the front and Van Impe little chance of taking either the stage or the yellow jersey. He sees Zoetemelk leading the trio home and Poulidor finishing the afternoon in yellow.

As Thévenet tracks towards the side of the road, taking the shortest line and all of his followers with him, Caput accelerates past the group in his Peugeot 504 and swiftly covers the 400 metres up to Van Impe and Zoetemelk. P'tit Louis believes history is within his team's grasp, but, as he summons up the image of Poulidor in yellow, he is on the verge of committing a very serious error.

THE MAN WHO PAINTED THE ALPE ORANGE

In all likelihood, the British tourist who had left his car on a roadside verge next to the seafront at Valras-Plage didn't understand the signs indicating a temporary ban on parking because the road was set to host the finish of a bike race. Yet no one was later able to explain why the car hadn't been towed away before the opening stage of the GP Midi-Libre finished in the resort.

That first day of the 1974 edition of that now extinct and widely missed stage race in France's southern province of Languedoc-Roussillon should have been mundane. The opening half of a split stage on a warm but blustery Ascension Day ran 96 kilometres from Carcassonne to Valras-Plage, the second half another 97 between Béziers and Montpellier, where Britain's Barry Hoban took the first of two stage wins on his way to second place overall, which his Gan-Mercier team leader Zoetemelk had been tipped to win.

During the early months of that season, the Dutchman had already won Paris–Nice and Catalan Week, dishing out some Cannibal-like treatment to Eddy Merckx at both. A subsequent success at the Tour of Romandy by a whopping five minutes had confirmed the belief that Zoetemelk, twice runner-up to Merckx at the Tour de France, was set to become the first rider to topple the all-conquering Belgian in July. Yet, sadly, that possibility was about to disappear in a 'what if…?' moment.

With only ninety riders in the pack, the field wasn't big. The clear favourite for overall victory, which would be decided in the wooded hills of the Gard and Aveyron in the days ahead, Zoetemelk was sitting well back in the peloton as it sped towards the Mediterranean resort, a massed sprint guaranteed. Only the first ten riders would be classified, the rest simply listed as finishing in the bunch behind them. However, a sudden turn into a headwind changed the complexion of the finale.

Previously happy to tool along in the pack, Zoetemelk realised there was now a chance of the bunch splitting. When teammate Jean-Pierre Genet came up alongside him and said, '*Allez*, Joop, follow me,' Zoetemelk jumped on his wheel, and started to ride full bore with his head lowered.

Bearing down the finishing straight, the first few riders in the peloton could see the abandoned car and were able to swerve away from it. But those charging along in their wake weren't so lucky. Bernard Labourdette hit it first, his body smashing the rear window, then rising two metres in the air before landing on the roof and sliding down onto the bonnet.

About a dozen more riders went down, including Zoetemelk and one of the other general classification favourites, Lucien Van Impe. The Belgian was up quicker than the Dutchman, whose first thought, as so often when riders crash, was for his bike. Zoetemelk was taken away with blood pouring from a wound in his head, his Midi-Libre over. There was no consolation to be had from the award of the 10,000-franc prize for the most unfortunate rider of the day.

X-rays taken at hospital in Béziers showed no apparent damage to Zoetemelk's head beyond the superficial. When his father-in-law Jacques Duchaussoy and Gan team manager Claude Sudres came to visit him the following day, they found the Dutchman vomiting into a bag. They insisted he needed to be kept in, but the doctors were adamant. Apart from a nasty gash in his head, Zoetemelk was fine, they said.

Duchaussoy and Sudres decided to move the ailing rider back to his home east of Paris by plane, but were unable to do so because anyone being carried on a stretcher needed to be accompanied by another person, and both men had their cars with them. This was extremely inconvenient at the time, but turned out to be absolutely vital with regard to Zoetemelk's wellbeing. The drop in pressure during the flight could have worsened the skull fracture that would only be diagnosed some days later. It could even have killed him. They organised, instead, for the Gan team leader to be transported back home in an ambulance, the trip taking ten agonising hours from the Midi to Zoetemelk's home, where his wife, Françoise, put him to bed and made an appointment for the local doctor to visit.

The next morning, Zoetemelk felt well enough to get on his home trainer, but his condition immediately worsened. Françoise resummoned the doctor, who checked the patient and his X-rays. The doctor confirmed that he could find nothing wrong.

Two days after the crash, Zoetemelk, by no means a heavyweight, had lost six kilos. Worse still, the pain in his head was becoming intolerable. 'I wanted to die. That statement has nothing to do with the expression used in the peloton when a rider goes on the offensive in the attempt to escape. Instead of escaping, mine consisted of putting an end to suffering that had become intolerable,' he revealed in his autobiography, *La Prochaine Étape*. 'I hadn't got enough strength to evade the blows that some kind of invisible jackhammer was striking my head with. My head threatened to blow apart at any moment under this infernal pressure. The root of every hair in my head already seemed to be ablaze. I attempted, as a result of the madness that had seized me, to pull them out. But in vain.'

He confessed he would have gone to get his .22 rifle if his legs had allowed him to stand up. Instead, he ordered Françoise: 'Get me the rifle! Get me the rifle!'

His wife got the doctor rather than the weapon. Then she called him again. And then a fifth time. Ultimately, the intervention of Gan directeur sportif Louis Caput led to Zoetemelk being admitted to hospital in Suresnes, in the western suburbs of Paris. The final diagnosis: head trauma on the petrous portion of the temporal bone and purulent meningitis. The administration of lumbar punctures to treat his meningitis increased Zoetemelk's torment.

At Suresnes, the doctors told Françoise: 'Your husband is now out of danger, but you have to prepare him: his hopes of going back to cycling are gone.' The consultant told Zoetemelk: 'Out of 100 people affected with meningitis like yours, ninety die, and of the 10 per cent who don't, nine go mad.'

After regaining the twelve kilos he eventually lost and the racing condition that went with them, Zoetemelk did return to competition in 1975 and went on to enjoy the greatest successes of his career, including the Tour title, the world championship and two victories on Alpe d'Huez. Yet, in spite of his astounding record, Zoetemelk, a taciturn man who has generally been defined by the words and actions of others, largely receives more criticism than praise, outside his native Holland at least. He is cast as that most derided of riders, *de aanklamper*, as Belgium's press and fans dubbed him – the wheelsucker. But this one-dimensional caricature fails to take into account Zoetemelk's character, the astounding ability of his principal rivals, setbacks like his 1974 crash and, as has more recently been revealed, the severe difficulties and pressures he was under in his personal life.

Born in The Hague in December 1946 to pig and poultry farmers Gerard and Maria, Hendrik Gerardus Joseph 'Joop' Zoetemelk was the eldest of six children. A modest student, he spent his spare time working alongside his father in the family business. Every day, Zoetemelk cycled the eleven kilometres to school in Leiden and back on rough and often wind-blown roads, but showed no interest in sport until well into his teenage years. Instead, his talent first showed in woodwork classes. Happier with a chisel than a pen in his hand, he worked towards becoming a carpenter.

When he was fifteen, he developed a passion for skating, where, surprisingly, this future mountain goat's sporting talent first shone through as a sprinter. Fluctuations in the winter weather meant training on icy waterways was never a certainty, so Zoetemelk stayed in shape by riding on his school bike. Soon caught by the cycling bug, he received his first racing bike as a present on his sixteenth birthday thanks to a promise he made to his mother that he wouldn't take up smoking. He joined a cycling club in Leiden and was persuaded into racing. Seventh in his first cyclo-cross race, Zoetemelk was soon racking up victories. His first earned him sixty-five florins, a pair of shoes and a chicken. 'The Little Redhead', as the local papers nicknamed him, raced another seven cyclo-cross races that first winter, winning them all, including the Dutch junior championship. As he continued to work towards becoming a fully qualified carpenter, the young Joop (pronounced 'Yop' rather than 'Yoop') fitted his cycling in around his other commitments until he started riding for the Amstel Bier amateur team in 1968. That year he rode the Tour of Turkey, where he encountered high mountains for the first time. No one was expecting much of him, but the suppleness he had gained in Holland from spinning low gears when his teammates were pushing bigger ones revealed a very unexpected benefit. On the first mountain stage, 'with his legs going up and down like pistons' according to one teammate, he shocked even himself by staying with the lead group.

'How are you feeling?' asked his team manager, Herman Krott, as that group went up the final climb.

'No problem!' Zoetemelk replied.

'Attack then!' Krott barked out. Zoetemelk rode the

final forty kilometres on his own to win the stage. Six punctures the next day put paid to his overall hopes, but a subsequent second place behind teammate René Pijnen at the Tour of Scotland confirmed the youngster's prowess on the climbs.

Selected later that year to represent his country in the team pursuit, road race and team time-trial events at the 1968 Mexico Olympics, Zoetemelk won a gold medal in the latter alongside Pijnen, Jan Krekels and Fedor den Hertog. But it was his victory the following year in the Tour de l'Avenir that aroused the interest of professional teams, three of them making him offers. On the face of it, opting to sign with Alberic 'Briek' Schotte's Flandria outfit, which featured the De Vlaeminck brothers, Jean-Pierre Monseré, Eric Leman and André Dierickx, was a poor decision. The Belgians weren't interested in much more than the Classics and sprinting, and the introverted Dutch climber who said little was very much an outsider, as he was soon made to realise.

When, after offering strong support to his teammates during the spring Classics campaign, he asked if he could be given a free role in the Amstel Gold Race, his home Classic, Roger De Vlaeminck answered for Schotte: 'There's absolutely no chance of that at all.' Even after Schotte had insisted on giving Zoetemelk protected status at Amstel, all of his teammates apart from fellow Dutchman Eddy Beugels refused to stop when he punctured early in the race.

But there was a significant benefit of being at Flandria. Few of their one-day specialists were interested in riding the Tour. They certainly had no desire to mix it with the best in the mountains, where Zoetemelk was happy to lead and they were content to leave him to it.

It is a little unfortunate to note, given subsequent accusations of wheelsucking, that Schotte's instruction to Zoetemelk prior to the 1970 TdF was: 'Force yourself to follow Merckx as long as possible. That's the best way to usefully continue your apprenticeship.' The Belgian press made much of the fact that all Zoetemelk did was follow Merckx, but the strategy paid off, as the young Dutchman finished a dogged but very distant second to 'The Cannibal'. This hugely impressive Tour debut led to the Dutch media talking him up as the successor to the nation's only previous Tour champion, 1968 winner Jan Janssen, which Zoetemelk later admitted did him no favours at all. 'It was as if Eddy Merckx himself didn't amount to much,' said the Dutchman, who would soon realise the power that the all-conquering Belgian wielded off the bike as well as on it.

The 1971 Tour is best remembered for two stages. Regrettably for Zoetemelk, he was portrayed as the villain after both. The first was to the Alpine resort of Orcières Merlette, where Luis Ocaña handed Merckx the biggest drubbing of his career. Victory by more than eight minutes gave the Spaniard the yellow jersey that Zoetemelk had held for the first time that day. Initially on the attack with Ocaña, Mars-Flandria leader Zoetemelk couldn't stay with the pace and eventually fell back to the Merckx group chasing some minutes behind.

As the yellow jersey, Zoetemelk should have been prominent in the chase behind Ocaña. But trying to stay on terms with the Spanish climber had all but finished him off. 'With a supreme show of pride which resulted, perhaps unconsciously, from the yellow jersey I was still wearing, but which Ocaña had already removed from my shoulders, I leaned over my machine to hang on to the Merckx group. I was naturally incapable of giving the slightest relay. I wasn't the only one to be in that state. With the exception of Merckx, no one else was really riding in that squad of vanquished men,' Zoetemelk said in his own defence.

Humiliated by Ocaña, Merckx hit out at Zoetemelk for his lack of assistance in the pursuit and blamed him for the extent of his defeat. 'Of all of the words Eddy Merckx used, the public would only retain the one of "profiteer" that he'd tagged me with ... It was going to stick to me and would have profound and incredible repercussions with the Belgian public,' Zoetemelk recalled. Ocaña later added fuel to the fire when he suggested that, 'Ordering Zoetemelk to attack is like ordering a paraplegic to get up and walk!'

Still under fire for this performance when the race went into the crucial Pyrenean stage to Luchon, Zoetemelk inadvertently swung the battle for the yellow jersey completely in Merckx's favour in an apocalyptic deluge on the descent of the Col de Menté. Without any heed to his own safety, Merckx attacked in torrents that had sent rocks tumbling onto the road. Trying to chase him, Ocaña overshot a hairpin and crashed. As he was being helped to his feet, Zoetemelk, his brakes next to useless in the conditions, delivered a full-frontal body check, complete with bike. When Ocaña failed to remount after the impact, Merckx rode on to complete a third successive Tour victory, with Zoetemelk his *dauphin* once more.

Looking back, these two second-place finishes behind one of the greatest champions any sport has seen merited praise, but Zoetemelk got little. To an extent this was down to his introverted personality, his inability to come up with a quotable line. According to his biographer, Fred van Slogteren, 'A large part of the press did not like Joop. He was boring, he never said anything. Time after time, his lack of charisma was widely reported. The press loves guys like Jan Janssen, Gerben Karstens and Gerrie Knetemann, who always had a good story. But with Joop you had to delve and decipher.' Even the Dutch press ended up frustrated with Zoetemelk's lack of quotability, which for many equated with a lack of ambition and excessive caution. His standard response to almost any question at the Tour, on good days or bad, was to dodge it by saying, 'Pfft, Paris is still a long way away...' With Zoetemelk offering little of himself, the press turned to riders who did. If they talked of 'wheelsuckers' and 'profiteers', then so much the better.

Zoetemelk's peers also recognise the Dutchman didn't

help his own reputation, Bernard Hinault once declaring, 'Joop was no Cipollini. *Au contraire*,' drawing a comparison with the Italian sprinter whose profile-raising antics included turning up at the Tour start line dressed like Julius Caesar, complete with golden laurel crown, and insisting he wanted to die in an orgy. Speaking to van Slogteren just before his death in 2004, Knetemann, Zoetemelk's teammate at Gan-Mercier and TI-Raleigh, said of his erstwhile colleague, 'Joop was not a dominant figure, he didn't beat his fists on the table. Joop spoke more with his legs than with his mouth… You can sum up Joop very quickly: the man is just like he seems. Everyone who knows him appreciates his value and he just does his own thing. I never caught Joop bullshitting about others. Never ever… It's always much easier to talk about Joop than to talk to him. If you say nothing, then Joop says nothing. Joop is the silent type. This is of course based on a certain degree of shyness.'

Those peers are also quick to defend Zoetemelk's apparent passivity at key points in races, and particularly at the Tour. 'He always had to deal with great riders,' said Knetemann. 'He started up against Merckx and ended up facing Hinault.' Lucien Van Impe, who was accused of currying favour with both of these great riders, says, 'We riders knew all too well that not just anyone could stick on Merckx's wheel. We all tried to do that but there was only one man who could and that was Joop. He is one of the best cyclists ever.'

The question that should surely be asked more often about Zoetemelk is whether he might have been even more successful if it hadn't been for the horrific injuries he sustained at Valras-Plage in 1974 and the difficulties he faced in his home life. On the first point, his then team-mate Raymond Poulidor, who with a record eight Tour podium finishes to his credit has one more than the Dutchman, insists Zoetemelk was held back by the crash, believing he was on the verge of a major breakthrough that year. 'Zoetemelk was soon the only one among us, myself included, to be able to stay on the wheel of the super Eddy Merckx. I know that he's been widely reproached, particularly in the Belgian press, for not showing himself as capable of relaying Eddy. But that's a bit like asking a 2CV to overtake a sporty saloon car,' said Poulidor.

'In my opinion, before his accident in 1974, Zoetemelk...had the same power as Merckx. He opened up extraordinary gaps on the passes and in time trials. He exited undefeated from all of the stage races he took part in. That accident, which I witnessed, has probably deprived us of one of the greatest champions of the modern era...The Zoetemelk of 1974 – and for me there's no doubt about it – would have shown himself to be at least at the level of the best Hinault. The latter, though, would undoubtedly have stifled his ambition, which was often lacking.'

Zoetemelk has himself suggested that he had cast off the label of 'wheelsucker' that many, and particularly

Belgian fans and the nation's media, ascribed to him. He insists that in 1974, which was shaping up as his best season, he had finally freed himself of what he described as his 'Eddy complex' and believes he could have won the Tour that year, that there were signs Merckx was physically spent. 'Often the only rider capable of staying on the wheel of super-Merckx, I had already achieved an exploit of a kind. Now it was his turn to hang on to avoid being distanced...I wasn't described any longer as the wheelsucker!' the Dutchman said of his early season exploits in 1974.

It is harder to assess what impact his marital difficulties had on his career. He married Françoise Duchaussoy, the daughter of long-time Tour de France publicity caravan director Jacques Duchaussoy, in 1971. It appeared a happy union, the couple taking over a hotel near Meaux and having two children. However, following his wife's death in 2008, Zoetemelk revealed she had battled against alcoholism for years. Speaking to journalists Joop Holthausen, Jacob Bergsma and Peter Ouwerkerk for a biography entitled – with an evident touch of irony – *Joop Zoetemelk, Een Open Boek,* he confessed that he still did not understand the reason for his wife's alcohol abuse and that racing had offered him an escape.

'When I was away at races, I could forget about everything. I didn't talk about it at all. Even my brothers and sisters didn't know. But I do realise that without her I would have had an even better career. That's naturally something that eats away at you,' he confessed following the book's publication in 2011. Perhaps not surprisingly, given his long-standing reluctance to say much at all about anything, Zoetemelk didn't describe how he managed not only to keep his career on track, but to challenge for the greatest prizes it offered. He did acknowledge that the pressure of running a hotel that was failing and on which he had a huge mortgage meant that he had to race more often than he wanted to, and that Françoise's illness became so acute that she was unable to look after their children. He contemplated divorce, but Jacques Duchaussoy threatened to prevent him seeing his children if he went ahead with it. 'I later told my father-in-law that if I hadn't become involved with his family my career would have been much more successful,' Zoetemelk revealed.

Holthausen suggests that the turmoil in Zoetemelk's personal life was why he changed from a regular guy who liked a laugh and joke into the retiring personality he became. It could also explain his devotion to racing, which became an obsession. He competed until he was almost forty-one, starting and finishing what was until recently a record sixteen Tours. 'Most people race in order to live. Joop just lives to race,' five-time Tour winner Jacques Anquetil said of the Dutchman. This is backed up by those who knew him well. Peter Post, his team director at TI-Raleigh, described him as 'someone who thinks about the bike twenty-four hours a day', and as a man who focused on 'eating, sleeping and exercising'.

Zoetemelk was always in the shadow of Merckx and Hinault, his brash, brutal and all-conquering rivals, off the road as well as on it. Yet he played a more fundamental role than either of them in establishing the legend of Alpe d'Huez. He was the magnet that pulled Dutch fans from their traditional spectating heartland in Bordeaux to their much more celebrated one at the Alpine resort.

Long overshadowed on the sporting front by neighbours Belgium and West Germany, Dutch teams and athletes became more prominent from the mid-1960s onwards. Following figure skater Sjoukje Dijkstra's victory at the 1964 Winter Olympics in Innsbruck, the country's first success at the Games, Ajax started to emerge as one of the great powers of world football with Johan Cruyff as their star, and Jan Janssen claimed the elusive first win in the Tour de France.

Zoetemelk was part of this new wave of talent, his gold medal-winning ride in the team time trial in Mexico City coming three months on from Janssen's yellow jersey success. Yet, while Janssen continued the Dutch tradition of producing riders who were strong in time trials and sprints and who could climb a bit, Zoetemelk offered something very different. As the Tour became increasingly focused on the high mountains in the early 1970s, his ability in that terrain made him Holland's perennial challenger and produced a nation of 'Jopie' fanatics. There were already thousands of them up at Pla d'Adet in 1975 when Zoetemelk served up the first high-altitude victory for the Dutch, that success providing the impetus for thousands more to head for Alpe d'Huez on the first holiday weekend of July 1976 to support him.

Although Hennie Kuiper insists his Alpe d'Huez victory in 1977 marked the real birth of the climb as 'Dutch mountain', and there's no denying the brilliance of the racing and finale that day, Zoetemelk remained the Dutch standard-bearer. Asked about his status in his homeland by *L'Équipe* prior to the double dose of the Alpe in 1979, he replied, 'I'm the most popular rider, the Poulidor of the country to some extent.'

About a month beforehand, Zoetemelk had spent a fortnight training on the climb. It proved a propitious choice. The stage starting and finishing on the Alpe was due to be preceded by one running between Les Menuires and the ski station at Vars, south of Briançon. A local developer had promised the race the use of his chalets and apartments at the resort. However, when his application for a new project at Vars was rejected three weeks before the Tour started, he tore up the agreement, which meant the re-routing of the stage. The mayor at Alpe d'Huez was happy to accommodate the Tour for an extra day, especially as the resort got the additional stage gratis.

Vilified once again for his perceived passiveness in the face of Hinault's dominance on this re-routed stage won by Portugal's Joaquim Agostinho, Zoetemelk responded with the cycling equivalent of a two-fingered salute on the one that followed. 'It was the last mountain [in the race], and I didn't want to leave my favoured terrain without leaving my mark. So, as soon as we left Bourg d'Oisans, I attacked,' he later explained.

With more Dutch than ever on the mountain and tens of thousands of French fans chanting 'Ee-no! Ee-no! Ee-no!' as the riders passed, there was no better place or moment for Zoetemelk to cast away his reputation as a wheelsucker once and for all. After accelerating right from the very bottom of the Alpe, the Dutchman quickly opened up a lead of forty seconds on Hinault, who was riding in typically relentless fashion, his bushy brows bristling furiously. Although his yellow jersey was not seriously under threat, the Frenchman was still determined to impose his rule and he trimmed his deficit back to twenty seconds. Most would have yielded, but Zoetemelk rallied, stretching his advantage to forty seconds over second-placed Van Impe, with Hinault another seven back on the Belgian.

'Knowing that you can't quit, even when almost everything seems lost, and provoking an adversary who is reputedly superior without taking into account the risks involved is one of the essential qualities of a champion, which Joop Zoetemelk can now take pride in being,' wrote Pierre Chany. 'It was an effort that was both an act of revolt and a cry of liberation at the same time... Because Joop Zoetemelk had fully committed himself to the dangerous challenge set before him, not by the wearer of the yellow jersey, but by a critical public that still persisted, even yesterday, in regarding him as a rider who is too economical with his effort.'

Chany's colleague Jean-Marie Leblanc described how Zoetemelk 'shook every little bit of effort out of his frail carcass' and related how his effort drove the very, very many Dutch tourists holidaying in the region and the 'Joopie... Joopie' [sic] to the edge of hysteria. The future Tour director signed off by saying the 'unforgettable climb towards Alpe d'Huez' was one of the best he'd seen as a race follower. 'To achieve this kind of little exploit, you need talent and to be a real racer. And, despite all that some people say about you, you are definitely that.'

Zoetemelk's victory on the Alpe that afternoon, which he still regards as his best at the Tour, set in place a key stepping stone towards his overall victory in the race the following year. During the race, TI-Raleigh manager Peter Post approached him with an offer to lead the Dutch squad, which was packed with *rouleurs* and sprinters who made it a powerful force in the Classics and team time-trials, but it lacked an obvious general classification leader. Initially, Zoetemelk was reluctant to take up Post's offer, fearing his objectives might conflict with those of Knetemann and Jan Raas. Ultimately, though, both team and rider got what they most needed. TI-Raleigh had a Tour contender; Zoetemelk had the most organised and best equipped team riding for him. The result was the yellow jersey in Paris the next summer.

Although it is still widely maintained that Zoetemelk's

was a lucky victory that came entirely thanks to the injury-enforced abandon of Bernard Hinault, the protagonists repeatedly insist this was not the case. When Hinault quit in the yellow jersey, with half the race still to run, he led Zoetemelk by a mere twenty-one seconds. The Dutchman admits Hinault's injury was hugely significant but points out: 'How did Hinault end up with that knee injury? He was under pressure, and keeping your body in shape is all part of the task at the Tour.'

As for Hinault, when he was once again asked about his famous night-time flit from the Tour – when he realised his knee was not going to hold up in the mountains – and the consequent loss of the Tour title to Zoetemelk, he replied: 'In 1980, he won the Tour and he completely deserved it.' Indeed, he went even further in his support of Zoetemelk's reputation. 'He was the one who made life most difficult for me. Contrary to what a lot of people say, he wasn't a follower. He was a fighter. He never gave up, but he simply didn't have any luck,' he told Breton paper *Le Télégramme*. 'He came up against Merckx, then he was knocked back physically and then he came up against me. Nevertheless, he was second six times in the Tour de France.'

The negative perception of Zoetemelk has stuck even into the modern era. In 2014, when *Procycling* ranked the top twenty-five winners of all time, Zoetemelk placed only twenty-fifth and out came that old Belgian joke once again about his paleness from being in Merckx's shadow. Yet, his 1980 success, plus those six second places at the Tour, three behind Hinault and two behind Merckx, underline the extent to which Zoetemelk is still defined by the words of others. As 'The Cannibal' and 'The Badger' are established unanimously among the top three riders of all time, Zoetemelk surely merits a place close behind them in the sport's pantheon, perhaps even right behind them, his supporters might insist with a smile.

6

Until Caput manages to find his way past the Thévenet group and up alongside them, Lucien Van Impe and Joop Zoetemelk continue to cooperate. Through bend fifteen, where the road ramps up again after a shallower run from La Garde, and then bend fourteen, their collaboration is still paying dividends. Their lead extends to fifty-five seconds. At bend thirteen, which sweeps them leftwards, they can see the next few switchbacks ahead, but sticking to the racing line on the right-hand side of the road right next to the cliff face denies them a glimpse of a spectacular view back down towards La Garde and Bourg d'Oisans, which is now a long way below in the valley.

Just before bend twelve, at Le Ribot d'Huez, their advantage goes beyond a minute. The road carries them over two streams that plunge down the mountainside and up to the tightest hairpin on the Alpe at Le Ribot. When Thévenet leads his little band around it seventy seconds later, the Frenchman is already climbing away from the corner as the last rider in the ten-strong line is coming into it.

Above bend eleven, where the huge overhang requires regular repinning work to secure the metal mesh draped over it to prevent rock falls, the stage takes an unexpected turn. As so often in professional cycling, the individual professional's interests often don't fit neatly with those of his team sponsor. In this case, Van Impe and Zoetemelk are Lowlanders riding for French teams – Gitane and Gan-Mercier, respectively.

Gitane's Cyrille Guimard is slightly surprised but delighted at what he's seeing. After months of coaxing and ultimately coercion, Guimard has convinced his leader that he can win the Tour and also of the plan required to achieve this. As the French DS looks on from the driver's seat of the Gitane car now tucked in just behind the two leaders, Van Impe is carrying out that plan to the letter, riding himself into a two-man duel for the title.

Gan-Mercier DS Louis Caput, however, has a dilemma. Realising that the gap back to the beloved Poulidor in the Thévenet group is now unbridgeable unless some catastrophic physical or mechanical failure besets the two pacesetters, Caput's challenge is to ensure that Zoetemelk wins, but not by so much that Poulidor's hopes of overall victory are extinguished on the very first day in the high mountains. Given the OK by the commissaire to advance, he stamps down on the Peugeot's accelerator and draws up alongside the Dutchman.

'Joop!' he calls out. 'Joop, remember not to press too hard.

*There are more mountain stages still to come and you also
don't want to embarrass Poulidor in front of the French
public by finishing five minutes ahead of him.' In trying to
keep the revered 'Poupou' in contention, Caput must know
that he's also preventing Thévenet from being finished off.*

*Zoetemelk knows this too and considers for a moment.
The next day,* Het Vrije Volk *will report: 'Unlike what a
potential Tour winner would have done, Zoetemelk listened
to his boss.'*

KINGS FOR A DAY

It is with good reason that Alpe d'Huez has been dubbed
the Tour de France's 'lucky mountain'. Thanks to its
southerly aspect and extremely temperate microclimate,
the weather has only ever been a concern when the sun
gets too fierce. More importantly, from the racing point
of view, the mountain has never failed to produce a memorable spectacle.

Generally, great champions or riders in the thick of the
battle for the yellow jersey have zigzagged their way up to
cycling immortality. But there have been surprise winners,
too. Taking advantage of stalemate between the major
contenders, a handful of unheralded performers have
managed to steal away and permanently raise themselves
from cycling obscurity with victory on the biggest stage of
all. More than the great champions, these lesser names
have become defined by their success on the Alpe, their
names permanently commemorated on the signs on the

twenty-one numbered hairpins and forever associated with those of Fausto Coppi, Bernard Hinault and, for now at least, Lance Armstrong.

After Coppi, Zoetemelk and Kuiper had initiated the climb's stratospheric rise from obscurity, the first rider to upset the favourites on Alpe d'Huez was Joaquim Agostinho, who won the 1979 stage that had initially been destined to finish in Vars. Burly, powerfully muscular and very dark of complexion, for Jacques Goddet the Portuguese was 'the bull with the tanned skin', while Pierre Chany described him as being 'of average height, but as solid as a rhinoceros'.

Agostinho's path to the pro ranks was more typical of professionals in the pre-war period, being accidental rather than planned. Born to peasant farmers in Torres Vedras, fifty kilometres north of Lisbon, he was one of six children who walked barefoot to school. At twelve, he started working alongside his parents in the fields, and would probably have stayed on that path if he hadn't been called up to undertake three years' national service in the mid-1960s. Sent to Mozambique, he fought in the front line. His fortunes changed, though, when a colonel in his regiment saw him playing football and noted his physical strength.

The officer gave the twenty-year-old Agostinho a bike and the task of ferrying messages back and forth between the front lines and HQ. Covering up to fifty kilometres on a hefty army bike, the first he'd ever ridden, he quickly made a name for himself by completing his missions in two hours when it took other soldiers five. When the 23-year-old Agostinho returned to civilian life in Portugal in 1967, his comrades pressed him to make the most of this innate ability.

Back home in Torres Vedras, he used some of the salary he had earned during his national service to buy a sit-up-and-beg bike to ride between the family home and the vegetable fields where he worked. One day, he crossed paths with riders from the Sporting Clube de Portugal in Lisbon. They encouraged him to follow them, and he did, responding easily to all of their attempts to drop him. Come back tomorrow with a better bike, they told him. Agostinho bought one on hire purchase and did exactly that.

Taken under the wing of former Tour of Portugal winner João Roque, Agostinho won his first race, lapping the field. But he saw no future for himself in cycling given his age, lack of experience in riding in a bunch and desire to marry his boss's daughter. Sporting's directors weren't convinced either, but Roque persuaded both sides to trust him. Selected for Sporting's *espoirs* team for the Tour of Portugal, Agostinho almost won the race.

Still an amateur, he claimed the national road and time-trial titles, which earned him a place at the World Championships. Knowing little of tactics or of the reputations of Eddy Merckx, Jacques Anquetil, Rik Van Looy and Felice Gimondi, Agostinho attacked right from the gun. Having blown the race apart, Agostinho was only caught on the last lap by eventual winner Vittorio Adorni and the group chasing the Italian. He was fifteenth of just nineteen finishers. Another devastating performance at a subsequent race in Brazil convinced illustrious French DS Jean de Gribaldy to offer the Portuguese his first pro contract the following year.

Unlike thousands of his compatriots making their way across Europe looking for work, Agostinho flew out first class. According to French magazine *Pédale*, Amalia Rodrigues, 'Queen of the Fado', was sitting next to him. 'Watch out for those French girls, Joaquim. A lot of them are going to try to seduce you.' Instead, it was the Portuguese public that was seduced.

He made his Tour debut that summer, winning two stages in a race dominated by Merckx. It has been said that the Belgian feared Agostinho, with his boxer's physique and huge calves, more than any other rider that year, such was the extent of his power. But Merckx may also have had concerns about the Portuguese's handling skills in the bunch, where he had a reputation for nerves and crashing. 'He didn't know how to control his own strength,' said his faithful mechanic Francisco Araújo. 'He couldn't turn when there was a tight bend. He finished his first Tour with his knees and elbows covered with plasters.'

Although often compared to bristlingly formidable animals, Agostinho was a gentle man who regarded the sport as his best means of maintaining and stocking the ranch where he lived with his family near Lisbon. Raphaël Geminiani, his DS when he was with De Gribaldy, insisted Merckx was far from the only leading rider who was fearful of the Portuguese. 'But he didn't have the vicious streak required to impose himself on them,' said Geminiani. His overriding thought was for his family and his animals, which in addition to cattle and horses included a chimpanzee he had brought back from Africa.

As the Tour was the best way of ensuring he could stock his ranch, he dedicated himself to it almost entirely, riding it thirteen times and finishing in the top ten on eight occasions. Third behind Bernard Hinault and Zoetemelk in 1978, he repeated that feat a year on, principally as a result of his solo victory at Alpe d'Huez. He started the stage without any set plan at all, deciding to see how the race unfolded. Descending the Lautaret pass towards the Romanche valley, he noticed that race leader Hinault was not getting his Renault team to chase down noted climbers who had clipped away off the front of the peloton. 'They had got their exit pass, so I said to myself why not me as well?'

He worked his way up to and through the small groups ahead of him on the road, until he joined the two leaders, Lucien Didier and Guido Van Calster, at bend seventeen. Fearing the expected rush of attacks from the yellow jersey group two minutes behind which could wipe out their advantage, the Flandria-Ça Va Seul leader did just what it said on his jersey and went off on his own, extending his advantage as he pummelled his bike.

'Agostinho tackled the climb in his very characteristic style, slumped over his machine, his hands firmly fixed on the brake hoods, sat on the nose of his saddle with his head bared. He had unzipped his jersey to its full extent on his muscular and hairy torso in order to counter the heat and lack of air,' wrote Jean-Marie Leblanc, who described the Portuguese and the mountains as having 'the same ruggedness, the same impression of solidity. The brute strength of the man seems tailor-made for this rocky landscape that we've encountered.'

The victory enabled Agostinho to add a few more head of cattle to his ranch at Torres Vedras. Five years later, having recently turned forty-one, he was still committed to that goal. Leading the Tour of the Algarve with a fourteenth Tour appearance in his sights, he crashed heavily on his head after two dogs ran into the pack sprinting into the finish at Quarteira. He walked away for treatment to his injuries and returned to his team hotel, only to fall ill later that evening. He was taken initially to the hospital in Loulé, but its X-ray machine wasn't working, before being moved to Faro, where the hospital didn't have a neurological department. With no helicopter available to fly him to Lisbon for emergency treatment, he had to endure a four-hour transfer to the capital in an ambulance. He fell into a coma en route and died nine days later.

By then a national hero to compare with legendary

footballer Eusébio, he received a state funeral attended by Portugal's president and prime minister. Hundreds of thousands of mourners lined the fifty-kilometre route between the Estrela Basilica in Lisbon and his final resting place in Silveira, many of them applauding as his funeral cortège passed, just as many thousands had done when he rode to his most famous victory, on Alpe d'Huez, just five years earlier.

As well as the traditional signpost commemoration, in his case on bend seventeen of the Alpe, Agostinho is also remembered with a memorial another three hairpins up the mountain, where he made his stage-winning attack. Cut from grey marble with a profile of Agostinho in relief, the stone was erected by his beloved Sporting Clube de Portugal, whose green-and-white hoops he wore as both an amateur and a professional.

By coincidence, the sign on bend fourteen pays tribute to another of the Alpe's lesser-known names, who also had an exceptionally long career. Nicknamed 'The Mountain Flea', Switzerland's Beat Breu could not have been any more different to Agostinho. Weighing just 57 kilos, the scrawny ex-postman, who had told his teachers he was going to be a clown when he left school, looked like he could have succumbed to a single squeeze from the Portuguese, but packed a massive punch on the climbs.

Never was this more notable than during his first two seasons as leader of the Cilo team. In 1981 he prevailed in his national tour. The following season, Cilo unleashed him at the Tour for the first time. Two mountain stage wins, the second of them at Alpe d'Huez, resulted in wide-spread acclaim for 'the new Van Impe' as *L'Équipe* dubbed him, with his 'morphology of a jockey'.

Looking back on his brief flowering at the Tour, Breu is always amused by the extent to which his victory at Alpe d'Huez overshadows the success he had taken four days earlier at Pla d'Adet. 'It was also a great victory and certainly just as hard, but Alpe d'Huez is much more important,' says Breu, also dubbed 'Pinocchio' for the obvious reason.

His victory on the Alpe is now remembered as much for the pared down Cilo bike on which he took it. The Swiss manufacturer had started using state-of-the-art Columbus tubing and constructed an extremely light-weight frame with a short wheelbase featuring a cutaway curve in the vertical seat-tube to accommodate Breu's rear wheel. They married this with several weight-saving devices, including plastic brake hoods, super-light wheels, tapeless bars, to which a gear changer was fitted to prevent an unnecessary movement that might have been required by standard downtube-fitted gear levers.

After his Cilo teammates had set an infernal pace up the Col d'Ornon in order to prevent a breakaway thwarting Breu's hopes, their leader switched to his climbing bike on the approach to Alpe d'Huez. On the opening ramps, Breu held tight during the initial burst, but stayed near the front of the lead group, as per the instructions of Cilo DS Auguste Girard, who had told his leader to wait until the final three kilometres of the climb before making his attack. His caveat was that Breu should move if he sensed one of the general classification contenders was in trouble.

Noticing Zoetemelk was grimacing and sensing this was something more than the Dutchman's perennially agonised look, Breu upped his cadence slightly, drawing ahead of the group. Without a glance back, he increased his pace a little more, gliding steadily away, the ease of his acceleration belying the chaos ensuing in his wake. The group was blown to smithereens. French climber Robert Alban responded, as did Zoetemelk briefly, before race leader Hinault brought the Dutchman back into line.

So began a game of cat and mouse between Breu and Alban, with the Swiss playing his rival all the way to the finish. In blazing heat and in front of a record crowd on the climb, the pair were rarely more than fifty metres apart. *L'Équipe*'s Pierre Chany was captivated by their contest, writing: 'On this climb of Alpe d'Huez that has become a tower of Babel where holidaymakers of every nationality had gathered in furnace-like heat, Beat Breu and Robert Alban, David and Goliath, served up an epic and poignant duel of the kind that only races in the high mountains are capable of producing.'

He described how Breu allowed Alban to close up to him, which gave the Swiss a few moments to recover. Then, having judged that the Frenchman had got close enough, Breu would accelerate again, forcing Alban to make another effort. Chany makes the strategy sound straightforward, but Alban's dogged pursuit had Breu worried. In the Cilo team car, Girard could see his rider looking back again and again. Concerned that Breu was focusing too much on what was going on behind him and not enough on the road ahead, Girard drove up alongside him and said he would honk his horn if anyone started to gain on the Swiss.

No sooner had Girard dropped back than Alban came again, and off went the horn. 'I noticed that I could quickly open up a gap on Alban, and then I would ease off,' said Breu. 'When he got to within five or ten metres of me, I could hear him panting. When he got that close I would up my pace and open the gap again. I had to do this because if he'd got onto my back wheel I would never have shaken him off.'

Lauded as the successor to Charly Gaul and Federico Bahamontes as well as Van Impe, Breu rarely reached these heights again. He can't explain why, but admits his head was turned by the success he had at such a young age. Hailed as a potential Tour champion, he was advised to work on his time-trialling and give more thought to feeding during races, as he often suffered sudden physical frailty. But Breu, who admits he was only ever really inter-ested in riding well in the mountains, liked to do things his own way and rarely took advice on board. Consequently, at twenty-four, his Tour heroics were already behind him. Although he rode and completed another seven Tours, he never finished in the top twenty or took another stage win.

Nevertheless he continued to win races, clocking up 242 by the time he hung up his wheels in 1996, most were in smaller races or in cyclo-cross, where he campaigned latterly with considerable success. Twice national champion in an era when Switzerland was blessed with considerable off-road talent, Breu became one of the biggest draws in the winter discipline, attracting substantial appearance fees, especially on home ground, where he remained hugely popular. But, even as his cycling star faded in the international arena, Breu began to gain notoriety in other domains, making headlines on the front rather than the back pages of the Swiss papers.

Breu invested all of his savings of 512,000 Swiss francs in a property scheme overseen by his elder brother, Urs, a director at a Swiss bank. But when the Swiss property market collapsed in the late 1980s, the two brothers lost everything. Urs Breu was imprisoned in 1990 after it was discovered he had embezzled sixty-three million swiss francs (£25 million) from his bank.

'The Mountain Flea' continued to compete with plenty of success until he was almost forty. To keep his family afloat, he then fulfilled the claim he'd made when he was at school and became a clown of sorts. He spent the next seven years working as a comedian and cutting the ribbon for anything that ensured a financial return. In 2001, he turned to a new venture, opening up the

Longhorn City Lust-saloon in Oberbüren. The sex club sank after a year.

Despite suffering a stroke in 2003 and requiring heart surgery a year later to correct a congenital defect, Breu announced his intention to return to elite-level racing in 2007. By then forty-nine and the owner of more chins than Tour stage victories, Breu returned to intensive training and claimed he had received a new lease of life thanks to a 'rejuvenating' water called H2O3. Working in a PR role for the product, Breu asserted the water could 'reverse the biological clock' and that he felt 'twenty years younger'. He determined to prove it by taking on the best of Switzerland's cyclo-cross racers.

But this was no fairy-tale return. Lapped by future BMC Racing team member Simon Zahner halfway through the thirty-kilometre race, 'The St Gallen Flea' finished with just two riders behind him. Worse still, tests carried out in a Swiss lab revealed that H2O3 contained an ingredient with a similar chemical make-up to caustic soda. Instead of swigging it, Breu should have been cleaning his bike with it.

Breu stepped away from cycling again but continued to be headline material thanks to his personal life. In May 2009 he married his girlfriend of six years' standing, Heidi Stampfli. One hundred and sixty-seven days later, the pair split. Stampfli complained in the Swiss tabloid press about Breu's overnight change into a chauvinist who wanted to dominate every aspect of her life. The ex-rider's mother,

Helen Breu, saw things differently, responding: 'Heidi is simply lazy. She refused to wash and cook for my Beat. It's no wonder he's been coming to me for months to get his underwear washed!'

Breu found a new girlfriend when he took his son to compete in a motocross event in the Czech Republic. But scandal blew up again when the Swiss press trumpeted her conversion to Islam. This was news to Breu and his girlfriend, who challenged the story, which turned out to have been lifted from a Czech newspaper and then mangled by online translation software. In 2013, three weeks after splitting with his Czech girlfriend, Breu and Heidi were reunited. His next act was to declare bankruptcy.

'I've been trying to pay the money off for more than twenty years. But it just was not enough,' he told Swiss paper *Blick*. 'Now we will finally be able to start again from zero. I could never repay the whole debt with ordinary jobs. That's why I was always looking for alternative jobs in which I was hoping to make more money. The debt has almost crushed me. Now I just want to be able to live normally again with my Heidi.'

Today working as a rep for a bike parts company, Breu admits he still keeps an eye on the cycling scene. But only ever watches live coverage of one stage, the day the race heads for Alpe d'Huez.

That is one stage more than 1987 winner Federico Echave ever sees of the race. Now living a very quiet life tending to his animals and vegetables on his farm near the

Basque town of Guernica, Echave is twenty-five kilos heavier than he was in his racing prime, when he became the first Spanish rider to triumph on the Alpe. Echave's success was unusual because he was supposed to be playing a support role to his team leader, who finished a very disappointed second.

In what was the most unpredictable of Tours, the stage began with Irishman Stephen Roche holding a narrow lead over Spain's Pedro Delgado. The yellow jersey had already changed hands seven times, and the only thing that was sure as the peloton left Villard de Lans was that Roche was going to have a tough time becoming the latest rider to maintain just a fleeting grasp on the lead. With the general classification contenders certain to be preoccupied with each, BH DS Javier Mínguez scented an opportunity for his unfashionable team to take advantage.

Mínguez's hopes rested on his leader and best climber, Anselmo Fuerte. His strategy was well tried. He ordered the other BH riders to infiltrate all of the early attacks with a view to at least one of them acting as a stepping stone for their leader on the Alpe. Consequently, when a twenty-five-rider break formed, BH had three riders in it including Echave, who that morning had told roommate Laudelino Cubino, 'This climb really suits me, "Lale", just you wait and see.' Although now remembered primarily as a climber, at the time Echave's rep was as an all-rounder. Like most Basques, he liked a climb, but he was no mug in a time trial and also packed a good sprint in a small group. He hardly seemed a potential winner of the Tour's biggest stage, but that was about to change.

The escapees reached the Col de Laffrey more than six minutes up on the peloton. Just before the top of this tough precursor to the final test, Echave struck out on his own. He increased his advantage on the descent and approach to the Alpe. He was still four minutes up on the yellow jersey group when he started to climb again. When the general classification leaders reached the Alpe, Fuerte fulfilled his part in Mínguez's strategy, breaking clear of it and riding past all of the flagging members of the earlier breakaway, all except Echave that is. By the time Fuerte forced his way up to the finish, almost falling off his bike as he crossed the line such was the effort he had made, Echave was already being wiped down by a BH soigneur, ready for his next ascent up onto the Tour podium.

A couple of minutes later, Delgado crossed the line to become the eighth rider to wear yellow in this maelstrom of a Tour. In almost any other year, taking it on the Alpe would be a guarantee of eventual success in Paris, but not this time. As was his habit, Delgado gathered himself before submitting to the media onslaught. '¡Eres líder! ¡Eres líder!' the frenzied Spanish hacks yelled at him, but although this was a great day for the Spanish, Delgado insisted Roche was still the favourite. He wasn't about to get carried away – with good reason as it turned out.

Having collected his victory bouquet and received the

crowd's acclaim, the beaming Echave tried to explain how an all-rounder had won cycling's most renowned mountain stage. It was, he said, down to his doctors, who had helped him improve physically. 'I don't know why but since this year I've been climbing well. It's probably because my backside doesn't weigh as much,' said the Basque rider, who would become one of Swiss star Tony Rominger's key lieutenants over the following few seasons.

One of the last riders to switch from downtube gear changers to automatic gear-brake shifters, and adopt clipless pedals to replace toeclips and straps, Echave retired in 1996. He bought a house in the countryside, invested some of his money in a sports shop that is run by his wife and his sister, and got on with enjoying life. He dabbled in amateur team management for a while, did a little bit of radio commentary work, but didn't really enjoy either. After spending so many seasons slogging on the pro racing circuit, he wasn't interested in working at all.

'Nowadays, my biggest responsibility is planting lettuces, going fishing for eels or taking the dogs out for a walk,' he said on the twenty-fifth anniversary of his Alpe d'Huez success. 'It's a long time since I set the alarm clock and life is good. I don't want to give the idea that my life is ideal. Some days seem very long to me, almost interminable, and on those occasions I have to break my routine and try to find myself some job that needs doing, but when I retired from cycling I said to myself: "Fede, you've spent too many years stressed out, years when you couldn't even allow yourself to be affected by a simple cold. You've earned your money, you've made your investments, so why don't you focus on living?" The reality is that since then I've not worked. I don't know if this is good or bad, but I do believe I can't complain: cycling gave me money and I knew how best to make use of it to live, to avoid submitting to a routine, to labour reforms that could have annoyed me...No, my life is something else and it's above all that.'

Echave said he still had some of his bikes but confessed he never rides them now. 'I prefer to go walking in the countryside and also I really panic when I go out on the road. I almost die with fear when I see all of the cars. It's not like it was in my era, they don't respect cyclists any more.' As for his most celebrated day on the bike, Echave revealed that he could remember very little about it 'because so much time has passed and I'm not a man who focuses on the past. I remember that it was a hard climb, especially at the start and the end, that it seemed like it was never going to finish. But in life you have to know when to end a cycle and focus on what is most important to you and I'm now a very long way removed from cycling.'

Like Echave, 1994 Alpe winner Roberto Conti was a wingman who ended up in the right place at the right time thanks to circumstance. However, while the Spaniard was opening the road for a leader who failed to make the junction with his domestique, Conti started his ride into the history books with no leader to support and only two teammates left on his Lampre squad thanks to injury, crashes and stomach problems. For once, Conti could ride for himself and his move was to infiltrate the thirteen-strong break that slipped away early in the day.

Conti, whose heavily bagged eyes gave him a doleful look that fitted well with his lugubrious nature, had two cards to play. He got on well with race leader Miguel Indurain, whose Banesto team had tried and failed to sign the Italian at the end of the previous season. He was also a strong climber and, thanks to the early departure of Lampre leader Maurizio Fondriest, was still relatively fresh. When the dozen escapees left up front reached the foot of the final climb with an advantage of almost nine minutes, it was evident one of them was destined to win.

In Lampre's distinctive blue and fuchsia colours, Conti stood out on the front of the group as they climbed toward the first hairpin. Quick to respond to a couple of early attacks, Conti led around bend twenty-one, chased down Spaniard Roberto Torres and just kept going. By bend twenty he had opened up a gap of 100 metres and never faltered. In the final straight, after marking the moment with the baby-rocking celebration made famous that summer by Brazil's World Cup-winning striker Bebeto, Conti broke into the broad smile that earned him the nickname 'Horse' as he became the first rider to take his debut victory as a professional on Alpe d'Huez. He would add just one more during a career that covered seventeen seasons at the top level.

Although the day should have belonged to Conti, Marco Pantani hijacked his place in the limelight in setting a record time for the ascent of thirty-seven minutes and fifteen seconds. Both hailed from Romagna, were training partners, good friends, and, in 1997, became teammates when Conti joined Pantani at Mercatone Uno. As Conti admitted, the two men were quite different personalities, but those differences brought them together on the road, where Conti's qualities as a *gregario* were fully demonstrated when Pantani completed a Giro–Tour double in 1998. Conti was absent when Pantani was ejected from the 1999 Giro two days away from a successful defence of his title, but, like so many of 'Il Pirata's' tightknit band, he insists the incident was the start of the end for Pantani.

In the aftermath of Pantani's drug-related suicide in February 2004, Conti described how he had tried to help his friend, but had been pushed away. 'He instinctively did that, pushed you away. He refused help from anyone. One day he told me directly: "Roberto, be kind and just leave me in peace, I feel better on my own." ... He loved to enjoy himself, he would get intoxicated by speeding in his car, on motorbikes, by discotheques. When I tried to share my family values with him, I could read in his expression the incomprehension of a world that wasn't his at all.'

Italy's unprecedented run of success during the 1990s, during which Andy Hampsten was the only non-Italian to win on the mountain, continued with another rider connected to Pantani, although he was one of his long-standing rivals. Giuseppe Guerini was one of Italy's illustrious class of 1970, along with Ivan Gotti, Wladimir Belli, Francesco Casagrande, Michele Bartoli and Pantani. Nicknamed 'Turbo' by his family because of his childhood obsession with the turbines at the power station near his home in Vertova, Guerini was the least renowned of this distinguished but ultimately tainted group.

In 1999, tempted by a big boost in salary, he made what was then an unusual move, from leadership of the Italian Polti team to a support role on the German Telekom squad led by 1997 Tour winner Jan Ullrich. However, when Ullrich was forced to miss that year's race due to a knee injury, 'Beppe-Turbo' was shunted back up to a more prominent role.

Although Alpe d'Huez arrived only halfway into the Tour, it had effectively ended as a contest the day before when Lance Armstrong steamrollered the field at Sestrières. Guerini had been crushed like the rest, and looked to be destined for the same fate again when he dropped out of the back of the yellow jersey group approaching bend twenty-one. Gradually, though, Guerini worked his way back up to the Armstrong group, realising as he bridged up with seven kilometres remaining that he was the only Italian in it. He sat tight until lone breakaway Stéphane Heulot had been reeled in with 3.5 kilometres remaining, then accelerated with everything he had.

Guerini's would have been a well-judged but pretty unremarkable victory as far as Alpe d'Huez is concerned if it hadn't been for a camera-toting French fan standing in the middle of the road just 700 metres from the finish. As the Italian climber sped towards him while he peered through his viewfinder, photographer Eric evidently thought Guerini was still a good distance away. Then, suddenly, he wasn't. Like two well-drilled line dancers, the pair went the same way, then again, before Guerini clattered into the young fan and hit the deck. To his credit, Eric did help the Italian get up but, with one hand still gripping his camera, quickly disappeared back into the crowd as another fan did the right thing and gave Guerini the shove he needed.

'In an instant I went from heaven to hell,' said Guerini. 'I was upset, convinced that I had lost the stage. I got up as fast as possible, but in my frenzy I couldn't get my feet back into the pedals. Then I felt someone give me a push. I looked back and saw the most beautiful sight in my life. I still had enough of an advantage to win. I didn't even see the guy's face. Would I like to have a picture of the incident? I'd prefer one of me crossing the line as the winner.'

Above: Fausto Coppi leads Jean Robic up the climb on the Tour's first visit to Alpe d'Huez in 1952.

Left: Lucien Van Impe's attacks on the initial ramps quickly left him with only Dutchman Joop Zoetemelk (right) for company when the Tour returned in 1976.

Below: Zoetemelk grimaces as he leads Van Impe away from La Garde en Oisans and towards bend fifteen.

Top: The bike-borne blackboard informs yellow jersey Freddy Maertens that his deficit on riders 11 (Van Impe) and 30 (Zoetemelk) has reached fifty seconds.

Above: Zoetemelk has good reason to smile as he outsprints Van Impe for the stage win.

Left: Moments later, Van Impe beams even more broadly having pulled on the first yellow jersey of his career.

Right: Bernard Thévenet is helped from his bike having endured the toughest day of his career and held on to his yellow jersey by a mere eight seconds in 1977.

Below: 1978 and Michel Pollentier is about to swap the polka-dot jersey for the yellow, only to lose both after his attempt to cheat the dope control is revealed.

Left: 'The Mountain Flea' Beat Breu, riding his pared-down Cilo bike, closes on what will be his greatest win, in 1982.

Left: The final fifteen bends from just above La Garde en Oisans to the famous resort.

Below: The aerial view from the south offers a perfect perspective on the twenty-one hairpins rising from Bourg d'Oisans to Alpe d'Huez.

Left: Having taken the yellow jersey from compatriot Pascal Simon on the mountain the day before, Laurent Fignon indulges the photographers on the rest day at Alpe d'Huez.

Right: Fignon eases away from Bernard Hinault in 1984, having rebuffed earlier attacks by 'The Badger'.

Left: Acting as teammate and race leader Greg LeMond's bodyguard, Hinault heads towards a famous victory in Alpe d'Huez, the final big climb of his career.

Left: Britain's Robert Millar shepherds Frenchman Ronan Pensec towards a successful defence of the yellow jersey on the Alpe in 1990.

Below: Having dropped his breakaway companions, Andy Hampsten climbs through the packed ranks of spectators in 1992.

Above: Italians dominated on the Alpe in the 1990s, and none more so than Marco Pantani, who won twice and set the fastest time for the climb.

Left: Lance Armstrong has passed Ivan Basso and is closing in on a second victory on the mountain in the 2004 time trial, which attracted almost a million fans.

Above: So often the lieutenant to his team leaders, Carlos Sastre turns towards Alpe d'Huez in 2008, when he took the stage win and the yellow jersey.

Above: Twenty-five years after Hinault last won for France, Pierre Rolland accelerates away from Alberto Contador and Samuel Sánchez to claim victory in 2011.

Above: Bend seven, *le virage des Hollandais*, Dutch corner. The Tour convoy edges through the orange throng.

Above: Christophe Riblon chases Tejay van Garderen and what will be a career-best win in 2013.

7

Boastful and brash, but widely regarded as the best motivator in the sport, Lomme Driessens has accepted there is now little he can do with regard to saving Freddy Maertens' yellow jersey. Even the race leader's regular pick-me-up of a bottle containing champagne mixed with caffeine isn't providing its usual lift. The motorbike-borne timekeeper who chalks time gaps onto a small square of blackboard has just brandished his work at Maertens' three-strong band of strugglers, completed by his team mate Michel Pollentier and Dutchman Hennie Kuiper. Two minutes. With the climb not even half done, 'Fast Freddy' is losing ground on Van Impe and Zoetemelk too quickly to have a hope of clinging onto the lead for even one more day.

Dubbed 'Cycling's Napoleon', the burly Fleming has a reputation for getting on well with his riders – as long as they do what he says. Maertens does precisely that, describing Driessens as almost a second father, who has *guided him to one major success after another in what has been a stellar season. But Driessens doesn't need to draw on the knowledge he's accrued over thirty years of management to realise Maertens is not the Tour contender some have talked him up as.*

Driessens acknowledged his leader rode well on the climbs at the Tour of Switzerland, but has repeatedly pointed out, 'But they weren't cols like those on the Tour de France.' The presence of Kuiper and Pollentier, the winner and runner-up in Switzerland, alongside Maertens only underlines Driessens' point. He has also refused to be drawn when it's been put to him that some believe Maertens will surprise everyone in the yellow jersey, others that he will be knocked from his pedestal. 'Some of them will obviously be wrong and the others will be right,' is all he has said.

Driessens has spent the past few days scoffing when asked about Maertens' rivals. 'What rivals? Where are they? If it wasn't for Freddy there would be no racing at all.' But he has known for days that Maertens and Flandria were sure to be found out at Alpe d'Huez. The big sprinter and several of his teammates went into the Tour fatigued by five months of almost ceaseless competition that have already yielded thirty-six victories for Maertens. Give him a rest, Driessens pleaded to Flandria boss Pol Claeys.

'We've had a jersey taken away that was too much of a burden for us,' Driessens will say. 'I wasn't holding out

any hopes for the yellow jersey. We've still got the green to think about and we can carry that all the way to Paris.'

At least Maertens has the consolation of the points title. For Pollentier, who came into the Tour with hopes of challenging for the overall crown, his prospects are collapsing at exactly the point he was hoping they would take off. Buoyed up by that performance in Switzerland and good sensations in his legs on the Luitel, he was among the quickest to counter Van Impe's initial accelerations. Like Kuiper, his rival in Switzerland and equally disappointed companion in the fading yellow jersey group today, Pollentier has succumbed to over-confidence. In believing he could respond to the pure climbers, he's been finished off by them. It is a lesson that he will have learned well by the next time he is in contention on Alpe d'Huez.

THE DARK SIDE OF THE ALPE

Like the colour orange and partying Dutch fans, the taint of doping has never been far away from Alpe d'Huez. The resort has been the setting for one of the race's most notorious and surely its most ridiculous drug scandal, the stage for some superhuman performances that have, in some very significant cases, been explained away by performance-enhancing excesses, and has frequently been the setting for the questioning of the physical demands required by the world's greatest race.

Long before the Tour's organisers considered setting

riders the challenge of high-altitude finishes, doping was already an issue for the sport. In its early years, when track racing was king, six-day races were exactly that, and riders resorted to all manner of potions and remedies to fend off fatigue and boost energy levels, strychnine and other 'stimulating' poisons among them. In the 1920s, the Pélissier brothers famously described how they raced 'on dynamite', revealing that cocaine and chloroform were among the products they used to get themselves through a typical Tour stage. In the post-war years, when the amphetamines that had been produced to keep troops alert were as widely employed in endurance sports as Smarties on a six-year-old's birthday cake, Fausto Coppi confessed to using them. 'How often?' he was asked. 'Whenever it was necessary,' he responded. Asked when it was necessary, he confessed: 'Almost all of the time.'

With his admission in mind, it is particularly interesting to note how *Miroir-Sprint* director Maurice Vidal viewed the introduction of Alpe d'Huez and other summit finishes to the Tour in that 1952 race, which was dominated so completely by the Italian. 'This Tour is instilling fear in us, because human effort, even when we're talking about "the giants of the road", has its limits. The numbers of those who finish each day discouraged to a degree, declaring that the work demanded of them drives them to their human limits, are legion,' wrote Vidal, one of the most respected cycling writers of that era.

Tour boss Jacques Goddet agreed with Vidal's opinion

to a degree, but his concern was more on the dampening effect these summits had on aggressive racing rather than the perceived threat to the health of riders. However, that action-is-everything attitude began to change when French rider Jean Malléjac suffered a near-fatal collapse when racing up Mont Ventoux in 1955. The incident caused a sensation. Tour doctor Pierre Dumas, who saved the French rider's life on the roadside, announced he would take legal action against anyone found to be giving riders 'stimulating pharmaceuticals' and took a lead in the campaign to introduce drug testing into all sports. Yet it took another twelve years and the doping-related death of Britain's Tommy Simpson on that same Provençal mountain to bring about a more comprehensive change in the mind-set of riders and the backroom staff on teams.

When drug testing had been introduced for the first time during the 1966 Tour, following the passing of an anti-doping law in France the previous year, the riders had gone on strike to protest. Simpson's tragic death a year later did at least result in an acceptance of testing being carried out. However, what it definitely didn't produce was an end to doping.

In 1969, five riders tested positive at the Tour, including prologue winner Rudi Altig. Another of the quintet, Frenchman Pierre Matignon, went on to win a stage after the test results had been released. Their punishment amounted to an addition of fifteen minutes to their time in the overall classification, emphasising the lack of concern on this issue. Fifteen minutes may have been a lot to a general classification contender, but it meant little to most riders and was therefore totally ineffectual as a deterrent. By 1971, when two more riders fell foul of the testers, this penalty had been cut back to ten minutes, last place on the stage in question and a small fine. Only in 1973, when Britain's Barry Hoban, the stage winner in Versailles, was one of a trio who tested positive, were riders handed a ban, but a month-long suspension didn't indicate any substantial change in attitude towards doping by the sport's administrators.

Consequently, the litany of positive tests continued. There were three more at the 1974 Tour, another three in 1975, including past champion Felice Gimondi. And yet another three in 1976, including stage winner Régis Ovion, whose positive test came after that victory at Saint-Gaudens, which was handed to Lucien Van Impe's Gitane teammate Willy Teirlinck.

Speaking in 2000 in the wake of the Festina Affair and Richard Virenque's tardy admission that he had used the blood-boosting performance-enhancer EPO, renowned French sports doctor Jean-Pierre de Mondenard said that he wasn't in the least bit surprised by the corrupt state of cycling. 'I've been in this milieu for thirty years and I know all too well how it works. I did three Tours: those of 1973, 1974 and 1975. Doping was already widespread and very organised for the most part,' he told *Le Soir*.

The prevalence of doping became incontestably clear in 1977, when a host of major names tested positive for Stimul, the brand name for the stimulant pemoline – in 2005, the FDA withdrew approval for its use in the USA because of its implication in liver failure among children prescribed it to treat ADHD. Eddy Merckx was caught out at Flèche Wallonne, and claimed he had never heard of it, which looked less likely when a Belgian journalist revealed the product had been the subject of his brother Michel's degree thesis, completed just three years earlier. Freddy Maertens, Walter Godefroot, Michel Pollentier and a host of other big names also popped a positive test for Stimul that season. In an autobiography produced in 1989, Merckx finally admitted: 'Those who weren't caught that year were lucky because practically the whole peloton was using Stimul.' Another half a dozen positives for Stimul at the 1977 Tour, where Joop Zoetemelk, Luis Ocaña and Joaquim Agostinho were among those caught out, support Merckx's judgement.

There was also support for The Cannibal's gloomy analysis from his regular journalistic collaborator, Marc Jeuniau. Dismayed that talk before the presentation of the 1977 Tour de France about 'humanising' the race had come to nothing when it was revealed to be just as tough as the edition recently won by Van Impe, Jeuniau lamented in *Miroir* that, 'The number of summit finishes has risen. The race organisers have shamelessly suppressed transition stages and [in 1976] transported the riders straight from the end of the Alps to the foot of the Pyrenees. It is difficult, inconceivable even, to carry out the job of being a professional cyclist in '77 without resorting to tonics...'

Stimul was only one of these tonics. In 1979, Bernard Thévenet admitted to Pierre Chany in *Vélo-France* that he'd used cortisone for three seasons, including the one when he claimed his second Tour crown. 'I'm in no state to get back on the bike again,' revealed Thévenet, who'd been prescribed what was at the time the completely legal anti-inflammatory and pain-killing steroid by Peugeot team doctor François Bellocq. 'We were all convinced we were doing the right thing and we were certain we were a step ahead of the rest in so far as what we were doing to prepare for competition.' Employing reasoning that later encouraged the management and medical staff at the Festina team to supervise the doping of their riders in order to prevent them coming to serious harm, Thévenet added: 'I had the feeling that he was taking us out of the continual experimentation to get us on a more methodical and scientific road... I was at ease with myself, satisfied deep down that I was doing my job seriously.'

Zoetemelk, meanwhile, had been drawing on the knowledge of a doctor he had met in the wake of his near-fatal crash during the 1974 Midi Libre stage race. Dr Henri Fucs was already working with the Sonolor-Gitane team managed by Jean Stablinski and led by Lucien Van Impe, and had noticed that their blood levels dropped during three-week tours. When he got the results of Zoetemelk's blood tests, he noticed that the Dutchman's levels were well below what he'd seen among Sonolor's riders. He diagnosed anaemia. Having been blasted by antibiotics to treat the meningitis that had developed as a result of his Midi Libre crash, Zoetemelk's bone marrow wasn't producing sufficient red blood cells. Fucs' solution? Transfusions of concentrated red blood cells.

Writing in *La Prochaine Étape* in 1980, five years before the IOC banned blood doping, Zoetemelk, who describes Fucs as 'a pioneer in this kind of treatment', says he received regular 'transfusions of concentrated red blood cells'. He then defends both Fucs and the process, which at that point was not prohibited, saying: 'By acting in this way, he only ever sought, and I always repeat this, to rebalance me using biological examinations as his guide. Rather than impacting on my current and future health, his treatment's only goal was to keep me in peak physical and physiological condition.'

Just in case that didn't clarify the correctness of this procedure, Zoetemelk, who stated publicly before the 1977 Tour that he wouldn't be using transfusions again, usefully adds: 'It should definitely not be confused with the method practised in certain Nordic countries and in the Eastern Bloc, which consists of trying to artificially multiply the athlete's number of red blood cells by reinjecting into them their own blood that had been removed some time before.'

Zoetemelk's defence might be a touch more credible if he hadn't tested positive on three occasions, the first for Stimul in 1977 two days before the Alpe d'Huez stage when he won the Tour time trial to Avoriaz. In *La Prochaine Étape* he attempts to sow doubt on the validity of the test by insisting he would never have been stupid enough to dope knowing that he was bound to be called to give a sample as the stage winner. He says the affair was 'as injurious as it was unjust', before going on to lay out a scenario in which he was handed a drug-tainted bottle either at dinner or while fulfilling his post-victory media commitments. He suggests this could also have led to the Mercier team's poor showing in the Alpe d'Huez stage won by Hennie Kuiper. He concludes in laughable fashion. 'Doped? Duped? It all seems bizarre, very bizarre.'

Just as odd were the rumours circulating at the end of that Tour that dozens of riders had tested positive. In *L'Équipe*, Pierre Chany said that Merckx's team manager, Raphaël Geminiani, and Van Impe's, Henry Anglade, had suggested that anti-doping penalties had not been implemented as fully as they should have been. Chany related that one race official had told him that fifty-four riders had failed tests.

Although only half a dozen riders' names appeared in the official communiqués, the media fully expected more to be announced. *Le Matin* summed up the general feeling of disillusion when it stated, 'Since its creation in 1903 the Tour de France has undoubtedly never finished in such a poisoned atmosphere.' Meanwhile, future Tour historian Jacques Augendre, writing in *Le Populaire du Centre*, described the race as finishing 'in confusion, resulting from the repression of anti-doping results that seems bizarre to say the least'. Commentators were united in their demand for greater clarity on anti-doping matters.

And so to the ridiculous...It is undeniable that the fact Alpe d'Huez became so quickly associated with Dutch riders and fans is to some extent down to Michel Pollentier being stripped of his stage win and the yellow jersey at the resort in 1978. The Belgian's long-range sortie began when he attacked near the top of the Luitel pass in the search for King of the Mountains points. With yellow jersey Jos Bruyère – for whom 'the climb towards Alpe d'Huez was a descent into hell where he ended up being burnt to a crisp', according to *L'Équipe*'s Antoine Blondin – already dropped and his most likely successors, Zoetemelk and Bernard Hinault, focusing on each other rather than the Belgian, Pollentier soon opened up a substantial gap.

With what Jean-Paul Vespini describes as 'his characteristic side to side sway, nearer in terms of elegance to a toad than to a cyclist', Pollentier didn't look efficient, but his method was effective. 'Lying flat over his bike, his back rounded, his elbows and knees sticking out, like a disarticulated puppet, determined to shake every little bit out of his carcass and torture his machine,' according to

Vespini, Pollentier judged his effort perfectly. He ended the day three seconds up on Zoetemelk and seventeen ahead of Hinault.

He later claimed he had pushed himself so hard on the ascent of Alpe d'Huez that he had been unable to control his bladder and had peed in his shorts and all over his bike. This may explain why, having completed the podium protocol, Pollentier went to his team hotel to change into clean clothes. The regulations required that he attend the dope control, located in a small white caravan alongside the finishing straight, within sixty minutes of finishing the stage. He arrived there just inside this limit.

The peloton was always well informed about the procedures enforced by the various testers carrying out the controls. During the opening two weeks of the 1978 Tour, the riders knew that the doctors carrying out the dope controls had not been adhering strictly to the testing protocol. Rather than asking riders to remove all clothing below the waist and watching them deliver the sample, the testers had been content to let racers keep their clothing on and turn their backs, making it possible to subvert the procedure. Pollentier, evidently believing that he might deliver a positive test, had decided to do exactly this. In addition to a change of clothes, he had used the time in his hotel room to fit himself with a device designed to enable him to deliver a third party's urine into the tester's container.

He had fixed a rubber balloon or condom containing

the urine into his armpit – his close friend Maertens has recently said it was a condom that was actually secreted into his anus with the help of Vaseline. From this pouch, a piece of tubing ran down (or up) his back, where it was secured with Elastoplast, to the underside of his penis, to which it was also taped. Although rather Heath Robinson in design, the kit was quite efficient when it came to execution of the task. As he prepared to deliver his sample, all Pollentier had to do was squeeze the reservoir of urine in his armpit and ensure his aim was true. That was the theory anyway.

While some reports suggest that Pollentier's ruse was uncovered when he started pumping 'one arm in and out as if playing a set of bagpipes' or when he tried to work out why the third party's urine wasn't trickling from the tube, contemporary accounts suggest otherwise. In fact, he was trapped by an official doing no more than implementing the correct procedure for carrying out a dope control.

New to the race that day, Dr Alain Calvez was a French federation representative from the Atlantique-Anjou region. Alongside Dr Calvez was UCI medical inspector Renato Sacconi. They had already caught one rider trying to cheat the control using a urine-filled 'pear' and insisted Pollentier follow the established protocol and deliver the sample stripped below the waist. As a result, the apparatus and intention to cheat the control immediately became apparent. The testers continued with the procedure, asking Pollentier to produce a proper sample, which took him almost two hours to deliver. When he left the dope control, he assured reporters that everything was in order, which was confirmed by Flandria DS Fred De Bruyne. The two men returned to room 32 in the Hôtel Les Cimes, where Pollentier's teammate Freddy Maertens had a bottle of Lanson already on ice to toast his friend's victory.

To an extent, everything was in order as far as Pollentier and De Bruyne were concerned. The rider had not used the device and had delivered the required sample. The testers had not mentioned the possibility of any sanction. However, they had informed the head of the UCI's race jury, Jean Court, who had in turn contacted his HQ in Switzerland to relate the details of Pollentier's attempt to cheat the control and request when the required two-month suspension should begin. The UCI's medical code seemed to allow some leeway, which could permit Pollentier to finish the Tour. However, UCI secretary-general Michał Jekiel informed Court: 'Apply the sanction immediately.'

As the press were writing their stories in Jaap Reuten's church, news began to filter through about Pollentier's long spell in the dope control caravan. Sensing something was afoot, L'Équipe's Noël Couëdel went to the Flandria team hotel to investigate. He found Pollentier reluctantly sipping the champagne Maertens had ordered, but apparently relaxed. The Belgian clearly couldn't believe that his short stint in the yellow jersey was soon to end. All he wanted, he said, was to shower, have dinner and sleep. He managed the former and was just starting on his yogurt dessert when the press returned having received the UCI's official communiqué detailing his sanction.

Back in room 32, Pollentier declared his astonishment at the penalty that had been imposed. He repeated his earlier insistence that all was in order, that he'd been told nothing by the UCI. 'It took me a long time to pee but the doctor didn't make any comments to me. I signed and counter-signed the usual papers. How can it be that an hour later they discover there's been a fraud? I don't understand that. What else do you want me to tell you?' Pollentier asked Couëdel, who admitted to feeling embarrassed at seeing the Belgian crumble in front of him.

As distress and anger gripped him, Pollentier, the first and still the only Belgian to win on Alpe d'Huez, declared: 'We're all going to go home tomorrow, that's decided, and I swear to you, and listen to me very carefully, I will never come back to the Tour de France again. You see that yellow jersey over there, well go and take it to Hinault, it's for him and that's perhaps what certain people wanted.' In 2011, Maertens reasserted this claim in an interview with journalists Les Woodland and Bill McGann, suggesting that Flandria DS De Bruyne had tipped off the testers about Pollentier's contraption. De Bruyne is not in a position to challenge this allegation as he died in 1994.

Flandria's claims of a conspiracy centred on the treatment of Lejeune's Antoine Gutierrez, the rider who had previously been caught attempting to cheat the control that day, in his case using nothing more complicated than a miniature from a hotel fridge filled up with someone else's urine. Initially, Gutierrez was set to continue in the race despite carrying out the sleight of hand/penis that Pollentier had only considered. Ultimately, although not disqualified until the day after the race leader, the Frenchman did not start the next stage.

Overnight and into the rest day that followed, Flandria's one-out-all-out stance eased. Flandria boss Pol Claeys, who had driven from Belgium to join the celebrations of Pollentier's victory, calmed his riders. They would continue. Even at this point, Pollentier believed there was a chance that he might be able to join them. His anger had turned to contrition, which was expressed publicly in the form of a letter addressed to the Tour's directors.

His apology for the stain he had brought onto the Tour was fulsome, but qualified. His defence was that he hadn't carried out any fraudulent act. 'In my opinion,' Pollentier wrote, 'the worst that could be said was that there was an attempt at fraud.' Coincidentally, thirty years later, Ivan Basso would employ much the same defence when it was confirmed that bags of his blood had been discovered during the Puerto investigation in Spain. Basso admitted he had given the blood, but had decided not to use it.

Pollentier went on to suggest that other riders in the top ten would have acted in the same way and that there needed to be consistency in the way controls were carried out – De Bruyne insisted others had probably got away with similar acts earlier in the race because of the laxness of the testers and insinuated this had led Pollentier down the same path. It certainly wasn't a one-off. At the Midi Libre earlier that season, Spaniard Pedro Vilardebo had been found with the same kind of contraption after sending teammate Eulalio García to do the dope control for him. Both riders continued in that race and both had lined up at the Tour less than two months later.

Yet, Pollentier and his team's claims of conspiracy were undermined by the Belgian's admission that he had been using a product called alupin designed to improve breathing. He confessed to using it previously in Belgium, where it couldn't be detected. He said it wouldn't show up in tests conducted in Italy or Switzerland either, but he feared it might be discovered in France. As it turned out, his sample didn't produce a positive result.

As he did so often, *L'Équipe*'s Antoine Blondin, crafting his prose in the nave of Jaap Reuten's church, summed up the affair in beautiful fashion, writing: 'The experts were saying that there must have been some kind of miracle...And there was a miracle in an unforeseen sense: Pollentier was thrown out of the race. The dragon with the bad habits had slain the archangel in this Michel. The shame was that if we'd had the news earlier, the priest could have rung the bells, because it's the Dutchman Zoetemelk who will be leaving this parish with the yellow jersey. But would it have been right to put out the flags when you've discovered there's a devil in the font?'

Just as he had done in 1952, Maurice Vidal insisted the Pollentier affair and other doping cases were the result of riders being expected to go beyond their limits. Writing in the *Miroir du Cyclisme*'s post-Tour issue, Vidal asserted: 'It is in any case difficult to ride the Tour *à l'eau minérale*. But it is completely impossible at its current speed.' That year Bernard Hinault averaged a touch under thirty-five kilometres an hour for the 3,900-kilo-metre route. A decade later, after Pedro Delgado had refused to quit the race despite a dope control showing that he had used probenecid, a known masking agent banned by the IOC but not at that point by the UCI, the Spaniard completed his Tour victory at an average speed that was four kilometres an hour faster than Hinault's over a 3,200-kilometre route. While the Tour route was shorter, the equipment better and training had improved, there is little evidence that there had been any shift towards a cleaner sport, despite regular claims of improvement made by the UCI.

A quarter of a century on from Delgado's probene-cid-tainted win, evidence of yet more systematic doping emerged concerning the PDM team of that year's Alpe d'Huez victor, Steven Rooks. In January 2013, Dutch newspaper *De Volkskrant* published images from a note-book kept by the Dutch team's soigneur, Bertus Fok, who had detailed the medical products given to seven of the team's eight riders. Fok, who had previously worked with Peter Post's TI-Raleigh team, confirmed the authenticity of the notebook.

The paper reported that Fok had taken on responsibil-ity for handling the team's medical programme in 1986. It included the provision of testosterone, corticosteroids and blood transfusions, although Fok made clear that he did not administer the blood-boosting product EPO. 'That was too much for me,' he said. Nevertheless, an image from the notebook suggests PDM's riders were well armed on 14 July 1988, when the Tour finished at Alpe d'Huez. Steroids and testosterone feature widely on the range of products listed under each rider's name. Beneath Rooks' entry, which indicates Fok gave him steroids and testos-terone, the soigneur has written: 'Incredible, 1st '. Under that of Theunisse, which features similar products, he's added: 'Brilliant, 2nd'.

Steroids, amphetamines and vitamin injections were, however, about to be dumped into the second tier of per-formance-enhancing products. In his 2009 autobiography *Het Laatste Geel* (The Last Yellow), Rooks admitted he boosted his arsenal considerably when he started using EPO in 1989. 'It was necessary to finish high up in the classification,' Rooks explained. As a test to detect EPO was not introduced until the Sydney Olympics in 2000, the Dutchman's claim that its use was widespread more than a decade prior to that is impossible to verify. However, performances on Alpe d'Huez during the 1990s point towards the use of EPO being as widespread and systematic during this period as that of amphetamines and steroids had been in previous decades. This is supported by the evidence that came out of the Festina Affair and subsequent trials at the end of the decade and the confessions of prominent riders during that period such as 1996 Tour winner Bjarne Riis and seven-time champion Lance Armstrong. In March 2015, the UCI-appointed Cycling Independent Reform Commission's report into doping within cycling described 'the late 1980s or early 1990s as the period when EPO was introduced, and when the pelaton started "flying"'.

When Fausto Coppi rode to victory on Alpe d'Huez in 1952, Jacques Goddet timed his winning ascent at forty-five minutes and twenty-two seconds. Almost forty years would pass, though, before the first officially timed ascent of the mountain in 1990. Fittingly, a Dutchman was quickest to the summit. Tissot timed the first thirty riders on the ascent and Erik Breukink set the best mark. His time of 43-19 earned him a gold watch worth 20,000 French francs (£2,000). By 1995, Breukink looked a slouch. His mark was a minute slower than the fiftieth fastest ascent of the Alpe.

A graph produced by the Finnish Ammattipyöräily (Professional Cycling) website highlights a surge in average speeds recorded for the 13.8-kilometre climb following the 1989 stage on the mountain. Using the five fastest times recorded in each year, the graph shows a sudden leap from an average of around 19.6 km/h in 1982, 1987 and 1989, to 20.7 km/h in 1991, 21.3 km/h in 1994 and 21.8 km/h in 1995, when ten of the fastest fifty all-time ascents were registered. This figure did not drop below 20 km/h again until 2011, in the aftermath of any number of doping scandals and confessions, combined with improved testing methods and the introduction of the World Anti-Doping Agency's biological passport.

A closer look at the stats reveals that none of the top 200 quickest rides occurred in 1992, when EPO use was, it is generally accepted, becoming very widespread within the pro peloton. The answer to this anomaly could lie in the previous stage to Sestrières. That day Claudio Chiappucci, who later admitted and then denied he had used EPO – but did twice fall foul of the UCI's 'health check', which was designed to check for EPO use in the absence at the time of a test for the drug – produced one of the great solo rides in Tour history, covering half of the 254km stage on his own. At the finish, Andy Hampsten, who was in the quartet chasing behind the Italian along with race leader Miguel Indurain, two-time Alpe winner Gianni Bugno and Franco Vona, says he watched riders finishing behind him that day and he could see that everyone was 'knackered'.

Hampsten, who doesn't have even the slightest taint of

doping attached to him and is universally regarded as having been clean throughout his racing career, says he was conscious of the significant change taking place within the sport. 'I was aware of riders going faster on the climbs and of riders who weren't climbers going faster on the climbs. But winning on Alpe d'Huez perhaps gave me a lot of false hope too that things were OK in our little world,' the American admits. 'But pretty soon after they really weren't.'

Hampsten acknowledges it quickly became more of a struggle for him to make a mark, but he persisted in trying based on his long experience in the grand tours and the backing of his team doctor. 'I don't know what my rationalisation was. In the hot weather, in the very, very hard racing well into the third week of a Tour de France I knew that I could still do what I set out to do. A lot of my battle with riders taking EPO was not allowing myself to get too wrapped up in what they were doing, because then I'd just be thinking about them. This was why my doctor, Dr Massimo Testa, was so good because he would stress that I should not be owned psychologically by thinking, "Oh my gosh, there's this rider and I saw him with that doctor, or he's on that team…" If I was too focused on what other riders might have been doing, then: the first thing is that I'd never know; and, secondly, it would be the end of me psychologically as I'd just be worrying about what other people were doing.'

It is significant that the one other year during the period

before the introduction of an EPO test when the average speed dropped was in 1999, when Giuseppe Guerini survived a close encounter with a camera-wielding fan on his way to victory on the Alpe and Lance Armstrong moved a step closer to his first yellow jersey. That day's stage also followed another epic mauling of the competition by one rider at Sestrières, in that case by Armstrong, who says in his first autobiography, *It's Not About the Bike*, that when he reached the foot of Alpe d'Huez the next day he joked with his US Postal directeur sportif Johan Bruyneel that, 'I could do this damn thing on a tricycle.' We would perhaps look back on that stage more fondly now if he had.

A further twist is added by the fact that Armstrong inherited Hampsten's position as leader of the Motorola team. 'I also had a good season in 1993 and I was very convinced by what I was doing with Motorola, with a very anti-drug policy, but not trying to be overly worried about what was going on, although we were concerned,' Hampsten explains. 'Getting the right results was a very good indication to me that I was doing the right thing, and I had a lot of conviction and belief in the training I was doing and the race programme I had.' Two years later, realising that he and the Motorola team he now led could not compete with their EPO-fuelled rivals, Armstrong successfully pushed for the introduction of a state-of-the-art doping programme.

Between Hampsten's victory on the Alpe in 1992 and Fränk Schleck's in 2006 two riders dominated on Alpe d'Huez, which became a showcase for cheats and fraudsters. Marco Pantani produced three startling performances on the climb. According to Ammattipyöräily's timings, his 1995 ride to victory was the fastest ascent ever (thirty-six minutes and fifty seconds), while his climb in 1997 was just five seconds slower and his debut appearance in 1994 was another twenty seconds slower than that. Only Lance Armstrong in the 2004 time trial on the mountain and Jan Ullrich when he was chasing Pantani up the climb in 1997 have also recorded marks under thirty-eight minutes.

Tour de France route director Thierry Gouvenou was in the break that also included eventual stage winner Roberto Conti when Pantani gave his first startling performance on the Alpe in 1994. 'It's one of my clearest memories as a rider at the Tour,' he says. 'I was actually a couple of minutes behind the leading break when we reached the climb. The mountains were never my strong point, so I soon fell back even more. I was shocked and surprised by the speed with which Pantani came up to me on a bend and shot away. It was incredible to see, really incredible.'

Pantani emerged on the Carrera team led by Chiappucci, but quickly eclipsed his compatriot. Third in the 1994 Giro, during the course of which he outclassed defending champion Miguel Indurain in the mountains, Pantani's unique brilliance and showmanship when roads steepled up into the Alps and Pyrenees soon won a legion of fans. For a sport that had become sterile during Indurain's crushing but dull dictatorship, Pantani was a godsend. Like Coppi, the *'uomo solo al comando'* to whom he was frequently compared, he raced with the intention of forcing everyone off his wheel. As Daniel Friebe described it in *Procycling*, 'The romantic in all of us couldn't wait for the cap to be tossed away, then the bandanna, then at last for Pantani's hands to fall onto his drop handlebars as he prepared to fly. The striptease was the prelude to art of utmost sophistication.'

Rarely remembered for his turn of phrase, Indurain offered a simply precise portrait of his rival following Pantani's drug-induced suicide in 2004. 'He was a tragic genius who got people hooked on the sport. There may be riders who achieved more than him, but they never succeeded in drawing the fans like he did,' said the five-time Tour winner. Those fans, principally Italian, flooded the Alpe in the mid-1990s. In what was the cycling equivalent of the Roaring Twenties when anything went, Pantani, with his tattoos, shaved head, goatee beard and bandanna, was the entertainer-in-chief. Styling himself as 'Il Pirata', his swashbuckling raids provided the antidote to Indurain's conservatism.

Like the fans, the media was also in raptures. 'Justice has been done! Marco Pantani has finally won a stage of the Tour de France,' *L'Équipe* crowed when the Italian's record-breaking ascent of the Alpe carried him to that first success in 1995. On the rest day that followed, he told the paper, 'I'm a cycling romantic. When I climb a pass it's with the aim of enjoying myself.' Who could fail to be won over by such simple bravado, especially when he added that he didn't use the computer Carrera's team of doctors had given him. 'I've never ridden with a heart-rate monitor. They don't really help all that much. I'm a rider *à l'ancienne*. Technology is important but it's not fundamental,' said Pantani.

The irony is that Pantani, who depicted himself as a Luddite getting by on talent alone, was taking full advantage of the world-leading scientific and medical knowledge relating to performance enhancement that was the focus of Dr Francesco Conconi and his assistant Dr Giovanni Grazzi at Italy's University of Ferrara. Conconi is widely believed to have introduced EPO into the pro peloton while trying, with IOC funding, to develop a test to detect its use.

Like the Roaring Twenties collapsing into the Great Depression, cycling's era of EPO excess ended suddenly and dramatically. The Festina affair of 1998 almost brought that year's Tour to a premature end, and the whole professional side of the sport with it. Pantani, briefly, resuscitated it with his Zorro-like dissection of Jan Ullrich at Alpe d'Huez's neighbouring resort of Les Deux Alpes, which won him the Tour. However, when the Italian was hauled out of the 1999 Giro d'Italia just two days from victory with an elevated red blood-cell count, the descent towards his tragic demise five years later began.

In 2000, an Italian public prosecutor's investigation into Conconi turned up computer files that showed Pantani's haematocrit (red blood cell) level had been 58 per cent in July 1994 when he made his first astounding ascent of the Alpe. That was up more than 17 points on his level just four months earlier. In July 1995, his haematocrit was recorded at 56 per cent. These hugely fluctuating levels are indicative of EPO use. In the end, Pantani was more lab rat than swashbuckler.

'We'll never know what type of champion Pantani would have been without that turbo-powered, poisoned blood,' Candido Canavo wrote in *La Gazzetta dello Sport* after Pantani's death in 2004. At that same time, Sandro Donati, head of research at the Italian Olympic Committee, surmised: 'Pantani saw that a world that had continued to build him up and urge him to push back the boundaries was able to turn on him and condemn him for the same practices it was endorsing. He probably felt that people in cycling used him to their own ends, then isolated him. It was a rejection he couldn't swallow.'

Two months on from Pantani's ejection from the Giro, the so-called 'Tour of Renewal' hailed a new hero. Untainted by the Festina Affair and eulogised for his inspirational victory against cancer, Lance Armstrong became, as *Procycling* magazine put it, the 'Fine Young Cannibal'. As driven and merciless as Eddy Merckx, on whose bikes he rode, Lance Armstrong was the revitalising figure the Tour and cycling needed. Or at least he was for the cycling establishment, who could hardly believe their luck when the brash Texan cantered into Planet Tour and swept everyone before him, attracting rave reviews and a new wave of fans. It was box-office magic until, in 2013, Armstrong finally admitted it wasn't. Like Riis, Pantani and so many others, he had been turbo-powered with EPO and other PEDs.

Stripped of his seven Tour titles and all of his post-1999 stage wins, including those taken at Alpe d'Huez in 2001 and 2004, Armstrong's demise has been almost unprecedented. His humbling was received gleefully by many, including some of those who had previously been his most vigorous defenders. His offences, which included pressurising his teammates to dope, were deemed so serious that he has been banned from all forms of competitive cycling for life. Once inspirational, he is now the greatest pariah in sporting history.

Yet, as far as the use of PEDs is concerned, it seems illogical and unjust to heap blame on one man in a sport where doping has long been systemic. Like Pantani, Pollentier and a host of others, Armstrong was competing within a milieu that has always been corrupt, where recourse to illicit assistance has been systematic and encouraged, as was so clearly demonstrated in Paul Kimmage's *Rough Ride* in 1990 and Christophe Bassons' *A Clean Break*, published in 2014. I have no particular regard for Armstrong, and he's made it apparent that he has none at all for me, calling me up on one occasion to angrily accuse me of running a vendetta against him and his then girlfriend Sheryl Crow in the pages of a magazine for which I was freelancing and over which I had no editorial control. Nevertheless, it is perverse to essentially blame one rider for every shred of rottenness.

In his illuminating book, Bassons recalls the Alpine stages of the 1999 Tour, the only one in which he rode. Already ostracised for penning a daily column in *Le Parisien*, in which he did no more than reveal his impressions of his debut Tour and what it was like to ride it à l'eau claire, the Frenchman describes the desolation felt by many of the peloton after witnessing Armstrong's demolition of his rivals in a long time trial at Metz and a brutal stage to Sestrières that ended in a mountain storm. On the eve of the stage to Alpe d'Huez, Bassons sensed mutiny among his peers.

'In our hotel and in many others, revolt was simmering. The opposition had been humiliated. French, Italians and Belgians crossed paths and exchanged the same disillusioned phrases. Some spoke of stopping, of leaving the Tour as a sign of protest. At the dinner table, everyone cried foul... But the discontent remained shut away behind closed doors. The next day the weather was back to normal. It was beautiful. I immediately realised that the race's barometer had also risen. The storm had passed. Nothing followed in its wake, not even a whisper. They held everything in behind a wall of silence. Seeing this, I thought to myself that a serious affliction was lying in wait for the riders in the shape of a festering ulcer.'

Soon after the stage to Alpe d'Huez began, Armstrong eased in next to Bassons. 'You know, what you are saying to the journalists is not good for cycling,' the Texan told him.

'I'm simply saying what I think. I'm saying that there is doping,' said Bassons.

'If you're here to do that, it would be better for you to go home and find another job.'

'I'm not leaving when I've not changed anything; if I have something to say, I will say it.'

'Then get the hell out!'

Instead of mutiny and Armstrong being ostracised, Bassons realises he is the one being shunned. Armstrong's attack on him is the best remembered, but others that came from his teammates, managers and, most damningly, cycling's ruling body said more about the state of the sport.

When, in December 2013, Armstrong and Bassons met again on the American's tour of retribution to apologise to some of those he had slighted in the past, Bassons ended up defending the disgraced champion. 'I don't agree with you taking the blame for the whole milieu,' the Frenchman tells him. 'I don't think you're responsible for everything that's happened. The UCI, the federations, the organisers also have to take some of the blame. We have to put an end to this hypocrisy.'

There are positive indications that this process is under

way. The UCI has a new president and perspective. Among riders and teams there has been a switch from depending on doping to enhance performance to seeking out marginal gains in all aspects of equipment, training and preparation for racing. Yes, there are still positive tests and drug scandals, but the sense is that these are the result of idiocy on the part of those involved and more successful targeting and testing by anti-doping bodies.

When, in 2000, Jean-Pierre de Mondenard was asked for his solution to damage caused by doping, he pointed to the need for more drug controls and for a complete change of perspective on the part of riders, team staff and race organisers. This, he insisted, would lead to the adoption of alternative methods to improve performance. 'If everyone stopped doping today, it would undoubtedly take about twenty years to get back to the levels that have been achieved thanks to doping,' he asserted. 'But I challenge 99 per cent of the fans who watch the ascent of Alpe d'Huez to spot the difference between a rider who is climbing at 27 km/h and one at 30 km/h. It's the contest that provides the thrills.'

8

Bend ten sits right above Le Ribot and bend twelve almost 200 metres below. A missing car-sized section of the parapet suggests that some poor unfortunate has recently made this trip in horrifyingly direct fashion, taking the signpost indicating the number of this hairpin with them.

Thanks to a substantial dressed stone foundation, the bend juts out from the cliff face just enough to offer a brief glimpse back to bend eleven. With the crowds slightly sparser, Van Impe has the chance to glance back at the terrain he's most recently covered and check on the progress of the chase group behind. But he doesn't take it. He's been distracted by Zoetemelk.

A willing collaborator for the last few minutes, the Dutchman is now refusing to come through. Van Impe is well aware of the instructions Louis Caput has passed on to his rider, but is bewildered by Zoetemelk's uncomplaining acceptance of them. He urges the Gan-Mercier rider to come through and provide another relay, but all he gets is *a shake of the head. In a brief but very agitated conversation conducted in angry Dutch, the Belgian warns his rival that he will attack if the collaboration doesn't continue. It makes no difference. Zoetemelk is staying faithful to team orders and the hopeless and romantic hopes Caput has for Poulidor.*

When the Dutchman again refuses to come through, Van Impe's anger provokes him into forgetting the orders he's been given by his team director, Guimard. Instead of maintaining a steady pace to the finish and stretching the advantage over the Thévenet group, he accelerates. But he can't shake his shadow.

Unsure of his next move, Van Impe calls up Guimard for instructions. The little Belgian climber wants to win the stage. For him, victory on any summit is cherished above all else and leading the Tour into Alpe d'Huez would be the most beautiful outcome. However, having bought into his team director's plan to focus everything on winning the yellow jersey, he knows he should play the longer game.

Sensing that his plan is in danger of going awry, Guimard quickly motors up alongside his leader and implores Van Impe to sustain his pace. The Gitane DS yells: 'Ride! Ride! You're going to take the jersey.' He knows this is a critical moment, that the Belgian's temperament is fragile, but also that it will be bolstered by taking the yellow jersey for the first time in his career. This, he knows, will confirm to Van Impe that he, and not Freddy Maertens, is the rider best placed to give Belgium its sixth Tour win in eight seasons.

Guimard, though, is also aware that Gitane are heading into dangerous waters. While he has faith in the reliability of experienced pros such as Van Impe's roommate Robert Mintkewicz, Sylvain Vasseur and seasoned Belgian Willy Teirlinck, young French riders Hubert Arbs, André Chalmel, Jean Chassang and Alain Meslet are all making their debut appearances at the Tour. Belgian René Dillen is making only his second. Guimard's team certainly has potential, but, in Raymond Martin, it has only a single rider capable of defending Van Impe's interests in the high mountains.

Guimard is already considering the unimaginable: having found a way to take the yellow jersey, he is weighing up how to let someone else have it without inflicting too much damage to his team leader's long-term prospects and, just as significantly, his mental focus. The arch-strategist, Guimard is already thinking several moves ahead but knows it will prove extremely difficult to have Van Impe do the same. He will later confide of Van Impe that, 'where tactical initiatives are concerned, let us say that his behaviour is still a bit evasive. I don't think he understands racing particularly well, because he has never tried to understand it.'

Will he be able to keep his leader pointed in the right direction?

THE GREATEST CLIMBER IN HISTORY

Alpe d'Huez lies at the end of a cul-de-sac in the flatlands of Flanders between Ghent and Brussels. Given the landscape, the beige-bricked house could hardly have a less appropriate name, the letters set out in flowing, gold script next to a grand neo-Roman facade around a solid, wooden front door. The half-dozen steps leading up to it form the only climb for miles around.

The name brings back bittersweet memories for the property's owner. Lucien Van Impe enjoyed both the greatest and most heartbreaking day of his career on the fourteen-kilometre climb that lies one thousand kilometres to the south of his home in Impe. In 1976, although beaten to the line by Dutch rival Joop Zoetemelk, he took the yellow jersey at the ski station perched high above the Romanche valley in the central French Alps and went on to win the Tour de France in Paris.

A year later, Van Impe reached the foot of the Alpe alone, with the Tour all but won for the second year in succession. The greatest climber of his, and arguably any, generation was entering his favourite terrain. Yet, instead of soaring, Van Impe fell apart, weakened by riding on his own in the wind, stricken by hunger knock, and, ultimately, shunted into the roadside ditch by a race follower's car. Pictures show Van Impe standing in the middle of the road in the red polka-dot King of the Mountains jersey, his useless bike in one hand, a mangled wheel in the other, tears streaming down his face.

As Van Impe waited for his team car, Dutchman Hennie Kuiper zipped by. The sign on the next bend confirmed there were five of Alpe d'Huez's twenty-one numbered hairpins left before the finish. Climbing through them, Kuiper rode over the painted letters of his name on the road again and again, his compatriots roaring him on. Van Impe trailed in minutes down, an early victim of the maxim that has it that the Tour is won – and, therefore, also lost – on the Alpe.

Meeting Van Impe, it's impossible not to be won over by his ever-present smile and absolute passion for cycling. Give him any theme related to the sport, and he's off, ideas, memories and analysis spinning out of him without pause. He is the perfect interview – a good talker, ready to answer any question, with a great memory for anecdotes. But it's not so easy to tease out the essence of Van Impe, who tends to talk up the high points of his professional racing career and skirt around the lows. For a deeper insight, you have to go back to the years he was the focus of the spotlight at the Tour and not the supporting artist who would swan away from his rivals on lofty peaks before disappearing into the background once again.

On the afternoon the 1976 Tour finished in Paris, French TV reporter Daniel Pautrat went to Lucien Van Impe's hotel room to film a brief interview and profile of Belgium's new yellow jersey winner. Broadcast that evening on the main TF1 news, it features Van Impe resplendent not in the fabled yellow tunic, but in a bright-blue towelling dressing gown, propped up on the headboard of his bed with his wife Rita at his side.

With less than a couple of minutes to fill, Pautrat gets

quickly to the point. 'It's said that Lucien's a big kid. Is he a big kid or is he a man?' he asks Rita.

'Yes, he's a big kid, that's true,' says the smiling Rita. 'He likes to be spoiled. How? He wants me to do everything for him. I wash his hair. I cut his nails. I have to look after him just like I do our two children.'

On the face of it, Van Impe appears to have taken Scottish climber Robert Millar's maxim 'don't walk when you can stand, don't stand when you can sit, don't sit when you can lie down' to its furthest extent. If he had had the time, would Pautrat have discovered that poor Rita had to carry her husband to the bath in order to wash his hair? It's possible she did, as in a newspaper interview published around the same time she revealed she had to mix the water for him before he would get into it.

In his ninety-second broadcast, Pautrat manages brilliantly to capture the essence of Lucien Van Impe. Beaming angelically, his eyes darting beneath a luxuriant monobrow, the diminutive Belgian looks a little bundle of mischief. At his side, as she so often was at races despite this being taboo for riders' wives, Rita is doing his talking for him. She's the schemer, the one who can see what's best for her husband and is determined to get it.

Cycling lore has it that the sport's specialist climbers are a breed apart. From Federico Bahamontes, who once stopped for an ice cream and to wait for his rivals at the top of a Tour pass, to Charly Gaul, who liked nothing more than to be alone and ended his days a hermit in the

Ardennes forest of his native Luxembourg, to Marco Pantani, the self-styled 'pirate' complete with bandanna and hooped earring, they are depicted, often quite rightly, as mavericks who live by a quite different set of rules to their peers.

Van Impe, often described as *l'ouistiti des cimes* – the oddball of the summits – by the French press, certainly had his own way of doing things. Having guided – although coerced might be a better way of putting it – the Belgian to victory in the 1976 Tour, Gitane directeur sportif Cyrille Guimard, one of the straightest talkers sport has ever seen, described him in typically forthright fashion. 'Having a Van Impe in a team was a guarantee of depression for a directeur sportif,' declared the Frenchman, who went on to guide Bernard Hinault and Laurent Fignon to another six Tour wins.

Guimard expanded on this throwaway put-down by explaining: 'The greatest climber of his generation – and one of the greatest of all time – didn't have the character to match his qualities on the bike...The Belgian Lucien Van Impe, with his air of inferiority and serious aspect and tendency to look away, had something shifty about him, a little guy whose utterances did not ring true. He always used to say "yes" but thought the contrary, without ever expressing himself openly.

'Let me reassure you that there's no sense of acrimony behind this unflattering portrait: the man didn't deserve to be a champion, that's all there is to say. Based on facts, gestures, words and acts, I know that Lucien was a pain in the arse. It was impossible to place any confidence in him. He was every directeur sportif's nightmare.'

Van Impe was brought up in Erpe-Mere, halfway between Ghent and Brussels. The third of seven brothers, one of whom died very young, he had bikes in his blood. His father, Jef, who had two sisters and five brothers, three of whom were professionals, owned the local bike shop in the back of the same building where Lucien's mother, Julia, had a café-bar. Jef Van Impe organised the coaching of his sons, who all raced even though some of them, Lucien included, didn't want to. 'I never really liked racing, to be honest. I did like working on bikes. In fact, when I was six years old I could build a wheel up from scratch. But I only raced because my father insisted on it and because I got paid for it,' he reveals.

Jef Van Impe's methods, which Lucien describes as 'very reasonable, very competent and very, very hard', were also extremely unusual in the Flemish flatlands. Until Lucien was seventeen, he used a fixed gear of 49x16 when training and racing – in theory, not big enough to compete on the flat, too big to cope with the region's fearsomely steep hills. 'He'd say to me, "Right, today I want you to ride to the Muur de Geraardsbergen and sprint up it thirty times." Sometimes it would be thirty-five times and always at a sprint, so not sitting in the saddle but up on the pedals to boost my *souplesse*. That's how I ended up becoming a racer, and also because when I was sixteen or seventeen I used to deliver newspapers on my bike around this whole area. The bike was very heavy, and it used to always weigh between sixty and a hundred kilos with all of the papers loaded on it. I used to be out delivering in the wind, covering thirty-five or forty kilometres.'

This regime proved hugely effective in the races on Flanders' cobbles and bergs. Van Impe gained the nickname 'Little Monkey' due to his ability to scamper up the steepest of these ramps, which often reach 25 per cent. 'When I was fifteen and sixteen I used to race at least once a week,' says the Belgian, who left school at fourteen to work as an apprentice carpenter with a coffin-maker before switching to newspaper deliveries. 'I used to win most of them, or usually finish second if I didn't. I could sprint a bit then, but I didn't like to do so. I preferred to attack right from the start and would often finish five, six or even more minutes ahead. Races would be about fifty, sixty kilometres long and my goal at the start would be to lap everyone.'

His talent as a climber earned him selection for the Belgian team that lined up at the 1967 edition of the Tour de l'Avenir, which was effectively the Tour de France for younger riders. Unfortunately, his opportunity to shine disappeared as the result of a serious crash on the descent off the Portet d'Aspet, which was unwittingly caused by his future team director Guimard, Van Impe's junior by exactly three months, who was on the French team and claimed the points title. 'It was actually on the same bend where Fabio Casartelli died when he crashed in the 1995 Tour de France. I was first to the summit and I started off down the descent quite steadily, waiting for the riders behind. Guimard was the first to pass me. He went by on my left. I clipped his wheel and fell into the trees in the ravine below, cutting my head right open. There was blood absolutely everywhere.'

Van Impe returned to the race the following year, winning a stage and the mountains title, but even then he felt his chances of becoming a pro were still very small. All that changed, though, due to the intervention of two illustrious former pros: Edgard Sorgeloos, a former racing lieutenant to the great Belgian Classics rider Rik Van Looy, and Federico Bahamontes, the Tour's all-time greatest climber thanks to his six mountains titles. Aware that Van Impe had a very different skill set to the archetypal Flemish rider who was the size of the brewery door and looked like he ate cobbles for breakfast, Sorgeloos took him to see former French champion Jean Stablinski, who was based just over the border from Belgium in Valenciennes and was team director at the Sonolor team. 'Stab' was impressed and said he'd keep an eye on Van Impe's progress.

Early the following season, Bahamontes was managing a Spanish team at the Vuelta a Navarra and was immediately smitten when he saw the Belgian romp away from the field every time the road went up in that amateur event. 'Bahamontes was staying in the same hotel and he came to see me to say what a great climber I was and that

I had to turn pro,' Van Impe recalls. 'It was quite something as he was my idol. He told me I could win the Tour de France, and of course all I could think was that there was no way I could manage that. When I got home I had all the directeurs sportifs ringing me up because the papers had picked up on what Bahamontes had said about me, that I should turn pro.'

Bahamontes also set about making that happen by ringing up several team directors and pleading the Belgian's case. One of those the Spaniard called was Stablinski, who already had the little man on his radar. Convinced by Bahamontes of Van Impe's incredible potential, the Sonolor-Lejeune DS offered him a contract with the promise that he would make his professional racing debut at the Tour de France.

'Stablinski sorted it all out with my father,' says Van Impe. 'On the Monday before the Tour started I spoke to Stablinski myself; the next day I went to Brussels to get a pro licence. I did a race at Valenciennes the next day as that was where Stablinski was from. I punctured and didn't finish. Then on the Saturday I lined up in the Tour de France. I couldn't believe I was there. It was a dream for me. It came very quickly for the team too as the bike they gave me was much too big. Everyone was joking with me about it. The first rider I saw was Rik Van Looy, who came over and said to me: "Hey, Pinocchio, what are you doing on that big bike there?" I couldn't believe Van Looy was talking to me, as were all of the other riders like Eddy Merckx.'

According to Tour director Jacques Goddet, Van Impe was 'very small and light, with angelic features, always smiling, always amiable'. Goddet also said he was 'gifted with a touch of devilry that contained a strong dose of tactical intelligence'. He was twelfth that first year, a good distance behind another Belgian Tour debutant, Eddy Merckx. Van Impe describes his compatriot as 'intimidating' and Guimard suggests that his Gitane team leader was so fearful of getting on the wrong side of Merckx that he went out of his way to help 'The Cannibal' whenever he could. Van Impe agrees that he was in thrall to Merckx, although he was far from alone in that. 'Eddy was a phenomenon already. He'd already won the Tour of Italy, and he was so strong. I spent as much time as I could watching him and trying to learn from him. That was the first time I'd raced against him. In that first Tour I did manage to stay with the big names in the mountains, but I didn't really take them on. It was all about gaining experience. But I wasn't afraid of anyone. When someone attacked, I would stay on their wheel.'

Guimard insists Van Impe let his fascination with 'The Cannibal' colour his tactics and attitude on the bike. He says of Van Impe that his 'Lilliputian body seemed very frail next to the solid carcass of Eddy Merckx', and questions whether the little climber was afraid of 'his cannibalistic compatriot'. Did this, Guimard later wondered, explain Van Impe's shattered psychology and brittleness?

'Van Impe aimed low. And he did so very well,' says the Frenchman. 'At no time did he want to be the "sporting enemy" of Merckx because of the risk of becoming unpopular in his own country. On the contrary, if "The Cannibal" was in difficulty, he would even help him. You never knew how that might help you. Effectively, Van Impe signed up for life insurance... If he'd had a directeur sportif alongside him who had been courageous enough to make him a rival to Merckx, to build a team around him that was capable of fighting for him, The Cannibal would certainly not have won five Tours...'

Van Impe doesn't accept this, insisting there was no point in targeting the yellow jersey while Merckx was in his pomp, insisting that the teams he was part of were rarely strong enough to enable him to challenge his compatriot. Indeed, he doesn't agree with very much of what Guimard has said and written in two books about his years in the sport. 'In both of them he's written stuff that's simply not true. He lies an awful lot; he just says what he thinks and believes it. It's always "me, me, me" – "Me, I did this, I did that, me, me, me!" It was him who won the Tour, not Van Impe, not Hinault, but him. But that's not true at all. It's the rider who wins.'

Van Impe does acknowledge it wasn't all bad with Guimard, but it's evident the pair don't seek each other out to discuss the good old days. 'As a directeur he was very good, but as a man he wasn't. He was a special one. Why? When I said something was white, he would say it was black. You couldn't discuss the issue with him. That's what he thought and he couldn't be shifted. Tactically, though, he was brilliant. He knew the races, the courses, and the riders because he'd been competing against them just the year before.'

A climber to his core, Van Impe has said that he got more pleasure from winning the Tour's King of the Mountains title six times than he did when he captured the yellow jersey in 1976, even though he describes the final day in Paris as the best of his career. His upside-down perspective is perplexing, although less so when his character is considered. Climbing mountains came easily to Van Impe, who loved nothing more than an easy life. He had his parents and then Rita looking after his every need at home; he bumped along very nicely with the big names in the peloton, his lack of threat allowing him a large degree of freedom when he reached his favourite terrain. As Van Impe saw it, there was no need to bring pressure on himself and stir his rivals by raising his sights to the biggest prizes. He acknowledges that his principal goal was putting his name alongside those others who had led the Tour to the top of its most renowned ascents.

Stablinski accommodated this attitude, while always feeling that Van Impe had much more in his tank. But the ageing French DS was never able to tap those resources, perhaps because three Tour de France mountains titles, four stage wins and a string of consistently high finishes were already a good return for one of the peloton's weaker teams.

Yet, long before Guimard's arrival in 1976 at what was by then Gitane, Stablinski believed Van Impe had the physical potential to win cycling's greatest prize. 'I am convinced Lucien has the makings of a Tour winner. Over the seven seasons that I've been with him...his progression has been constant. He's a rider who wasn't worn out as an amateur and whose athletic maturity has been confirmed over the course of several years,' 'Stab' told *L'Équipe* towards the end of the 1975 Tour, where the Belgian finished third overall and, to most people's surprise, won the third week's forty-kilometre time trial to Châtel, beating Merckx, Thévenet and Zoetemelk by a distance.

'Could Van Impe win the Tour?' asked *L'Équipe* in a post-stage headline. Stablinski was convinced he could. 'I've always thought that he would have the make-up of a Tour winner at the age of twenty-eight. That's the age that he is now, but he lost a year last year because of his accident at the Midi Libre,' said the Gitane DS. Like Zoetemelk, Van Impe had also been a victim of the crash at Valras-Plage. Although nowhere near as badly affected as the Dutchman, the little Belgian struggled for many months to regain his form, and only achieved that well into 1975.

Having competed against Van Impe throughout his own shortened career, Guimard, one of the most perceptive of riders and team directors, was extremely aware of his new leader's strengths and weaknesses when he took over at Gitane. He was sure, though, that the leader on his new team could win the greatest prize in the sport, despite his deficiencies.

The problem, as Guimard immediately recognised, was that because almost everyone accepted Merckx was invincible, they also regarded Van Impe's never-say-win outlook as legitimate. So how was the French director, who had been racing against his new charges just a few months earlier, to instil a very different attitude in his team and its leader?

He began by humiliating them. In January 1976 he had won the French cyclo-cross title. With a little bit of luck he could have added the world title a couple of weeks later. Consequently, when, at the very end of that same month, he oversaw Gitane's first training camp on the Côte d'Azur, he was at the peak of his form. He took his riders out on their first ride together and gave them a two-wheeled hiding. His aim was 'to impose group discipline'; in other words, to establish his own authority.

Guimard depended on three team members to achieve this: his assistant DS Maurice Champion and road captains Robert Mintkewicz and Willy Teirlinck. He explained to them how Gitane would head to the Tour, not with the aim of defending Van Impe's King of the Mountains title, but targeting the major prize. The difficulty Guimard and his confidants faced was getting Van Impe to believe the yellow jersey was a realistic goal.

'He only did what he saw fit. It was quite clear he hadn't

taken on the new spirit that was animating our group,' says Guimard, who had been pre-warned of Van Impe's stubbornness. 'But the portrait that had been given was nowhere near the reality.'

Along with his reputation for almost unparalleled brilliance on the climbs, Van Impe was known for being exceptionally fussy about his bike and acknowledges that some of his prima donna tendencies meant he could come across not only as a big kid but a spoiled one too. 'I need someone to be with me and take care of everything. I need them to talk about and only be interested in me. That's how I am,' he once confessed. At home, Rita played that role. Within the Gitane team and most especially at the 1976 Tour, Mintkewicz took it on, cleaning his leader's shoes, pinning his race number on his jersey, running his bath and bringing him food and drinks in bed, all so that Van Impe could spend as much time as possible lying down and resting. 'He was the best teammate I ever had. He did everything I ever asked did dear old Robert,' Van Impe acknowledges.

According to Guimard, in the weeks leading up to the Tour, Van Impe took 'a malign pleasure' in contradicting his team director, persistently pushing his patience. At the same time, Guimard was doing all he could to convince the Belgian that he could win the Tour, that the target was overall victory in Paris and nothing else. As Guimard saw it, 'I knew that he couldn't lose it as long as we didn't commit any strategic errors.'

Ultimately, two events changed Van Impe's perspective, at least to the extent where Guimard could believe that they both shared the same objective of winning the Tour de France. The first was a furious row between the pair during the Midi Libre stage race a few weeks before the Tour was due to start in Saint Jean des Monts. Convinced that Van Impe was still set on 'a cushy life with the polka-dot jersey as his focus' and exasperated at his lack of interest, Guimard cracked. He threatened the Belgian with exclusion from the Tour team. L'Équipe reported that, 'This psychological ploy hit the bull's-eye,' although it added the caveat that, 'Guimard still had trouble getting him back on the rails. Van Impe stuck very much to his habits.'

However, Guimard's task in getting Van Impe to believe his objective for the Tour was possible was made a good deal easier when, just a few days after that heated encounter, Eddy Merckx announced that he would not be starting the Tour. After finishing eighth at the Giro, it had become increasingly apparent his physical dominance was waning, although a finger-length saddle sore was his more immediately painful concern. For Guimard, Merckx's absence was a clear pointer towards Van Impe winning the yellow jersey, and on this at least Van Impe is in agreement with his former team director.

'I realised that a Tour victory was within my reach the previous year, especially after my victory in the time trial to Châtel, and I was even more convinced of it when I saw how mountainous the route was,' the Belgian confirms. 'There were lots of summit finishes and then of course we heard that Merckx wasn't going to ride and that boosted my morale even further, even though I still had to deal with Zoetemelk, Thévenet, Poulidor and lots of other great riders. But it was a good route for me. I also had Guimard as my directeur, and there's no doubt he was very good in that role.'

Guimard's strategy for the first half of the race was to ensure Van Impe didn't fall out of contention for the yellow jersey. This meant remaining within four minutes of defending champion Thévenet going into that first mountain stage. Fresher than he often had been in the past as the result of a pre-season operation to resolve a long-standing problem with a hernia, Van Impe, said *L'Équipe*, still 'pranced around without worrying too much about what was happening at the front of the peloton'.

However, lifted by the race's passage through Mere on the third stage, when banners urged him to forsake polka-dot red for Tour-winning yellow, and prompted regularly by Guimard, he didn't lose a substantial amount of time on race leader Freddy Maertens. Better still, he went into the first rest day at Divonne-les-Bains a second to the good on Thévenet and with eleven in hand on Joop Zoetemelk. With an individual and the team time trial already completed and all five summit finishes still ahead, Guimard's remodelled Van Impe was now a genuine contender for yellow.

Like so many riders, Van Impe's career can be divided into the period before they took the yellow jersey and the one that followed. It was this second part that best high-lighted Van Impe the rider and man.

Guimard recalls Van Impe being 'drunk with delight' having donned the yellow jersey. One of his teammates said he was like a kid who found his favourite present under the Christmas tree. The problem, they all realised, would be persuading Van Impe he had to relinquish it to someone else, if only for a few days.

Guimard's plan was to encourage a well-placed rider to attack and take the jersey on the stage to Pyrénées 2000. This, he hoped, would free Van Impe and, more impor-tantly, his mostly inexperienced team of domestiques at Gitane from the pressure of defending a very narrow lead on the brutally hard stage that followed to Pla d'Adet. Guimard informed his sponsors of his controversial plan, and they approved it. Later, he called Thévenet's Peugeot teammate Raymond Delisle and hinted that there might be something to gain if he attacked on the first Pyrenean stage. Guimard knew that if Delisle ran with the bait, Thévenet and Peugeot would not chase him down. He was equally convinced Gan-Mercier leaders Zoetemelk and Raymond Poulidor would sit tight too.

The plan worked a treat, although only after some of the Belgian teams had tried to give chase behind Delisle, apparently at Van Impe's instigation. He couldn't see why he had to release the yellow jersey, his consternation

– Guimard describes it as 'idiocy' – prompted by Rita, whose ambition for her husband far exceeded his own.

Van Impe admits his career would have been totally different without her, and that she had given him a rocket when he came back from the 1975 Tour with the polka-dot rather than the yellow jersey, which was within his reach. 'She's always had a considerable influence over me,' Van Impe confessed. 'She phones me every day. If by chance she doesn't, I sleep badly. On big days, she calls me twice, in the morning and the evening…I love seeing her on the race. I don't have any worries when she's around.'

The fact that Rita was such a constant in Van Impe's life exasperated Guimard on occasions, especially those when he would find himself up against both of them. This was one of those moments. When Guimard went to his leader's hotel room after the Pyrénées 2000 stage, he was confronted by both husband and wife. Rita harangued the Frenchman, who responded by saying she should pack her bags and leave if she didn't calm down. He added Van Impe could leave too if he didn't like it.

The story of Van Impe's epic ride back into the yellow jersey at Pla d'Adet is one of the Tour's most renowned. Climbing the Col du Portillon, with eighty kilometres still remaining to the finish, Guimard instructed first Raymond Martin and then Alain Meslet to tell Van Impe he needed to attack. Both returned to say he was refusing to. Guimard then drove up himself to pass on his orders.

An apocryphal account suggests the Frenchman threatened to drive the Belgian off the road if he didn't obey, but this has never been made clear. What is certain is that Van Impe did respond, but not fully, admitting that he was only riding at 80 per cent of his capacity when he first attacked. Climbing the Peyresourde in the company of Luis Ocaña, who was happy to contribute to any move that would sink Zoetemelk, whom he detested, Van Impe's lead was almost two minutes. *L'Équipe* reported that Guimard drove up again and said: 'You've taken 1-50 from Delisle and Zoetemelk. Do you want to win the Tour de France? Yes or no?' Van Impe's subsequent acceleration won him the stage and the Tour. 'For committing the same error Lucien might have committed without Cyrille Guimard's prompting, Joop Zoetemelk lost the Tour on this key stage,' noted *L'Équipe*.

It was a second Christmas for Van Impe, who was so overcome that he promptly told an interviewer at Pla d'Adet he didn't need anyone else in order to win the Tour. Guimard was apoplectic and threatened to kick him out of the race. He forced the yellow jersey to apologise to the whole team before the stage to Tulle, Van Impe, his face bright red with anger, doing so with obvious reluctance and much Flemish muttering.

Guimard says that by the time the race reached Paris he was on the edge of a breakdown. It was clear then and remains so today that Lucien Van Impe would not have won the 1976 Tour without the Frenchman's tactical interventions. Guimard, though, suggests, 'The real masterstroke, the only masterstroke in truth, was getting a rider to win the Tour who didn't want to do so.'

With Bernard Hinault fast emerging and some bad feeling between Van Impe and some of his teammates, Guimard didn't back down when the Belgian demanded a large pay increase to cement a new contract. He brazened out the negotiations, then let Van Impe leave. Finding few teams were interested in signing a notoriously difficult personality, even one who had just won the Tour, Van Impe eventually secured a deal with Lejeune, but for less money than Guimard had been offering him.

The new deal put Van Impe together with DS Henry Anglade, who adopted Stablinski's less confrontational approach with his leader, which ultimately suited neither rider nor director. Van Impe effectively ran the team on the road, Anglade defending that approach by saying, 'It's the team leader who's the one in the peloton and he must know how to react. If he doesn't know how to do that then he's not really a leader.' His method worked to an extent, but ultimately failed at the most critical point, when Van Impe rode alone towards Alpe d'Huez. 'At the foot of the climb Van Impe had won the Tour. Over twenty-one bends he definitively lost that opportunity,' wrote Jean-Paul Vespini.

At the time, Van Impe blamed the Matra in the Tour convoy that knocked him into the roadside ditch at Huez. But, by that point, Hennie Kuiper was almost on him. The incident was significant in his defeat, but not crucial, as Van Impe now acknowledges. 'I don't think I attacked too early that day. When I'd won the Tour in 1976 at Pla d'Adet I'd attacked eighty kilometres from the finish. I always liked going away on my own in the mountains. The problem was that I didn't eat after the Glandon and that was my own fault. When I was on Alpe d'Huez I could tell that I was running out of juice. I ate on the climb but it was too late by then. That was my big mistake because if I had eaten earlier I would probably have finished five minutes clear. I was still a minute or so clear about three kilometres from the top, but then they started pulling the cars out from between Kuiper and me and one of them hit me. I ended up standing there with my bike in one hand and the wheel in the other, waiting for my director, who wasn't there. Normally, I would have won the Tour again in '77. I was a lot stronger than I had been the year before,' he says with a smile and a shake of the head.

It should have been a footnote, but much continues to be made of the incident, particularly in Belgium, where a documentary, *De Val* (*The Fall*), appeared as recently as 2011. Van Impe harks back to it too, suggesting that it would never have happened had Anglade not decided to replace Van Impe's preferred mechanic, Chris Van de Gehuchte, with another member of Lejeune's support staff in his team car just moments before that stage began.

'I always liked Chris to be close by on the mountain stages because he was almost like a brother, and we're still close today. After the stages he would take my bike and sleep with it in his room. He knew me so well and he'd watch me and say, "You need to eat something," and stuff like that. He knew me much better than the directeur,' Van Impe explains. 'Anglade changed things at the last minute that day and had a friend of his in the car, and this guy did nothing. When you ride up a mountain, the mechanic would be standing in the back door of the car with a bike ready on his shoulder. But this guy left it strapped onto the rack at the back, fastened with two straps. So when I crashed and the car stopped, he had to undo those first before he could help me. I lost a lot of time waiting while he got the bike out for me.

'That day in '77 was my worst day as a rider. Every time I go back to Alpe d'Huez I feel a little unhappy because I never won there. It makes me sad because it's a climb that suits the best climbers and they all want to win there. It's special, even more so now.'

The situation has at least resulted in Van Impe re-evaluating Guimard's ability. 'In all honesty, he helped me considerably…If he hadn't been there [in 1976], I don't know whether I would have won, but what I can say for sure is that if I had still been with him in 1977 I would have won my second Tour de France. You always need good advice at a certain moment, and Cyrille knew when to give it. He knew me perfectly as a rider and as a man.'

For Guimard, whose assessment of Van Impe and his achievements is no less cutting than his analysis of Eddy

Merckx, Greg LeMond and many others, Van Impe may have been 'a pain in the arse', but he concludes: 'His reputation as a climber was well deserved. I believe he remains one of the best of all time, the greatest in this category alongside Charly Gaul and Federico Bahamontes.'

In the latter part of his career, as his form became more erratic, the teams he rode for more ordinary, and Bernard Hinault was dominating the peloton as Merckx had once done, Van Impe switched his focus back to the climbs. He all but writes off the four years between 1977 and 1981, saying he was consistently dogged by bad luck. Poor judgement was also apparent in his choice of teams, but a second Tour stage win at Pla d'Adet in the 1981 Tour signalled a renaissance in his career, just when it seemed his only claim to fame would be sporting the most cele- brated perm in the peloton, which came thanks to a cousin of Rita's who was the Belgian hairdressing cham- pion for seven years in succession.

'The mountain classification is for me the most impor- tant thing. I'd rather have a bird in the hand than two in the air,' he said in 1981 when asked if he would attempt to challenge Hinault for the yellow jersey. Without Guimard to prop him up, having gone back to being 'a big kid who makes his way through life without being too concerned with it' as *L'Équipe*'s Robert Silva put it, Van Impe was content to stick to his patch and avoid goading 'The Badger'.

His only racing goal was to equal, but not beat,

Bahamontes' record of six mountains titles, which he achieved in 1983, when he also claimed his sixth solo victory at a summit stage finish. Looking back, he has some regrets, but mostly good memories. 'In addition to the finish in Paris, my favourite is of that day on Alpe d'Huez in 1976 when I first got the yellow jersey. But a year later, that same climb also gave me the saddest day of my career,' he says, looking wistful for a moment. But the smile's soon back. 'I think about those two days almost every time I walk in my front door,' he chuckles. 'I'll never forget that mountain.'

9

Once Cyrille Guimard has dropped back into the convoy of vehicles tracking the two leaders, Van Impe sticks to the orders he's been given. Fuelled for the past year by his astounding victory in the final time trial of the 1975 race, when he beat a field containing Merckx, Thévenet, Zoetemelk and Poulidor, he draws on that memory now. Riding just below his limit, but going hard enough to discourage Zoetemelk from attacking, he surges up to and around bend nine.

The road steepens noticeably coming out of this hairpin, which comes halfway up the climb to Alpe d'Huez. Van Impe's rhythm is relentless. Sensing the gradient tugging him back, he springs up out of his saddle. His pedal cadence picks up slightly to maintain his speed, but his body remains almost stationary as he dances on the pedals, his slender arms swinging the bike smoothly from side to side as his legs, sculpted like a thoroughbred's, with the valley between his vastus medialis and vastus lateralis muscles in his thighs *so deep and defined that it is lost in shadow, send almost every watt of power down through his pedals.*

Watching from his following car, Tour director Jacques Goddet is captivated. 'Van Impe was no longer the little blue-eyed boy who contents himself by making flea-like leaps in order to be crowned best climber,' he will write in his editorial in L'Équipe *the next day. 'Yesterday he was a resolute man, carrying the fight directly at the point where it was most advantageous. He exploited the rising terrain to the maximum, carving out gaps so substantial that from this point on the rivals that he conquered will have to train their sights on him and attempt to rough him up away from the high passes.'*

Van Impe leads Zoetemelk through the little chicane coming into bend eight. Their lead is now 1-12 over the chasing group, where Thévenet is in full nodding-dog mode, his upper body bobbing like the arm on an oil derrick, pumping out every little bit of resource, 'looking like he was trying to tame his bike', according to Pierre Chany. Race leader Freddy Maertens and Michel Pollentier, his personal St Bernard, are almost three minutes in arrears.

Exiting bend eight, the spire of Saint-Ferréol church is just 300 metres away, standing proud from the ash trees, although the background greenery of the mountainside on the other side of the Sarenne gorge initially makes it difficult to pick out. Far easier to see is the road sign that announces 'Panorama Saint-Ferréol 300m'.

Still doing all of the work on the front, Van Impe stays

on the racing line on the left-hand side of the road, missing what is undoubtedly one of the best views back down the mountain, over several hairpins and the church at La Garde, all the way to Bourg d'Oisans. Horseshoeing to the left around the front of the eleventh-century Église Saint-Ferréol d'Huez, which sits on the Alpe's second 'landing', the Belgian glances up to get a first sight of the pretty village of Huez. Above it, like 'a row of giant beehives against the skyline' according to the Observer's Geoffrey Nicholson, sit the blocks and oversized chalets of the resort of Alpe d'Huez, which is now less than half a dozen kilometres away.

The proximity to Huez combined with the stunning grandstand perspective has drawn a considerable number of fans to this bend, which, like the one far below in front of the church at La Garde, turns ninety degrees into the mountain as the third and final part of the climb commences. For Van Impe and Zoetemelk, who switch down a couple of sprockets in order to pick up speed as the gradient eases passing around and beyond the church, this bend isn't any more significant than any others on this mountain. However, 1,000 or so kilometres due north, the name Alpe d'Huez is quickly increasing in import.

In Belgium, bike fans are listening in to Théo Mathy, whose TV and radio commentaries have described the many exploits of Eddy Merckx and, in the absence of the country's most celebrated athlete, are now detailing Van Impe's push for glory. At the same time, Dutch wieler volk are tuned in to the Tour coverage on the national network NOS, *where Theo Koomen, excitable even when there is no need to be, can barely contain himself as Zoetemelk closes in on a potential double – a stage win and the yellow jersey. Even better, his final victim will be a rider from Belgium, the country that loves to hate Holland's beloved 'Jopie'.*

It's been eight years since Jan Janssen was crowned as the Tour's first Dutch champion. In the interim, there have been some great days, mainly thanks to Zoetemelk, but Merckx's defence of the yellow jersey has been close to remorseless. Now, though, there is hope. Merckx is absent, Freddy Maertens is quickly losing his grip on yellow, and Van Impe is a one-trick pony, a mountains specialist who is sure to stumble.

As Koomen paints a picture of Alpe d'Huez, rippling in the heat haze high above bend seven, the mountain is already gaining mythological status among the hundreds of thousands who have stopped working and are listening in back in the Netherlands.

A LITTLE CORNER OF HOLLAND

The origins of the tale of how the Dutch came to adopt a road on a French mountainside lie in wine and dykes. The story begins back in the Middle Ages, in the vineyards of Bordeaux on the other side of France. From the fourteenth century onwards, the Dutch had acquired a taste for the wines from this region. However, by the early seventeenth century, demand for Bordeaux's production exceeded supply, which could only be increased by bringing more land under cultivation. The difficulty was that much of the land in the Gironde delta region was marshy and unusable.

Searching for a solution, Dutch merchants turned to engineers who had drained coastal land in the Netherlands, principally Jan Adriaanszoon Leeghwater, an architect and hydraulic engineer. Leeghwater oversaw the construction of dykes and pumping stations in this marshland, draining the water in newly dug channels to create more agricultural land and increase the cultivation of grapes for wine production. Given their nation's extensive trading links, Dutch merchants were then well placed to take advantage of this boost in production.

Holland's traditional links with France's south-west took on a two-wheeled perspective in the years after the Second World War. Dutch holidaymakers flocked to the region over the summer months and were always enthusiastic supporters when the Tour passed by. According to *L'Équipe*, it was 'a time when habit gave birth to a kind of aphorism: the Bordeaux stage was the stage of the Dutch'. Between Hans Dekkers' victory in 1952 and Jo de Roo's in 1965, Dutch riders won half of the fourteen stages to finish in the beautiful riverside city.

Always overshadowed as a cycling power by its neighbours, particularly Belgium but also by Germany and even Luxembourg, the Netherlands began to rise from relative obscurity in the mid-1960s. Leading the way was

Jan Janssen, world champion in 1964 and three times the points champion at the Tour before he rode off with the yellow jersey in 1968. Right on his heels were a pack of youngsters, led by Joop Zoetemelk, who was undoubtedly the best climber the country had ever produced. From the mid-1970s onwards, almost all of the most prominent Dutch riders at the Tour were specialist climbers. In the vanguard were Zoetemelk and Hennie Kuiper. Behind them came Peter Winnen, Johan van der Velde, Steven Rooks and Gert-Jan Theunisse.

There is little doubt that the Tour's change of emphasis from valley to summit finishes encouraged the emergence of riders of this type and turned them into sporting heroes in the Netherlands. While they were not at the same level as footballing icons such as Johan Cruyff, Johan Neeskens and Ruud Krol, they were not far behind. When Zoetemelk returned to the Tour in 1975 after his horrific crash the previous season and took what he has often claimed was the most satisfying win of his career at Pla d'Adet in the Pyrenees, the TV and radio audience back home was in the millions. Consequently, the appearance of Alpe d'Huez on the Tour route in 1976 was very much the right kind of climb at the right time as far as the Dutch were concerned. If a successor to Janssen was to appear, he would surely emerge on summits like this.

Although not as iconic as the Galibier, Tourmalet or the Izoard for the sport's purists – it has been described as a *parvenu* – Alpe d'Huez has changed the complexion of professional cycling in the same way those legendary passes did in the early twentieth century. As it has done so, the Dutch have been ever-present and hugely influential, perennially turning this superlative natural arena into the closest cycling gets to a football stadium.

Just as Bradley Wiggins' 2012 Tour de France victory further boosted the popularity of cycling in Britain on the back of successes achieved by its track riders and road stars such as Mark Cavendish, Holland's attachment to Alpe d'Huez increased when Hennie Kuiper won on the Alpe the year after Zoetemelk and, just like his compatriot, missed out on taking the yellow jersey by a mere eight seconds. Indeed, Kuiper insists that was the year that Alpe-mania first revealed itself. 'Actually, all the euphoria around Alpe d'Huez started with me. Joop had already won a year earlier, but when I won in 1977, all hell broke loose on the climb,' he told Dutch newspaper *Het Vrije Volk*.

As had been the case in 1976, that year's stage to Alpe d'Huez was the point that the Tour came to life. Having tackled the Pyrenees in the first few days, the race had lolled in the doldrums for two weeks, German debutant Dietrich 'Didi' Thurau holding the yellow jersey as his TI-Raleigh team kept his rivals in a vice-like grip. But on a stage that took in the 2,000-metre ascents of the Madeleine and Glandon passes in addition to the Alpe, time-trial specialist Thurau knew he was doomed.

Van Impe, Thévenet and Zoetemelk played key roles

once again. The little Belgian breezed away from his rivals halfway up the Glandon pass. With eighty kilometres to the finish, it appeared a premature and foolhardy move. But at the foot of the Alpe, his lead was more than two and a half minutes. Once again, Thévenet was forced to lead the pursuit of Van Impe with no help at all from Zoetemelk and Kuiper. The Frenchman chipped away at Van Impe's lead, until, just below bend seven, Kuiper accelerated clear. As he rounded the Saint-Ferréol church, Kuiper was speeding between thin rows of spectators and an unbroken line of Peugeots, Citroëns and Renaults as he closed in rapidly on Van Impe, who was desperately trying to fend off 'the man with the hammer'.

Soon after, Van Impe suffered a double blow. The first was figurative. As many have subsequently found, riding into the headwind that often blows down the Romanche valley is not ideal preparation for an assault on the Alpe, and he started to run out of gas. The second was physical. Just above Huez, when there was just a hundred metres between Van Impe and Kuiper, the Belgian was shunted into the roadside ditch by a car in the Tour convoy. As Van Impe floundered, Kuiper swept by.

Urged on by DS Peter Post's shouts and frantic slapping on the side of the TI-Raleigh team car, Kuiper looked to have the stage and the yellow jersey won at the bottom end of Alpe d'Huez, where huge crowds had gathered, many of them exuberant and celebrating Dutch fans who had transistors stuck to their ears blasting out Theo

Koomen's frantic commentary. But over the final three kilometres, the French fans managed to draw a last cussed response from Thévenet. With a lead of forty-nine seconds over Kuiper to protect, their 'Nanar' ceded forty-one. Lifted from his bike, he was still gasping several minutes later when French TV interviewed him. 'I confess I really thought I wasn't going to keep it,' he said of the yellow jersey. 'I had to take on the toughest pursuit of my career... I had to battle alone like a convict...'

Just as it had done in 1976, the climb up to Alpe d'Huez had provided an epic contest, with the Dutch at the very heart of it. Over subsequent years, that pattern continued. Although Kuiper's second success is tainted by the disqualification of stage winner Michel Pollentier for attempting to cheat the dope control, a year later the 'Jopies' were exultant once more when, having been vilified yet again for his passiveness during the first of two stages on the Alpe, Zoetemelk responded in the ideal manner with victory in the second. Zoetemelk admits, 'That victory in 1979 was my favourite stage win at the Tour.'

After a year's enforced absence from the Alpe due to roadworks, the Tour returned in 1981 and the Dutch fans came with it in unprecedented numbers. Just before the race, the *Limburgsch Dagblad* predicted 'an invasion of Alpe d'Huez from Limburg'. Describing the climb as '*de Hollandse berg*' – the Dutch mountain – the paper said that many locals were taking a week off to travel to the Alpe. 'You see real racing on Alpe d'Huez,' one Limburger bike fan told them. He also revealed that he and other fans provided a little more than just vocal support to Dutch riders. 'Whenever possible, we help the Dutch riders by pushing them. But you have to make sure there's not a commissaire around as pushing them can result in them receiving time penalties.'

The Alpe phenomenon was also picked up in national paper *De Telegraaf*, which labelled Alpe d'Huez as 'the Tour's Dutch city', adding that the resort had taken this status from Bordeaux thanks to the exploits of Zoetemelk and Kuiper. The paper estimated that a quarter of a million people had made their way to the mountain, and that many of the Dutch fans had been there for several days before race day. 'None of the other gruelling mountain stages such as the Puy de Dôme, Aubisque or Tourmalet can compete with Alpe d'Huez. They want to be here at all costs,' *De Telegraaf* said of the Dutch fans.

One member of the Fortuna cycling club told the paper he'd arrived at bend seven four days before the Tour was due and was passing the days pouring cold water over the heads of cyclists grinding their way up the climb in the summer heat. 'I've already poured about 150 litres of water today,' he said, before rushing into the road to douse another ruddy rider.

There was plenty of a different liquid flowing too. Three of the Fortuna clubman's neighbours at bend seven had brought 360 bottles of beer with them from the Netherlands. 'The beer in France is simply too expensive,' they said, complying with the stereotype their neighbours have of the Dutch being tight with money. They also had come with a hacksaw, just in case the gate allowing access to the pump-operated tap at the back of the church was chained up. Intended to water the flowers left by those visiting the graves of friends and relatives in the small cemetery that sits between the church and the road, that pump was the only source of potable water on race days and would creak around almost constantly. 'Last year someone put a lock on the cemetery gate. We had to saw through it because the riders need the water [from the tap],' they said in mitigation of this act of vandalism.

That year, when Peter Winnen gave the Dutch their fifth win out of a possible six since the Tour's reacquaintance with the Alpe, a substantial part of the huge Dutch contingent had settled on bend seven, with its spectacular view back down the mountain, ready access to water and, just as importantly, 'a landing' on which hundreds of tents could be pitched, some of them perched frighteningly close to a huge drop down into the Sarenne gorge. Some, though, made the trip in rather more style, and none more so than Frans and Corrie Siemons, who drove the one thousand kilometres south in a 37-year-old London double-decker bus, which guzzled a litre of fuel for every two kilometres it climbed and sported eye-catching promotional images for their business, the Sauna Diana, a high-class brothel in Zundert, just on the Dutch side of the border with Belgium.

Enthusiastic backers of a semi-pro cycling team, which would later bring through the 1992 Tour's best young rider, Eddy Bouwmans, as well as their own son Jan, who would ride the Tour five times and now runs the Sauna Diana along with brother Ruud, the Siemons became one of the great attractions on the Alpe. Having first come to see Zoetemelk's second win in 1979, the owners of what was probably the first team bus to grace the sport used to bring several members of their bike team with them, although – sensibly keeping business and pleasure apart – none of their two dozen female employees.

When Winnen, with legs as pale as his white cotton socks and eyebrows so blond that it made his ashen face almost featureless in the blinding heat, won on the Alpe in 1981 it had been estimated there were 100,000 Dutch fans on the mountain. After he emulated Zoetemelk and Kuiper by claiming a second success in 1983, giving Jaap Reuten yet another opportunity to set the bells ringing at Notre-Dame-des-Neiges, their numbers had grown again, and continued to do so. By 1986, when Hinault became the first Frenchman to win at Alpe d'Huez, leading some French papers to declare that the Breton had finally put the resort on the map, Reuten affirmed that it already was, telling *Het Vrije Volk*, 'The Tour has made Alpe d'Huez famous, especially in Holland. Ten years ago, hardly anybody had heard of it, but now it's a household name.'

Since Gert-Jan Theunisse claimed the eighth Dutch victory on the Alpe more than a quarter of a century ago, the orange-clad hordes have barely had a sniff of a win on the Alpe, but that has not stopped 'the thousands of blond heads and red bodies', as one Dutch journalist described them, from descending on the mountain. The mania still continues. According to Fabrice Hurth, director of Alpe d'Huez Tourisme, in 2013 the first Dutch camper van arrived twenty-six days before the Tour peloton were set to take the first double ascent of the Alpe. By race day, every possible camping space in the proximity of bend seven had been filled, the kerb stones painted orange, the road plastered with the names of a new generation of cycling heroes, principally 'Bau and Lau', Bauke Mollema and Laurens ten Dam.

For these fans, the trip to Alpe d'Huez is Spring Break and the X Factor combined, mixed up with a good measure of Amstel Gold and dosed with a touch of the Tour de France. It's more about partying than it is about cycling, until race day at least. Techno blasts out from myriad sound systems and continues well into the night. Fancy dress is almost de rigueur and often hugely entertaining.

When race day comes, the partying continues, but the focus is on those making their way up the road. Firstly, the thousands of cyclists, who get cheers, pushes and dousings. Then on the media and other race vehicles, whose occupants are advised to keep windows firmly shut in order to avoid soakings by the foul-smelling contents of water guns. Then, finally, comes the race itself. The fans create an orange corridor of noise that riders say is the closest they get to experiencing the atmosphere at a major football match. It's their Wembley, Amsterdam Arena or De Kuip. The noise is deafening, the quickening of the peloton's pace very distinct as they are pushed on by adrenaline and, perhaps, a touch of fear, their route ahead determined by the gap that always just opens up in the midst of the baying masses.

British ex-pro David Millar describes racing through this mayhem as an intense and even unpleasant experience. 'On a lot of climbs, when you get dropped you can enjoy the serenity of riding up, of being in your own space, but on the Alpe d'Huez there's a cacophony of noise. For us, it's a bit feral really. It's a bit like riding through a big village fair where everyone is drunk.'

Like a number of his peers, Laurens ten Dam's first encounter with the Alpe came as a fan rather than as a rider. In 2003, having won the Marmotte sportive that finishes on the climb, he decided to stay on for the main event with his girlfriend. 'We stayed at Bourg d'Oisans for a week,' he recalled. 'We were at Dutch corner, naturally, and the atmosphere was amazing... When I was there in 2003 I dreamt of riding up Alpe d'Huez in the Tour one day. But that's all it was – a dream... The Alpe is definitely my favourite climb, it's every Dutchman's favourite.'

It is certainly Aart Vierhouten's favourite, although he has plenty of reason to think the opposite. In 2004, having struggled all the way up the climb, illness putting him through every kind of torture, Vierhouten rolled into the finish after taking almost fifty-four minutes when most of his peers were taking around forty-five to complete the 15.5-kilometre time trial from Bourg d'Oisans. '*Jezus Christus!*' exclaimed the sweat-soaked Dutchman as saliva ran off his chin. A few hours later, as he lay on his bed looking at the ceiling of his hotel room, Vierhouten was told his effort had been in vain. He had been eliminated from the race after finishing outside the time limit established by Lance Armstrong's near-record ascent of the Alpe.

Rather than shedding tears as many of those left by the Tour tend to, Vierhouten listened to his Lotto team leader Robbie McEwen. 'Come on, Aart, let's go and do some boozing in the village,' the Aussie urged him. Vierhouten had already knocked back a few when he remembered he had agreed to go on Dutch post-stage TV programme *De Avondetappe*. He stumbled onto the set and conducted an interview with beer in hand. During the course of it, his eye caught that of a woman in the audience. They chatted, got on and spent the evening dancing in the Igloo nightclub. Aart and Miriam Langedijk are now married and run cycling clinics together.

For two-time Alpe winner Kuiper the climb is 'the Dutch equivalent of the Eiffel Tower', and for another ex-winner Theunisse it's 'a bit like Holland in France', – and there's no doubt large numbers of the local population have benefited from this, particularly in what used to be the low-season summer months. 'In the summer around

50 per cent of the foreign visitors to the resort are Dutch,' says Alpe d'Huez tourism director Hurth.

'We know that each day between mid-June and mid-September around 800 people ride up to Alpe d'Huez, and across the year the total is 116,000. It's like Mecca for people on two wheels. If you ride a bike, you have to do it, and it doesn't matter whether it takes one hour or three. The important thing is that you make it. Even though it's not so hard when compared to some other mountains, even some of those in the Tour, Alpe d'Huez has become mythical, the most famous climb in cycling, and that's largely thanks to the Dutch, who come not only to see the race, but also to enjoy the party, particularly on *le virage des Hollandais*. They have a bar there and in 2013 they brought 100 barrels of beer. It's an incredible thing to see.'

There is, almost inevitably, a downside to this invasion, described by Belgian journalist Stéphane Thirion as 'a grotesque orgy', particularly for the local environment. Although the Tour organisation fulfils its obligation to clean the road and the metre of verge either side of the carriageway, the commune of Alpe d'Huez has to remove the detritus left in all of the areas beyond this. One local described the mess left in 2013 as '*catastrophique*'. At Dutch corner, where thousands camp out in and around the cliff-top garden dedicated by Raymond Mauchamp, the former mayor who agreed to finance the Tour's return in 1976, the extent of this clean-up is considerable and requires three days of work after the race has moved on.

Yet, most locals insist that what is an onerous and often disgusting task, given the fact there's only one mains-connected toilet on Dutch corner, is worth it as the Tour's passage raises takings by between 10 and 20 per cent for the year.

There are also plenty of Dutch who don't appreciate the perspective bend seven gives of their nation. Chief among them is TV journalist Mart Smeets, who covered forty-two Tours, latterly as presenter of *De Avondetappe*. 'I hate Alpe d'Huez. It's too crowded, people are too drunk, too noisy, people do things that I don't like,' says Smeets. 'I remember waking up one morning and we had three or four broken wing mirrors, all done by Dutch fans. I remember getting back to our car and seven or eight Dutch guys, who were drunk like skunks, were dancing on the car, standing and urinating on the car. Is that something to be proud of? It's worse than football hooliganism.

'The last couple of times that I did my show on Alpe d'Huez we didn't stay there. We stayed on the other side of the mountain in a calm village, where you can work easily and no one tries to rob you, or break your car or urinate on it, which is the kind of thing that was happening.'

Smeets admits that he wasn't always so opposed to the mountain, explaining, 'It was completely different in the 1970s. There weren't as many people as there are now. People behaved differently. The whole world was different. Now it's rowdy and it's vulgar. I don't like it.'

Smeets' grumbles may be dismissed as a veteran's yearning for halcyon days in the past, but the extremely experienced Dutch journalist insists he still loves being on the Tour. 'I'm just not very fond of Alpe d'Huez. A Tour de France without Alpe d'Huez is heaven for this journalist,' he affirms, before going on to dismiss the mythology that has grown up around 'Dutch mountain'.

'The Tour de France lives on stories, and one of those stories is Alpe d'Huez and it's a made-up story. It's just one day. Yes, a couple of Dutch riders won over there, that's all, but it's still "Our mountain"!' he says with disgust. 'What does that mean, "Our mountain"? Why isn't it a Danish mountain or a German mountain? It's a typical made-up story that we try to believe in. How long is it since a Dutch rider did well over there? Twenty-six years! So let's not talk about "Dutch mountain". It's a Dutch mountain in terms of colour on certain bends, and there are certain people of Dutch ancestry who act like drunken fools, but should you be proud of that? No. I said in my broadcasts that it was disgraceful, but lots of people don't like to hear that. It's not something to be particularly proud of. I won't be back at Alpe d'Huez this year, and I won't be missing it. Not at all! Not at all!'

Since 2006, the Dutch link to the mountain has taken on another aspect in the form of the Alpe d'HuZes charity event, which takes place in June each year. Combining the Dutch word for 'six' with the name of the resort, the event sets riders the challenge of completing half a dozen ascents of the Alpe over a weekend. Run by volunteers with a no-overheads policy, all money raised by participants goes to the Alpe d'HuZes fund and the Dutch Cancer Society.

Just sixty-six riders took part in the first edition, but numbers ballooned to 7,800 in 2013, when almost €30 million was raised. Although numbers dropped significantly in 2014 in the wake of a scandal prompted by the revelation that the management company behind the event had reportedly been paying itself substantial fees, it still raised another €13.5 million.

'It is an incredible event,' says Hurth. 'I call it "the little Amsterdam", because we give the key to the resort to the organisation and then let them get on with it. It's very impressive to see how they put it together to support these anti-cancer charities. They even have live coverage on Dutch TV, where it's the most popular programme of the year. We get groups of firemen, nurses, police and many more, who all take holiday to come and take part in the event. It is very inspiring.' Ex-pros have taken part too, most notably Zoetemelk and Bernard Hinault, who finished together having completed the climb at a rather more sedate pace than they had three decades and more ago.

From his final resting place on the top level of the cemetery behind the Église Saint-Ferréol d'Huez, Georges Rajon, who was never the mayor of Alpe d'Huez, as is often stated, but was undoubtedly one of the key drivers behind the long-lasting bond between the Tour and the Alpe, would no doubt have mixed feelings surveying the race on the Alpe today. On the one hand, he would be dismayed to see his beloved Hôtel Christina, named after his daughter and host to Coppi, Hinault, LeMond and many more, boarded up and neglected, its tennis court surrounded by waist-high weeds, as the building awaits demolition and redevelopment as Les Chalets du Christina.

On the other, he would be pleased with how his plans have raised the profile of the resort he loved. Lying at the point where you get the first clear sight of Huez and Alpe d'Huez above it, and next to his father Maurice and their wives, Rajon fully achieved his objective when he brought the Tour to the mountain in 1952 and when he brought it back again in 1976. It has become world famous, although more renowned for cycling than it is for skiing. What he hadn't foreseen, though, was that he would end up in the one part of it that will be forever Dutch.

10

Van Impe starts to ride harder as the pair rise through the hairpins in the village of Huez. He's still setting a pace fast enough to all but ensure that Zoetemelk can't attack, but he's also got insurance in the form of a muttered agreement from the Dutchman that he won't go on the offensive until they get into the final straight and battle it out for the stage win.

They round bend six, from which there is a magnificent view up the Sarenne gorge, with the sound of the river surging downwards far below. Turning back towards the upper part of Huez, they pass the turn to Villard Reculas and the Pas de la Confession, which offers a longer, but easier route to Alpe d'Huez that's popular with local riders thanks its eyrie-like 'balcony' section.

Sitting next to the end of a downhill ski run, bend five has a longer and steeper sweep than most on the Alpe and delivers riders into the grassy meadows below the resort. In the summer months, cattle are driven up from Arles down *in the south of the country to graze in these pastures. But, for the past few days, the herdsmen have moved them well away from this part of the mountain and the clamour of the Tour.*

The road steepens noticeably above this bend and just beyond Huez's final chalets. Ninety seconds after Van Impe has flashed by with Zoetemelk sitting half a bike-length down and slightly to his side, Spaniard Francisco Galdós takes advantage of this rise in the gradient to accelerate away from Bernard Thévenet, who is still hauling another half a dozen riders up the mountain.

At almost a kilometre, the gap between bends four and three is the longest on the Alpe. Now that it's running through grassland rather than carving through rock, the road widens substantially, passing the right turn that offers an alternative 'Entrée Est' route to Alpe d'Huez and up still further to the heliport and the little-known back road into the resort via the Col de Sarenne.

The leading duo, the pursuing Galdós and the group being dragged upwards by Thévenet are now above 1,500 metres. The effects of altitude become ever more pronounced, impacting more noticeably on the cardiovascular system's ability to transport oxygen around the body. The growing numbers, closeness and excitement of the fans further exacerbates the detrimental effect of altitude on performance. Many have trooped down the eastern route into Alpe d'Huez to watch the riders ascend the 'Entrée Ouest' into the resort. What becomes a never-ending human funnel keeps some of the wind out, but the fans are so close and unpredictable that even the most confident of racers gets edgy. More than the riders, it's the fans who decide the line that needs to be taken, the erratic pulsing of this boisterous corridor of humanity impacting on their rhythm, drawing a little more on their reserves.

The narrowness of the unbroken line of bellowing bodies benefits Van Impe and, now almost two minutes behind him, Thévenet, who know the riders tracking them are unlikely to attack given the unpredictability of the fist-shaking, yelling, water bottle-brandishing masses around them. It's bedlam and even frightening, but also rousing and inspiring. It delivers a final rush of adrenaline, which compensates for the increased physiological stresses. Van Impe draws on this, pushing a bit harder now that the finish is less than three kilometres away. Zoetemelk remains half a bike-length down on the Belgian as they head into bend three.

Rounding it, the two leaders can glance the best part of a kilometre back down the road. The cars tracking lone pursuer Francisco Galdós are less than 500 metres behind the Belgian and the Dutchman. On the short run up to bend two, where the church in Huez is now a very distant landmark, both can see that the Spaniard is closing the gap, but know that the Kas leader has misjudged his counter-attack. There is not enough of the mountain left for him to bridge up to the two leaders before the finish.

HOW TO WIN AND LOSE ON THE ALPE

The beauty of any mountain stage from the racing perspective is that the best rider is very evident. This is especially true at Alpe d'Huez where all but four of the twenty-seven winners (not including the 2004 time trial) have ridden alone onto the final straight on the Avenue du Rif Nel.

Those twenty-three successes have all been constructed in different ways, depending on the opposition, the wind and weather, and the situation of the race. Some of the winners attacked before the Alpe, but most held back until they reached it. Once on those slopes, a few of the better and braver climbers made their winning assault in the hardest kilometres near the foot of the climb. Again, though, most held back, often because previous knowledge of this unparalleled natural arena suggests caution is required before glory can be achieved.

On 19 July 1992, Hennie Kuiper was about to head back to the climb where he twice savoured victory as a rider. By then a directeur sportif with the American Motorola team, the Dutchman had been waiting two and a half weeks for this stage. Once his riders were up and out of bed, he went to see his team leader, Andy Hampsten, in his room. 'Today is your day,' Kuiper told the American climber, adding that he should attack halfway up the Croix de Fer pass, the final climb before the Alpe.

As it turned out, Kuiper's instinct was almost spot on. The winning break did form on the Croix de Fer and

Hampsten was in it. However, the tale of how he managed to achieve that and what happened once he had done illustrates why mountain stages are so difficult to judge for those aiming to win them and why successes on the Alpe d'Huez are prized above all others by those who excel in defying gravity.

Hampsten, best known at that point for becoming the first American winner of the Giro d'Italia, partly thanks to a legendary performance in a blizzard on the immense Gavia pass, already had plenty of experience of Alpe d'Huez going into that stage in 1992. His best performance was his first in 1986, when he placed sixth on the day of the 'Eagle with Two Heads', that bird comprising his La Vie Claire teammates Greg LeMond and Bernard Hinault.

That day, Hampsten finished more than six minutes down on that Tour's dominant performers. He had got closer to victory in 1990, finishing in seventh place, forty seconds behind Gianni Bugno. But 'Little Rabbit', as Hinault nicknamed him for his ability to scurry up climbs, had also experienced one of his worst moments on the bike when he had tackled the Alpe in 1989. Part of the yellow jersey group at the foot of the climb, the Ohio-born, North Dakota-raised Hampsten, whose racing career started with his brother, Steve, around the English city of Cambridge where his parents were teaching, lost a quarter of an hour and more to the other members of that group.

'I'd ridden it so many times and had some spectacular

failures, which I kept in mind when I was feeling good,' says Hampsten as he recalls that stage in 1992. 'It was always the plan for me to try to win on Alpe d'Huez. Hennie Kuiper was very eager for me to get up there and savour a victory because he had won it twice. I knew going into it that I had a good chance. But on a day like that you need everything to fall into place. If one element is missing you can end up nowhere.'

Sizing up the opposition

'Looking back, it was an odd Tour, although back then it was normal. There were only really three stages in the mountains that year. The race didn't really take in the Pyrenees. There was one stage early on where we crossed the Pyrenees but ended up finishing in Pau on the flat. Then we wandered all over the north. The day before the Alpe d'Huez stage, Claudio Chiappucci had that fabulous day over seven climbs to Sestrières.

'I worked fairly hard in the break chasing him with the aim of moving up on general classification. I finished fifth after being a member of the four-man chase group with Franco Vona, Miguel Indurain and Gianni Bugno. I was the last of that group to finish and didn't work overly hard, but being a rider who was looking to finish well up overall I didn't want to just sit on, even though my general classification wasn't high compared to some of the other guys in the group. Although I wanted to put in a big effort in the mountains, I didn't want to be foolish. But being strong in the mountains was my primary goal.

'Winning stages was also very important, and it's often the case that the riders who win mountain stages are good riders but are just out of the picture a little bit in terms of the general classification. So, after I had finished exhausted at Sestrières, I stopped just after the finish line to catch my breath and to wait to see what the riders in the next groups were like because I knew that the Alpe d'Huez winner would probably be a very good climber who had perhaps taken it easy in a following group. But every one of the next ten or fifteen riders I saw come across the line was absolutely knackered. They were shattered even though they might not have been chasing as hard as we had been, because it had been such a tough stage, so that made me feel better about how tired I was. I just thought, "Look, I need a great night's sleep and to feel relaxed about the next day."'

The breakaway

'The key thing about that stage in '92 was that I was already in a breakaway when I hit the base of the climb, and it was a very good breakaway too. I wasn't in that many breakaways as a pro where everyone worked well together. They were very rare beasts, especially at that point in my career. For many years I had stopped going for King of the Mountains sprints and trying to win stages and was just focusing on the general classification. A lot of that was down to the fact that I was on a list of riders who were just not allowed to get into breakaways. There were many years when I could try to break away in the last hour of a race, but no GC riders' teammates would ever work with me, so I had to relearn my game a little bit, to just wait and make my move for general classification riding, which is a lot more boring than trying to win stages. I'm not complaining, it wasn't a giant sacrifice, but it took a lot of enjoyment out of stage races by making me look only at how I could move up bit by bit in breakaways by keeping with the other general classification riders.

'But that day I did get the chance. It was an aggressive stage almost from the off because Laurent Fignon attacked going up the Lautaret. It all came back together, but the racing was still pretty aggressive over the Lauteret and Galibier. After what had already happened a day earlier, I really thought I'd wait until the last climb of Alpe d'Huez. That all changed, though, when an attack went at a steep part of the Croix de Fer on the first quarter of the climb. I remember two or three people jumped – it turned out it was Éric Boyer, Jesús Montoya and Franco Vona. That move went earlier than my grand plan for the day, but my legs took off. They weren't listening to my grand strategy, thank goodness. I had quickly realised that the other three weren't going to be chased down so I jumped after them with Jan Nevens and caught them pretty soon after.

'All five of us in the break knew that because we'd gone at a good place, and because we were working well together, the winner was going to be one of us. I think we were all pretty confident because we all had pretty good reputations as climbers, and whoever had the best day would probably win. That was one of the real joys of the whole day – that everyone understood that they had a good chance of winning and that the politics ended up being pretty agreeable between all of us. The only exception was when Éric Boyer made a big attack further up the Croix de Fer. I showed my cards early by dragging everyone else back up there to him – so silly! I'd already ruined my little plan of pretending I wasn't really, really very excited.'

The Alpe's early ramps

'Even on the dozen or so kilometres of flat before Alpe d'Huez, we continued to open up a good gap because we were cooperating so well. We were the best part of four minutes ahead of the yellow jersey group containing Indurain and Chiappucci.

'Going into the base of Alpe d'Huez I had a few things on my mind. I really wanted to win. I was the highest placed on GC so I wasn't hammering the breakaway exactly, but I was taking a really good pull, a generous pull, at the front in order to encourage everyone to keep it going. I really don't like the first mile of Alpe d'Huez. It's the steepest part and I'd run into trouble there when I hadn't been in great form, so I remember I was a little nervous about it. But I wanted to keep the pressure on all of us. I was willing to take the lead as there's really not much drafting on the first quarter of Alpe d'Huez. I was willing to put myself in front and force a pace that I was comfortable at. Éric Boyer was also very keen to lead up the climb, so we had this stupid little half-wheeling battle for the first few kilometres of the climb.

'Hennie Kuiper, of course, had been watching all this from the follow car, and I thought we'd have to get into a conversation about tactics three or four kilometres up the climb. He came up in the car and I was expecting him to have probably a very clever plan – perhaps that I should pretend I wasn't feeling that well and then attack at the end, something that was more complicated than I'd already come up with. But what I really didn't want to do was to lose time by pretending that I wasn't feeling well, so I was really dreading what he was going to say.

'But lo and behold he came up and said, "Andy, you're looking great. Keep the lead the whole way and then attack in the last third," which was exactly what my plan was. It was a relief not to have to come up with another tactic.'

The winning attack

'Franco Vona had been second the day before and I was fifth, so one could argue that he was the stronger rider at that moment than I was, but I just kept on with that tactic of keeping the pace up and trying to open up time on Indurain and Chiappucci behind us, which we did. With three k's to go, I thought, "OK, I'll do three attacks very hard, but not quite 100 per cent because I know Alpe d'Huez." It's a wonderful climb – it's not the hardest, it's not the longest, but I would guess the best description I could give it is that it's perhaps the most exciting for a racer to be on. It's the most theatrical. I hate to compare climbs, because when you go into the Pyrenees there are a trillion fantastic Basque fans who come across the border, but Alpe d'Huez is the greatest theatre in terms of a mountain being transformed into a stage and an atmosphere of absolute madness. So it's very easy for a rider to get overly excited and go too hard too early and fall flat on their face in the final kilometres.

'I certainly didn't want to do that, but since I'd been leading up the climb, perhaps foolishly or very obviously, I also wanted to make sure that my first attack didn't really look like an attack. I think Montoya and Nevens had dropped away earlier and I had Vona on my wheel with Boyer just behind, and it was down to the three of us. Going around one of the bends, with about a third of the climb left, I attacked but only by maintaining my speed and staying sitting down through it, so that I accelerated. I like to sit and spin and it looked like I just forgot to feel the gravity, which I knew could be sort of demoralising for the other two riders, who were sitting behind me and were getting some draft at that point.

'They might have been very excited and were waiting for me to fade so that they could take off. But, as it turned out, I got a little bit of a gap. Without turning my head I could see that Boyer had conceded and Vona was two metres back having previously been right on my wheel. I tried not to stand up and get excited, but just kept on with the pressure and gradually pulled away from Vona. And then I was very, very excited and thought I would sprint to the top, but I managed to calm myself down and told myself to wait for the barriers at three kilometres.'

Riding through mayhem

'The fans were almost insane and it was a mad situation, a little bit funny. I've been in a couple of situations on the bike when I felt I was losing my equilibrium. This was one of them. My balance is actually pretty good, but it really does depend on having a horizon. Usually, racers look at the road and the nature of the climb, studying which grade and line we want to take. But that was out. I somehow couldn't get my bearings. I can only compare it to being out in downpours when there were sheets of water coming down the road, the downpour becoming so intense that I started to feel a little light-headed because visual clues and balance were lost. So I ended up relying on secondary balancing cues to make sure my bike kept heading the way it was supposed to be. It felt the same trying to get through this vertical forest of people.

'It's very exciting, it's why we racers love Alpe d'Huez. But the fans closest to us are the drunkest. I don't want to get too graphic, but there is an absolute stench of alcohol, of people who've drunk too much alcohol. They've got so much of it in their bodies that you can smell the odour of them sweating it out, the stench of digested alcohol. It's like the yeast in bread. You think, "Oh my gosh, there's just so much alcohol coming out of these people's pores." They're out of their minds, so drunk that it turns into a bit of a guessing game. Instead of deciding which line I want to take on the road, it's like trying to go through a group of lizards that surge three-quarters of the way across the road, then retreat instead of just going across to the other side. There is definitely an element of danger.

'I did end up lashing out a couple of times. When I pushed myself that hard mentally on a climb, it would create a fair bit of a rage, which is not a negative thing at all, as it helped me to keep pushing myself. It got to the point where so much mental energy was being expended on pushing myself physically to go uncomfortably hard that I ended up really on edge and not wanting to deal with all this mayhem at all, but at the same time it was also incredibly exciting. The upside to it is that, as long as someone didn't knock me over, the huge amount of energy coming out of the crowd matched the rage that I had pushing myself to go faster. It was a potent combination.

'The other factor is that the fans are so close to you that you feel that you're going much faster than you are. You get the impression you're riding into a small hole among the fans. It becomes so easy to doubt how fast you are going because there's no longer a static road surface against which to judge relative speed. I had the impression I was going incredibly fast, but it was just down to people jumping out of the way at the very last moment. It's very, very confusing as a racer to deal with. But it's a lot of fun – one of the most beautiful things I've seen in my life.'

The final three kilometres

'When you get into the barriered section you can focus much more, but I missed the crowds instantly. But once you're in between the barriers you can focus fully on getting to the top. I was focusing on going 100 per cent there. I know we racers talk about "100 per cent" and "almost everything" and "110 per cent", and it ends up being a little bit of a ruined mathematic. But I did consider both that morning and when things fell together on the climb: "How hard will I push myself when I get to that point at three or two kilometres to go? How hard can I motivate myself to go, with everything working well, absolutely as hard as I possibly can?"

'I thought back to three years earlier when I was trying to win at Alpe d'Huez in the Tour and I had food poisoning – my entire team had food poisoning. Eddy Merckx was our bike sponsor and he chose to be in our team car that day. He could have chosen to be in any car on the race, but he said, "No, no, no, I'll watch Andy win on Alpe d'Huez from the team car." It was a huge honour to have him there but I hadn't been able to eat anything all day long. When we hit Alpe d'Huez, which was the third climb that day, there was a breakaway up the road, but I was with Indurain and all of the GC leaders. I finished that stage in sixtieth place. I completely bonked, got the knock, whatever you want to call it. I was crying I was going so hard, and I knew there was nothing there. I was saying to myself, "I have to bounce back, I have to try to keep something down, I need some energy, Eddy Merckx is in our car to watch me and..." – sixtieth place! And I felt so bad every inch of the way. I had that memory in mind and decided that, with everything working well, I was going to make sure that I hurt as badly as I did three years before. I knew exactly what I had to give, exactly what 100 per cent was, so it worked out very well.'

Winning on Alpe d'Huez

'I did say that winning on the Alpe was better than winning the World Championship and I'd stick with that now – if you're a climber. I'd amend that, though, and say that winning Paris–Roubaix feels the same way. As a racer, just about every one of my colleagues would say they'd rather win Paris–Roubaix than the Worlds. But, for a climber, for someone who had been focusing on general classification, Alpe d'Huez is the ultimate goal.

'If I'm objective about it, my victory there had a lot to do with my age. When I was young I was very fast going uphill. I remember one race just after I turned pro in '85 when I missed the breakaway. It was two minutes up the road with seven very good riders and I bridged the gap on one climb, but then blew up. So I was very swift going up hills, but didn't have the stamina. When I started getting good results and working on increasing my stamina, I listened hard to advice about being patient, being less explosive, having less fun in order to do better in general classification, which was my goal. At the same time, I lost some of my climbing speed in my later twenties and certainly into my thirties. But that day in 1992, when I was thirty, I was a mature racer, not old but in my prime. I was absolutely ready to win that stage, the one stage that meant the most to me.

'I also think experience does help a lot on Alpe d'Huez. It's a funny climb. There are nearly flat sections in the middle. If someone's being clever and sitting on, it can provide quite an advantage. And it is so easy to get carried away by enthusiasm on Alpe d'Huez and lose track of what your body is actually doing. Experience is crucial at that point.

'It's always great to go back there. It's become a pilgrimage point for most cyclists, which makes it fun. When I'm on bike tours with my company I love riding my bike slowly and enjoying the view, but I would have to say it's the least scenic mountain that I see over months at a time. I love coming down the Col de Sarenne on the far side of it, but all I can say about the route up is that it's a good road to get to a ski area. I think it's a pretty dull climb. Sure, there's all the history of it, but in my mind it's more of a cycling stadium than a beautiful road through the gorgeous French Alps. In all honesty, the climb is ugly and the town's not spectacular, although it's such a fun place to go to because there are so many cyclists. It's really at its best when all of the spectators are on it to see the Tour go by. It really is out on its own then.'

11

Aware that Francisco Galdós is trying to bridge the gap up to the two leaders, Joop Zoetemelk is pricked into a response. Unwilling to allow Galdós the chance to make the final sprint any more complicated, the Dutchman finally goes to the front and relays Van Impe for a few moments. His move electrifies the many Dutch fans, who know from listening to Theo Koomen's by now completely hysterical radio commentary that such a move will almost certainly yield both the stage win and the yellow jersey.

But Zoetemelk isn't ready to leave Van Impe. This is just the first day in the mountains and the Dutchman, who is cooler and cannier than his rival, and also reluctant to take the initiative, knows it is far too early to be weighed down by the pressure that the yellow jersey brings. He is sure the Tour title is within his range, but he doesn't want to make a grab for it yet. His inspiration is not Eddy Merckx, who is still the sport's dominant figure in spite of his now evident demise, but the last man to win the Tour before the advent of Merckx, the Dutchman Jan Janssen. 'He took the yellow jersey on the very final day, which seemed like the perfect option to me,' Zoetemelk will later admit.

Van Impe takes the lead again as they ride immediately below the chalets on Alpe d'Huez's southern edge. Approaching bend one, the fans are massed in even greater numbers, largely thanks to a misguided attempt by the local commune to charge fans five francs to enter a temporary car park just below the resort, resulting in a traffic jam blocking the road almost as far back as Grenoble as fans attempted to access it. A quickly taken decision to shut it and encourage fans to pull in at the roadside has allowed the riders an unhindered passage, but this is still the most densely packed section of the climb so far.

Bend one is the widest on the mountain. The netting on its top side is to prevent downhillers plunging to the tarmac, and it allows some of the more daring fans a bird's-eye view as Van Impe leads Zoetemelk around it and onto the last of the Alpe's steepest ramps. It brings them up into the oldest part of the resort, the Vieil Alpe quarter. After the twenty-one hairpins, they reach the short platform of the Route d'Huez. Any rider or group that is clear at this point is almost certain to stay clear. There is now no way back to the front for Galdós and the rest chasing behind.

The long ramp up from bend one carries Van Impe and Zoetemelk through a mass of fans into the resort. On the landing between the shops and restaurants, where in the current era the Rapha store and Cycles Huez are neighbours to bakeries, restaurants and cafés, they both change up into the big ring and are stomping on the pedals as the road takes them past the front of the Office du Tourisme and into Place Paganon, now the site of a monument to the victims of the 1985 Armero disaster in Colombia, where they veer hard left under the wooden flyover that brings skiers into the heart of the resort.

Re-emerging into bright sunlight, they are climbing again as they pass the back door of the tourism office, then the post office and the modest town hall. There is still one more unnumbered hairpin to negotiate in amongst the oversized chalets. Still in the big ring, they climb on the Route du Signal past the banner announcing the start of the final kilometre. Once under the ski lift at the top of the rise, the packed crowds send them right into Place Jean Moulin, where Zoetemelk gets frisky once again. He sprints to the front and maintains this position as the pair swish down onto the flat expanse of the Avenue de l'Étendard. For a few moments, the heliport and the wild magnificence of the Sarenne pass can be seen over the crowd-lined barriers, but all the two Lowlanders are interested in is the best line into the final corner of this eight and a half-hour stage.

SILVER AND COAL

The D211F, the road that enters Alpe d'Huez on its eastern side, tracks around the southern edge of the resort, below the Quartier Éclose, where the first ski lift was constructed in 1935. As this road turns in a northerly direction, it passes a seldom noticed reminder of this mountain's industrial past in the form of a sole pylon that once formed part of the lift that carried coal mined at l'Herpie, where a large private house now stands high above the heliport and the road towards the Sarenne pass.

It is incongruous to consider this quite pristine location as a centre for heavy industry, even on a small scale, but as long as eight hundred years ago intrepid miners realised that the rippling of the layers that has produced nature's dazzling display of rock art on the cliff faces on both sides of the Romanche valley also resulted in valuable minerals and metals being deposited very close to ground level. These minerals and metals are most easily accessible where the terrain is less precipitous, just above Alpe d'Huez and higher into the Grandes Rousses massif, the huge rock barrier to the north-east on which several of the ski station's most renowned pistes originate.

Georges Rajon may have claimed that his father, Maurice, was Alpe d'Huez's first resident, but there were already plenty of indications back in the 1930s of human occupation many hundreds of years before winter sports began to offer locals a different lifestyle choice. The Romans used the valley as a trading route following their subjugation of the local tribe, the Ucenis (from which the word Oisans is derived), in the early part of the second century. There is also some evidence of the Romans exploiting natural resources in the area, notably sulphur from Uriage, iron from the lower Romanche region and perhaps lead and silver from Brandes, where they had a small fort on a route across the mountains.

Located on a prominent bluff above Alpe d'Huez, not far from the modern resort's heliport and terrifyingly angled landing strip and just below the road that the Tour peloton took in 2013 to the Col de Sarenne, Brandes is a hugely significant archaeological site. Forgotten for several hundred years after the Romans had been forced out of Gaul, the settlement was re-established in the early thirteenth century thanks to the investment by the dauphin, as the count of Albon, the ruling noble in the region, was known. Like the Romans, the dauphin was interested in seams of argentified lead, which came to the surface near Brandes and also a thousand metres higher up in the massif.

The first archival mention of *l'argentaria de Brandis* dates from 1236, when the dauphin, Guiges VI, used the revenue that came from the mine to establish the Collégiale Saint-André church in Grenoble which became his family's private chapel and mausoleum. However, the extent of, and yield from, the mine workings suggests that industry had been going on there much earlier in that century and perhaps well into the previous one. What is clear is that Brandes' location at 1,900 metres and its population of around 200 people made it the highest permanently habited place anywhere in Europe at that time.

Once the seams near the surface had been exhausted, the miners began to tunnel into the ground, using fires to loosen the rocks before hacking away at them and, later, by blasting them with jets of water powered by hydraulics. This was accomplished by the construction of a 250-metre-long reservoir fed by a 700-metre canal running from Lac Blanc above the settlement. Once the water had been fed into the reservoir, it was released to wash away the top layers of rock, exposing the prized seams below. The workings also had machinery to crush, grind and wash the ore, enabling the extraction of the precious metals.

At that time, the settlement, which covered an area of approximately three hectares, comprised a 'château', a church with a cemetery and numerous stone houses with sheepfolds and gardens. Constructed using whatever large stones were lying around, the gaps between filled with smaller stones and clay, these buildings were arranged in rows and half-buried into the ground to protect them from the elements. However, by the early fourteenth century the population of Brandes, where life expectancy was less than thirty, started to dwindle for two significant reasons. Firstly, the resources being mined became exhausted. Between 1313 and 1319, the mines produced nothing at all. In 1320, the yield was a mere two ounces of silver. Secondly, based on evidence derived from pollen and peat bag samples, archaeologists have discovered the area was affected by a mini ice age, which made year-round habitation extremely difficult.

Towards the middle of the fourteenth century, the dauphin continued to fund the diggings for another decade or so, but the miners struggled increasingly against worsening weather that flooded the workings. It is believed that by 1336 all work at the mines around Brandes had ceased. In 1339, there was no mention of the Saint-Nicolas church or the settlement's château in an inventory ordered by the dauphin, Humbert II, with a view to selling off some of his possessions to the pope to offset his debts. The area subsequently fell under papal control until 1349.

Four hundred years later, miners returned to this same flank of the Grandes Rousses massif. Deforestation of surrounding mountainsides by lumberjacks supplying fuel and building materials had put Huez and other nearby mountain villages in danger of being hit by avalanches. The belated imposition of a ban on tree-felling resulted in a new impetus for mining, with anthracite, a very high-quality coal, now the mineral they were after. Production was small scale, for local use, and perilous. In 1749 six miners were engulfed in an avalanche, as was Huez, where forty inhabitants died.

In the early part of the twentieth century, the concession to mine anthracite was held by a resident of Huez, a Monsieur Borry Borret, who trekked up to the seam at l'Herpie, 300 metres above Brandes and the Col de Sarenne, with his two mules and picked up what he could by hand, then sold it to his neighbours. In 1905, a local mining company bought out Monsieur Borret and increased production, transporting the coal down to Bourg d'Oisans via a cable car built that same year from which only that single pylon standing beside the lower road into Alpe d'Huez now remains. The weight of the full wagon going down into the valley would enable an empty wagon to do the trip in reverse.

In 1914, the company built a dormitory at the 2,200-metre-high mine for German prisoners of war, who dug galleries into the coal seams, creating the highest working mine in Europe. In the post-war depression years, local men worked the mine alongside Russians and Poles, all attracted by the prospect of making good money during a period when jobs were scarce. Working in teams that were three- to eight-strong, the miners laboured around the clock, ensuring the Compagnie Minière du Dauphiné, based in La Mure, made impressive profits.

Although the existence of the dormitory and the work being underground meant the miners were able to avoid the worst of the weather, they still lived with the constant threat of avalanches sweeping down the flanks of the Pic Blanc high above them. At five o'clock on the morning of 9 February 1950, their fears were realised when an avalanche struck, fatally trapping half a dozen men in the mine and killing half a dozen more in the dormitory, where the braziers lit to keep them warm were knocked over and caused a fire that burned them to death. Contemporary reports say that the miners who escaped from the dormitory attempted to rescue their colleagues but found only two survivors from the mine, one of whom escaped only after cutting his trapped hand off with a knife.

The Compagnie Minière du Dauphiné never reopened the site, claiming that the seams were close to being exhausted and, therefore, the mine was no longer profitable. However, locals have suggested that fear of another avalanche was the more likely reason for the closure. The dormitory, which has something of a Bond villain's lair about it, has since been turned into a private home. Totally isolated and almost unreachable, it lies close to the Combe Charbonnière, one of the mountain's best known black-rated ski runs whose name recalls this spot's coal-mining past. L'Herpie has some of the most spectacular views anywhere in the Alps, more than a thousand feet above the hotels, lifts and skiing paraphernalia of Alpe d'Huez and the rugged beauty and isolation of the Col de Sarenne.

This remoteness should ensure that the l'Herpie site will avoid the fate of Brandes, which is under increasing threat from rapid development of Alpe d'Huez. As pictures taken at Tour finishes on the mountain over the last six decades demonstrate, there has been significant development in this area adjacent to the Tour's finishing point on the Avenue du Rif Nel on the eastern side of the resort. The most direct path to the archaeological site passes a nine-hole pitch-and-putt course, a beach volleyball court and a tennis complex, as well as the heliport, with the resort now little more than 200 metres away from Brandes.

The Musée d'Huez et de l'Oisans, which is located in the Palais des Sports building that hosts the press room during the Tour's visits, has highlighted the importance of the site via a number of exhibitions and the work of its founder and curator, Marie-Christine Bailly-Maître, who has written extensively about the locality. The support of the local *mairie* has also been crucial in safeguarding Brandes from the encroachment of yet more pine lodges.

Any visitor will quickly understand why more investment is needed to ensure that this remarkable settlement can be seen and appreciated by future generations. The lack of footpaths to and around the site is resulting in damage of the settlement. Although there is a track of sorts around the remains of the various buildings, it is accidental rather than planned. In places it is easier and less perilous for visitors to walk over the ruins, which is speeding up the degredation of the site.

In addition, the settlement's astounding setting, high above the Sarenne, constrains ongoing attempts to save it. There are precipitous drops from some of the ruins into the gorge below. Further weathering and erosion are sure to lead to the permanent loss of these ruined, but historically significant structures. These buildings are also inherently difficult to maintain because they were half-buried in the natural slope, which has resulted in structural weakness and collapse.

This is very unfortunate because Brandes tells us so much about the people who first climbed and made their home on the Alpe eight centuries ago. Like the riders commemorated on the twenty-one bends leading up to the resort, these pioneers, who no doubt endured every kind of suffering, made and left their mark on these lofty slopes and should not be forgotten. A place of staggering beauty, enlightenment and quiet contemplation, and especially so when the Tour de France is in town, Brandes is just as much part of this mountain's history as the epic battles fought on the road leading up towards it.

12

Swinging left onto the Avenue du Rif Nel, where meadows climb steadily through now grassy ski fields and up towards the Grandes Rousses massif with its trio of 11,000-foot peaks, Zoetemelk and Van Impe are caught out by the sharpness of the bend, the Avenue du Rif Nel turning back at more than ninety degrees. The speed they've gathered in the big ring sprint down the Avenue de l'Étendard sends them both across to the right-hand barriers, before they can straighten up and begin to think about the 300 metres running up to the line.

Later, Van Impe will claim that he almost touches Zoetemelk's wheel as he negotiates this high-speed turn, forcing him to ease off his speed a touch and giving his rival the opportunity to open a stage-winning advantage. Yet the claim is no more than typical Van Impe bravado. Both men know that Zoetemelk will win this match sprint over and over again. He simply has too much speed for the Belgian and releases it almost immediately. The Dutchman 'makes for the line as if it was the last seat in the lifeboat', according to Geoffrey Nicholson, and in doing so he opens up a gap that is stretching even as he passes under the Poulain chocolate banner fifty metres from the finish, before thrusting his gloved right hand high in the air, his grin finally a little less rictus-like. Van Impe finishes three seconds in arrears.

The scenes beyond the finish line are just as chaotic as they had been when the pair rode through the human corridor further down the mountain. Officials, soigneurs and gendarmes swarm in around the two men, who know they have no hope of savouring the moment, not a chance of getting their breath back. Even as a human barrier is forming around each of them, the reporters, photographers and TV cameramen mob in around them. Zoetemelk and Van Impe have ridden everyone else in the race off their wheels, and the world insists on finding out as soon as possible how they managed it.

As microphones are brandished and swatted away, the two corralled riders are edged towards the presentation podium. Guided through the barriers, they finally find shade and sanctuary in the tent behind the podium.

Other riders are finishing now. Francisco Galdós is third home, the only rider to finish within a minute of Zoetemelk and Van Impe. Almost two minutes pass before Thévenet is the first Frenchman over the line. He's eighth and still has Raymond Poulidor right on his wheel. The two Frenchmen could hardly look any more different. While Poulidor looks *fresh and has clearly not ridden to the edge of his capacity, Thévenet slumps over his bars. The Peugeot leader has ridden to his absolute limit and is so spent that he needs to be lifted off his bike by two gendarmes, who carry him away for a medical check-up.*

Speaking to the press a few minutes later, his stomach distended by gulping down carbonated water, Thévenet confesses that his legs all but exploded when Van Impe delivered his first two accelerations at the foot of the Alpe. 'I was in the group behind but had to ride on the front of it for several kilometres because no one would help me,' he says, before praising Van Impe for his performance.

While the French press are grilling Thévenet, Maertens rolls across the line with Michel Pollentier and Hennie Kuiper, whose GC prospects have gone, having finished with the peloton's top sprinter rather than its best climbers. The despondent trio are almost five minutes down on stage winner Zoetemelk. Maertens' hopes of carrying the yellow jersey as far as the Pyrenees have evaporated on the first stage in the Alps. Having suffered that fate, Maertens has to suffer a final humiliation. In the mayhem behind the finish line, race director Jacques Goddet misreads his watch and thinks the bulky Belgian has done just enough to deny his elfin compatriot the yellow jersey.

Fortunately, the official timekeepers manage to convince the Tour boss of his error before Maertens can be led up onto the podium to be presented with the yellow jersey. With an angry gesture and a great deal of guttural Flemish muttering, Maertens stomps away. The Tour may be won on the Alpe, but it won't be by 'Fast Freddy'.

When one Belgian storms away from the victory podium, another takes his place. As Lucien Van Impe takes the bouquet that was almost handed to Maertens and acknowledges the crowd's applause, his teammate Willy Teirlinck crosses the line, sees Van Impe in yellow and shakes his head. 'That's a real shame,' he says. 'He's got the jersey a week early. We don't have a strong enough team to defend it for two weeks.'

Cyrille Guimard's scheme has worked, but too well. Even Van Impe acknowledges that when, after saying he has been waiting for this moment since 1969, he admits of his narrow lead: 'Merckx would hold the jersey to the finish with a three-second advantage, but me?' It's one thing planning for the Alpe, but, as Maertens and many others have just discovered, racing on the Alpe is something entirely different. 'What I hadn't expected was that by the evening only Zoetemelk would be able to stay with Van Impe, who suddenly found himself in the yellow jersey,' Guimard later confesses. 'Contrary to appearances, it was the worst thing that could have happened to us. My team couldn't defend a leader's jersey in the high mountains...I knew that we were on the verge of suicide. My plans had been sent awry.'

Described by Gitane DS Cyrille Guimard as 'drunk with delight' with his first-ever yellow jersey, Van Impe's mood quickly turns as he heads away and spies Zoetemelk in the throng. The Dutchman has spent the last few minutes with the press, principally defending his tactics and not doing so with a great deal of success. He himself acknowledges, 'Caput came up to me to say that I should not take the lead, which is a terrible shame because I felt very strong. You need to exploit opportunities like this when someone like Thévenet is struggling because you don't get them too often.' The next day even the pro-Joop Het Vrije Volk will headline its stage report 'Zoetemelk saves Poupou' and has a subheading 'The Belgians are unhappy'.

Zoetemelk can see that already. Van Impe is the image of unhappiness. 'Lucien was rather put out, to put it mildly!' he later recalls. 'He was literally furious. Red like a fighting cock, he came towards me with his fists clenched. He was usually so courteous, so amiable. Hadn't he got ample compensation for his defeat with the yellow jersey?'

Infuriated by the Dutchman's tactics, Van Impe is quickly moved on by his entourage before anything much can be said, but he is soon disparaging Zoetemelk. He spits out words like 'wheelsucker' and 'profiteer'. 'I can finally understand Merckx's anger every time he heard Zoetemelk's name before his own,' he mutters, sowing the seed for yet more Joop-bashing in the Belgian media.

Half an hour after Zoetemelk has won the day, Thierry Bolle from the Miko ice-cream team rolls in 120th and last. Battling illness, the Swiss has fought a lone duel with the Alpe and just about survived. There's little reward for finishing, though, beyond a massage, a meal and a bed in one of Alpe d'Huez's dorm-like chalets. He won't even get the perverse bonus of publicity given to the race's lanterne rouge. That honour goes to the appropriately named Frenchman Henri Fin. While the end is nigh for Fin, a Tour debutant who will fail to finish the following stage and won't ride the Tour again, this day has seen the renaissance of what will soon become cycling's greatest stage.

THE TOUR IS WON ON THE ALPE

The title of Jean-Paul Vespini's book states it baldly – *The Tour is Won on the Alpe*. Vespini affirms that, 'Alpe d'Huez has become the rite of passage, the key stage, the queen of all climbs, and the day of reckoning on which the Tour is won or lost. That is the true secret of the Alpe's success. It is a climb that delivers a verdict – absolute, impartial and final.' Statistics back up his assessment. Of the twenty-eight riders who have been presented with the yellow jersey on Alpe d'Huez, twenty-one have gone on to top the podium in Paris.

However, Vespini isn't content to support his argument with statistics alone. In his book, published in 2008, he points out that only two riders have prevailed on the Alpe and gone on to win in Paris: Fausto Coppi and Lance Armstrong, the latter doing so twice. In the subsequent period Carlos Sastre has joined them, or at least joined Coppi as Armstrong has now been stripped of his victories. 'Should we therefore conclude that Alpe d'Huez rarely determines the eventual winner of the Tour?' Vespini asks. He immediately responds: 'Definitely not. To truly gauge the significance of this climb in determining overall victory, we must focus our attention on the yellow jersey...In general, Tour winners must make a supreme effort there to either save the jersey or consolidate their lead.'

Vespini goes on to describe the exploits of every stage winner and wearer of the yellow jersey on the Alpe, from Fausto Coppi in 1952 through to Óscar Pereiro in 2006. His evidence is compelling, but closer examination reveals flaws in his case. The most fundamental can be highlighted by analysis of Coppi's victory in 1952. The Italian went into the tenth stage from Lausanne to Alpe d'Huez lying fourth overall, five minutes and four seconds down on his teammate Andrea Carrea, a domestique so loyal to the career and glory of 'Il Campionissimo' that he wept tears of disappointment and shame when he discovered that he had taken the race lead in Lausanne. In his distress, Carrea went to Coppi to excuse his presumption. 'You must understand that I did not want this jersey, Fausto. I have no right to it. A poor man like me, the yellow jersey?'

Carrea's reluctance to wear the yellow jersey, even on the historic day that the Tour made its first visit to Alpe d'Huez, speaks volumes. In reality, he was doing nothing more than keeping it warm for his leader. With Fiorenzo Magni, another Italian, holding second place, the primary obstacle to Coppi taking the race was Italian-born French national team member Nello Lauredi, who was a good climber but nowhere near Coppi's class. To underline that, Lauredi arrived at the foot of the final climb in the big leading group that included the Italian leader, but took seven minutes longer to reach the top.

In fact, a glance at the general classification that morning suggests that Coppi already had the Tour all but won before the Tour's first-ever summit finish. He began it more than eight minutes up on Stan Ockers. When the race paused for its rest day in Alpe d'Huez, the Belgian was more than thirteen minutes in arrears on the Italian. Ockers' final deficit when he finished runner-up in Paris would be more than twenty-eight minutes. So, while his victory on the Alpe undoubtedly contributed to Coppi's overall success, it wasn't the standout factor.

Of the nine Tours since the 1952 race that have similarly featured a visit to Alpe d'Huez before the final week of the race – and, therefore, ahead of the critical mountain stages in the Pyrenees – none provide substantial support to the suggestion that the race is decided there. In 1976, for example, Lucien Van Impe undoubtedly took a significant step towards winning the race when he finished with Joop Zoetemelk on the Alpe. But even as he was being presented with the yellow jersey, Van Impe's directeur sportif, Cyrille Guimard, was mulling over how quickly his Gitane team could rid themselves of the leader's tunic and who best to cede it to. Convinced by Guimard that he had to let it go, Van Impe regained and all but won the race on the Pyrenean stage to Saint Lary Soulan.

Pedro Delgado's performance on the Alpe in 1988 was in a similar mould, the Spaniard taking the yellow jersey, but not putting his rivals out of sight. Those of us who can't erase three weeks of race action from our minds despite what the Tour's official *palmarès* might tell us, will also remember Lance Armstrong's travails on the mountain in 2003. His moment of EPO-fuelled triumph came in the Pyrenees at Luz Ardiden. Other winners of these clockwise Tours that tackled the Alpe before the final week had to ride very well at the Alpe, but ultimately excelled in the time trials that preceded and followed the climb, notably Greg LeMond in 1990 and Miguel Indurain in 1992 and 1995.

The tendency for Alpe d'Huez to appear on the Tour route in alternate, and therefore often the race's anti-clockwise years has meant the mountain has featured in the race's final week on no fewer than nineteen occasions. These encounters with the Alpe later on in the race provide much more substance to the assertion that the mountain has had an outstanding part to play in deciding the identity of the Tour winner. However, on the majority of occasions the race leader has, as Vespini puts it, had to make a supreme effort to either save the jersey or consolidate their lead. In other words, they could have lost the Tour on Alpe d'Huez but rode well enough to ensure they didn't.

Particular mention in this instance should go to Bernard Hinault, who successfully defended the yellow jersey at

Alpe d'Huez on four occasions and to Miguel Indurain, who, in addition to his successful defence of the jersey on the clockwise Tours of 1992 and 1995, also managed the feat in 1991 and 1994.

Of those stages on the Alpe that did have a more decisive effect, a handful stand out and no fewer than three of these concluded with Laurent Fignon donning the yellow jersey. The Parisian, whose spectacles and donnish air led to him being nicknamed 'The Professor', inherited the lead in 1983 following Pascal Simon's injury-enforced abandon, and fought a short but memorable battle with Hinault in 1984 that, for many French fans, finally put Alpe d'Huez on the racing map. In 1989, he came out on top against Greg LeMond, with both riders slugging and reeling like boxers in the final round of a championship bout. Of those three, the 1983 contest provides the best support to Vespini's argument; in 1984 Fignon delivered a more significant blow with victory the next day at La Plagne and in 1989 the Frenchman took yellow on the day but ultimately ended up losing it.

In the end, two years stand out in backing the contention that the Tour is won on the Alpe: 1977 and 2008. On the first occasion, just as had been the case in 1976, Van Impe and Zoetemelk played key roles. Having fallen out with Cyrille Guimard over his salary and left Gitane, Van Impe had soon realised teams had tagged him, not as a Tour champion and potential second-time winner but as a troublemaker. Consequently, he ended up on a lower salary and with a weaker team at Lejeune. The little Belgian wasn't expected to put up much of a defence of his Tour crown, but he insists he was stronger in 1977. Even without Guimard to guide him he went into the Alpe d'Huez stage just thirty-three seconds behind race leader Bernard Thévenet, with Kuiper and Zoetemelk right on Van Impe's heels.

Halfway up the Glandon pass, the final climb that day before the Alpe, the yellow jersey group didn't react when the Belgian darted away, looking to do much more than simply boost his lead in the King of the Mountains competition. This was a very different Van Impe to the one his rivals were accustomed to. The coup he had achieved in distancing Zoetemelk and Thévenet with an eighty-kilometre raid to Saint Lary Soulan the previous year had changed this previously timid mountain goat. That victory at Saint-Lary had yielded the Tour title, and his attack on the Glandon was designed to emulate it. 'Van Impe's acceleration was so abrupt and vicious that I couldn't respond to it,' Thévenet croaked at the stage finish.

Van Impe increased his advantage on the lethally fast drop off the Glandon and, much more surprisingly, along the valley to the foot of what the French TV commentator described as '*la terrible Alpe d'Huez*'. Starting up it, he led the yellow jersey, Zoetemelk and Kuiper by more than two and a half minutes, largely thanks to the two Dutchmen refusing to give Thévenet the slightest assistance, instead hitching themselves to his rear wheel and quietly allowing him to take up the chase alone, encouraging his demise as he continued the pursuit.

Once on the Alpe, the inevitable occurred. The two Dutchmen immediately sprinted away from Thévenet. But the Frenchman wasn't the off-form rider who had floundered on the same climb twelve months earlier. In his characteristic ungainly style, bobbing metronomically, Thévenet relentlessly chewed up the deficit. Once he was back on terms, the French yellow jersey was allowed to take the pace and the wind, Kuiper and Zoetemelk sticking limpet-like to his back wheel. Cursing the Dutchmen under his breath, Thévenet chipped away at Van Impe's lead, until, just below bend seven, Kuiper accelerated and quickly gained fifty metres as he rounded the Saint-Ferréol church at what has since become the most celebrated spectating point in professional cycling.

As Kuiper chased up through Huez, he closed rapidly on Van Impe, who was desperately trying to fend off 'the man with the hammer'. Just above Huez, there were just one hundred metres between them when that infamous media car shunted the Belgian into the roadside ditch.

As the Belgian floundered, the Dutchman flew by. Urged on by TI-Raleigh DS Peter Post's shouts, Kuiper appeared to be destined for the yellow jersey as he reached the bottom end of Alpe d'Huez, three kilometres from the line. Over the final 3,000 metres, the crowds were huge, very much reminiscent of what we see today. Many were Dutch. Yet, as Thévenet neared the top, still dipping and swaying as he forced the final dregs of energy from his bull-like torso, the French fans drowned out the shouts for Kuiper as they urged their 'Nanar' on.

'About 700 metres from the finish I saw a friend of mine who told me, "You're going to keep the yellow jersey by one second." After that I did one hell of a sprint,' says Thévenet. 'I've always said that once I'd got to the line I had absolutely nothing left to give. I couldn't have taken another pedal stroke. It was the day that I managed absolutely every little bit of energy I had in order to go as far as I physically could.' With a lead of just forty-nine seconds over Kuiper to protect, Thévenet ceded forty-one. Lifted from his bike, he was still gasping several minutes later when French TV interviewed him.

'On my wheel I had two guys who were thinking more about me losing the Tour than about themselves winning it,' the Frenchman declared once he'd found the breath to spit out his reaction. 'Added to that, those assholes, they flicked me. Zoetemelk initially. He came to me and said he wasn't in the position to be able to relay me. Kuiper took his cynical approach even further by going on to win the stage. They're little riders. That's what they are! I gave every last bit of the resources I had to defend the jersey. But above all I was looking for victory in the Tour de France.'

His anger at the two Dutchmen was understandable. However, in Kuiper's defence, his TI-Raleigh teammate Didi Thurau, who had held the yellow jersey for two weeks, was only eleven seconds off the lead going into the stage, so working with Thévenet was hardly an option for him. As for Zoetemelk, he trailed in almost five minutes down and was so spent that he fell coming around the final corner. His verdict: 'It was a disaster. A veritable Waterloo.'

Speaking more recently, Zoetemelk defended his tactics that day. 'For a long time Thévenet reproached me for my reaction on the early slopes of Alpe d'Huez. To see if I was still capable of changing speed, I effectively attempted an attack – on pure instinct. It was a kind of uncontrolled reflex. But it was so feeble that Thévenet had no difficulty in overtaking me,' he says. 'Just like Lucien Van Impe and Didi Thurau, I had been completely floored on the elevator ride up to Alpe d'Huez. I wasn't a bastard, a cheat or an idler. I was simply an athlete beaten down by so much iniquity. It is also important to understand that I also wanted to win the Tour! Even in normal conditions, which was far from being the case, it wasn't up to me to carry my principal rival to the foot of Alpe d'Huez in an armchair.'

Thévenet sealed his second Tour victory with a success in the final time trial, where he pushed his advantage out to thirty-five seconds over Kuiper. Four decades on, he insists that he could have died on his bike that day, such was the intensity of his effort and determination. 'I ended up riding the best stage of my life on the climb of Alpe d'Huez. I really managed my effort well; I fought with everything that I had, I went right into my very depths in order to keep my yellow jersey, which I only managed to do by eight seconds, despite having to deal once again with the coalition of Zoetemelk and Kuiper,' he says. 'It was at Alpe d'Huez that I enjoyed the greatest moment of my career.' And this, it should be remembered, from the rider who had downed the invincible Merckx in 1975.

As affable now as he was unwavering that day, Thévenet maintains that the conviction the Tour is won on the Alpe stems from his resistance to Kuiper's challenge. 'It's usually been the case that whoever has the yellow jersey at Alpe d'Huez wins the Tour de France. That means that everyone really fights to get the yellow jersey there, to have this slightly superstitious belief working for them. If the stage was going to another unknown ski station, they wouldn't have that thought in their heads at all. Alpe d'Huez instils the mentality, the desire to fight with all that they have.'

Carlos Sastre is less convinced by the superstitious aspect to the Alpe's notoriety. In his case, it offered him his final hope of outwitting and outriding his rivals in the 2008 race. Looking back now, in common with most winners at Alpe d'Huez, Sastre asserts that previous experience of the climb is critical to success there. He tackled it first in 2001 as a domestique on the powerful ONCE team led by Joseba Beloki and Igor González de Galdeano that was aiming to challenge Armstrong's supremacy. 'I remember it well because it was my first big mountain stage at the Tour de France,' says the Spaniard. 'I could see that Armstrong wasn't going so well, but it turned out he was acting, pretending he was suffering and getting dropped and looking like he was in trouble. As a result of that, Team Telekom's Kevin Livingston was on the front going full gas trying to make things more difficult for him.

'But just before we got to Alpe d'Huez, Armstrong said to [his US Postal teammate] Chechu Rubiera, "Come on, Chechu. Let's go!" That was about one and a half to two k's before the start of the climb. They went full gas at the front and Chechu started onto the climb very fast. Just after we got onto it, Joseba Beloki's chain unshipped and it was my job to help him to get back to the front. I was pretty tired after that because I'd been working all day, and I ended up riding close to Laurent Jalabert, who was in his first year with CSC. It was just after that day that Bjarne Riis came to have a talk with me. Jalabert had told him that I was a good climber and that I could be a useful rider to have on the team. After some discussions, I ended up signing with CSC for 2002.'

Given more of a protected role at CSC, Sastre's results improved with Riis's team, including on the Alpe. He finished twentieth in 2003, although more than five minutes behind the untouchable Ibán Mayo, and tenth in the time trial on the mountain in 2004. 'We spent a lot of time training at Alpe d'Huez that year, trying to work out what was the best equipment to use,' says Sastre. 'In the end, I went to Bjarne and told him, "Just let me stick with what I'm already using because I don't want to mess around with changes to my equipment during the Tour de France. I don't want to try anything that will feel different." He was pretty upset with me because I wasn't willing to tinker with things, but it worked out fine because I did a good time trial, and that was after a bad crash earlier in the race when I cracked two ribs. We had a good physio, though, who used acupuncture to relieve the pain.'

While Sastre stuck to what he felt comfortable with, CSC team leader Ivan Basso did opt to change his set-up for this one-off test, with demoralising results as he ended up being overtaken high up on the climb by Armstrong, who had started two minutes behind him. 'It wasn't a good day for Basso,' Sastre recalls. 'He tried different things and used some smaller rings. He ended up being very blocked on the bike. He was putting out a lot of power, but he couldn't take proper advantage of it as his legs were just spinning round. But I was happy given the problems I'd had and because of the crowds that day. They said there were a million people on the mountain. It was absolutely amazing.'

More crucial to Sastre's 2008 victory, though, was his ninth place in 2006, when his CSC teammate Fränk Schleck won the stage. 'It was a strange Tour because all of the scandals before the race meant that a lot of the big names didn't start. I was going to the Tour with the aim of helping Basso, but he ended up sitting it out, so I had to change my mind-set,' says the Spaniard, who, thanks to the post-race disqualification of winner Floyd Landis, ended up on the podium for the first time.

'I tried to be up at the front every single day and go for the podium. That was a hard day, but a beautiful day for us because Fränk Schleck won the stage and I came in with the best riders. It was the first time I'd shown I could handle the responsibility of leading a team, of being with the best riders, of knowing what it would take to win the Tour in the future. I learned an awful lot during that Tour. When I won the Tour in 2008 I drew on a lot of the experiences I'd had two years previously.'

In 2008, CSC boss Riis opted for a three-headed attack. Sastre and Schleck had been joined by the latter's younger brother, Andy. However, hit by hunger knock during an important stage in the Pyrenees, Andy had dropped right out of contention. By the start of the final week, Fränk Schleck was in yellow, with Sastre sixth overall, forty-nine seconds down on his teammate.

During the rest day at the Italian resort of Prato Nevoso, Riis summoned Schleck and Sastre to his hotel room. 'They both had to accept that they might have to sacrifice their own chances for the other,' Riis later explained. 'I told them, "If you want to win the Tour, you have to work together and not be afraid if the other rider attacks." Since Fränk had the yellow jersey, it meant that Carlos would be the one to attack first.' That attack should have come on the stage into Jausiers, but a strong headwind nullified those plans. That left the Alpe d'Huez stage as CSC's last opportunity.

Although his racing career and 1996 Tour victory are tainted by his admission of doping, Riis is renowned as a supreme tactician and motivator. But the Danish team boss was worryingly unsure about the best option for his two leaders going into the stage over the Galibier and Croix de Fer to Alpe d'Huez. 'Before the stage Bjarne came out with twenty different sets of tactics and everyone was chipping in with their own thoughts,' Sastre reveals. 'After ten minutes I said, "I can't do anything with all this, with everyone wanting to use their own tactics, so the best thing I can do is wait." After ten minutes Bjarne came to me and said, "Carlos, what do you want to do today?" I said to him, "Bjarne, I need one tactic and for you to make it work. That's all that I ask."

'He then said to me, "Are you talking about winning the stage, for example? Do you want to win the stage? OK, we have the yellow jersey and we'll try to win the stage. Is that simple enough for you?" Everyone went quiet for a few seconds and Bjarne was getting a little bit angry with me because I wasn't saying anything. But it was what I wanted in as much as we had one tactic and because of that the team knew exactly what they had to do and were really impressive in carrying it out.'

CSC's domestiques set about controlling the race, keeping the pace high in order to ensure none of their principal rivals could attack before the final test on the Alpe. 'Seeing them doing all of the work gave me a lot of motivation because every one of them was giving all the energy they had for a common goal, which was winning the Tour de France. They didn't care whether it was Schleck or me who won the Tour de France. They just wanted to win,' says Sastre.

'They showed me a lot of respect in terms of the way they performed and I'll remember the atmosphere within the team that day forever. Even now I can feel energy starting to come into my hands and body just talking about it because it was very, very special. Seeing riders like Fabian Cancellara, Stuart O'Grady, Kurt Asle Arvesen and Volodymir Gustov climbing the Croix de Fer, pulling full gas with only twenty riders in the group, was unbelievable. We honestly couldn't believe they would be able to do that. Having Fabian lead over the Galibier, Télégraphe and Croix de Fer was like being a child receiving the best gift in the world. On the road between the Croix de Fer and Bourg d'Oisans, they were pulling full gas and we were all in a line. Nobody was able to do anything until we got to the bottom of Alpe d'Huez, where everyone knew we were going to attack from the bottom.'

Writing in the race diary he kept in *Procycling*, Fränk Schleck explained: 'The deal was that Carlos would attack first at the bottom of Alpe d'Huez, and that they would have to make an effort to chase him, and then I would attack them.' Sastre's memory of events at the foot of Alpe d'Huez is essentially the same. 'The Schlecks were in front of me with Volodymir Gustov pulling on the front. I waited a few seconds for the Schlecks, but they didn't want to attack and I said to myself, "Now is the moment. I've got to go now or never." I attacked and did a hundred metres deep, deep, deep, but Denis Menchov came after me. When I saw him on my wheel I said to myself, "This is not good at all." But suddenly he went over to the left and started to ride strangely, just sitting beside me, so I got my breath for a moment and then, just before the rest got back up to me, I attacked again and Menchov wasn't able to follow.'

After he had swept around bend twenty-one, Sastre pushed his lead over the yellow jersey group to about twenty seconds. It remained at around this mark for the next three kilometres – well short of the advantage Sastre needed to give himself any hope of winning the Tour. With a long time trial to come, the Spaniard needed an overall lead of a minute on specialist time triallist Cadel Evans. It was estimated that his teammate Schleck, a much weaker time triallist than Sastre, needed at least three times that, which was borne out in the fifty-three-kilometre test at Saint-Amand-Montrond.

Relaying instructions to his riders through their ear-pieces, Riis encouraged Andy Schleck to attack and join Sastre at the front, where the pair could then work together to forge a gap. But, as was so often the case, the younger Schleck was reluctant to leave his brother in the yellow jersey. Sastre, meanwhile, wanted to do things his own way. 'I knew there was a big battle going on behind me and thought, "Today, I can't afford to wait for anyone."

Attacking at the bottom was the only chance I had of getting a good advantage over Evans and the other leading contenders. So it was very important to press for as long as I could. After that point, every 500 metres or so I was gaining another fifteen to twenty seconds. Bjarne was telling me, "Forty-five seconds, Carlos... fifty-five seconds, Carlos... one minute, Carlos... one minute thirty... one minute forty-five... two minutes... two and a half minutes..."

'By that point I was near the top. I could tell that Bjarne and the other guys in the car were delighted with the way it was going. I picked up on that and, although I was very tired, I was still very motivated. I was enjoying that day more than any other in my career. I went into that Tour with my focus very much on myself. That day I knew I had an opportunity and when I took it and it started to come off, I enjoyed the suffering more than I ever had.'

Sastre eventually finished more than two minutes up on Evans, which gave him an advantage of 1-34 on the Australian, who ended the day only ten seconds behind second-placed Fränk Schleck. Not too surprisingly, the Luxembourgish rider didn't enjoy the day as much as his teammate. He was nonplussed by the lack of intensity in the chase behind Sastre, confessing: 'Carlos won a beautiful stage. But I had expected Evans to go after him and not just stay in our group, and of course it was a little disappointing to have to just stay with him while Carlos rode away with the yellow jersey.'

Sastre, who admits he hadn't expected to finish that stage in the lead, confirms that it was plain to see that the Schlecks weren't happy with how things had turned out, but has little sympathy with them, insisting they had tried to split the team into two, with them on one side and him on the other. 'They thought they were ready to win the Tour de France, but they weren't. They didn't have the experience then and there was a lot of monkey business going on. They didn't behave correctly,' he affirms. 'I'd sacrificed myself for many riders before, for Beloki and Igor González de Galdeano, for Jalabert, for Tyler Hamilton, for Ivan Basso. I supported many leading riders with the sole objective of getting experience, with the idea that one day I would be leading a team and would know how to use them correctly. But they didn't know how to use the team.

'I controlled the team from the start of the race to the finish. I wanted to keep everyone motivated. I didn't want different factions in the team or to favour some riders over others. I wanted to give everyone the chance to shine, whether it was for one minute, ten minutes, a day, a week. It's best for everyone if everyone is happy. When I won, I felt that everyone was a part of that victory. The Schlecks didn't know how to do that and today they still don't know how to do that. Without them in 2008 it would have been a lot more difficult to win because they were strong and they're very good riders. But they were not correct and honest with me and other members of the team.'

Sastre, who now devotes his time to his family and to a

number of bike-related charities and foundations, describes himself as being serene rather than elated at the finish that day. 'I was delighted, of course, but more than anything I was very calm. I felt satisfied at having given everything that I had, having waited right through the Tour for that moment to do so. I felt like a child as well. I got the yellow jersey and I was on the podium with Sarah Jessica Parker and Michael Douglas, who were there promoting a film. I wasn't immediately thinking about whether I could win the Tour de France. But I knew that if the others wanted to take it from me then they would have to be better than me. Bjarne kept encouraging us to attack so that I could gain some more time on Evans, but I told him, "Bjarne, we've got a minute and a half. If he wants to win the Tour, he's going to have to show that he's better than us."'

In the time trial, Sastre, who throughout his career consistently proved his endurance over three weeks, yielded just twenty-nine seconds to the flagging Australian, giving him the overall victory of fifty-eight seconds. While Thévenet had saved his yellow jersey by producing one of the grittiest performances in Tour history on the Alpe in 1977, Sastre had scooped the entire jackpot there. He won the Tour on the Alpe, and is determined not to forget it. 'I went back there again in 2012 for a charity event but I only rode up as far as bend seventeen, which is the one with my name on it,' he says. 'I didn't ride any further because I didn't want to fuck up the memories I have from 2008. It was such a beautiful day.'

CYCLING'S
GREATEST CLIMB

Spend a few days riding in and around the Romanche valley, which I would encourage any cyclist to do, and it soon becomes apparent that there are many climbs in this region that are much more beautiful, scenic and enjoyable than the fourteen-kilometre grind up to Alpe d'Huez. The ride up towards the Croix de Fer and Glandon passes from the valley is among the most majestic in the whole Alpine range, the 'balcony' roads to Auris en Oisans and Villard-Reculas are breathtaking, and, if you want to get away from it all, the road up the Ferrand valley to Clavans – Haut and on to the stunning desolation of the Sarenne pass is outstanding. Yet, of course, the climb up to Alpe d'Huez is the one ascent in the Oisans region that no cyclist would want to miss.

Just as the monumental Tourmalet and Galibier passes did in the early part of the twentieth century, Alpe d'Huez has altered the nature of professional cycling, and in doing so has also changed what all riders and fans expect from it. During the Tour's first half-century, the mountains were hurdles that the riders had to negotiate on the way from one stage town to the next. But ever since that first summit finish on Alpe d'Huez in 1952, when Fausto Coppi demonstrated so consummately how summit finishes provide such a simple means of dividing the best from the rest, high-rise finales have become the most critical of rendezvous for any stage race contender.

Oddly, this scenario is exactly the one that Tour director Jacques Goddet wanted to avoid when he included high-altitude finishes at Alpe d'Huez, Sestrières and the Puy de Dôme in that 1952 race. Expecting a tight contest between Coppi, defending champion Hugo Koblet, former champion Ferdi Kübler and French star-on-the-rise Louison Bobet, Goddet's showdown never materialised after Koblet, Kübler and Bobet were no-shows. As Coppi strolled towards victory, winning at all three of those summits, the desperate race director had to boost the prize on offer for second place in the hope of providing a contest to excite fans. Nineteen years would pass before Goddet included three summit finishes on the Tour itinerary for a second time. Although three or even more summits featured subsequently on every route, the race director remained unconvinced despite the enthusiastic popular response.

The day after the Tour returned to Alpe d'Huez in 1976, Goddet noted in *L'Équipe* that, 'The fourteen kilometres climbing the rock wall to Alpe d'Huez told us more than the 1,400 kilometres covered over ten days across our beautiful landscape in the pursuit of pipe dreams that filled our minds. That's how the Tour goes! The high mountains take even greater command now that the number of summit finishes is increasing.' But don't take this for an indication of him warming to the format. He went on to ask whether the top climbers had become the only potential Tour winners. Why, he asked, didn't those who don't climb so well at least attempt to put the climbers on the defensive on flatter stages? On his retirement in 1987, by which time the Alpe and its high-rise brethren were a fundamental part of every Tour, Goddet was still warning that, 'The Tour should not become a championship of the mountains.'

Yet, that is precisely what the race has become. When its route is unveiled in Paris each October, the most important stat is not its length, or the distance of the time trials, but the number of summit finishes. The Tour has always been a title that only a handful of riders can realistically target, but, more than strategic nous and power on the flat, it's speed on the climbs and the ability to sustain it that counts above all else. Ultimately, as Goddet feared, the advent of the summit finish has made for rather one-dimensional racing. As Daniel Friebe put it in his exceptional guide to the sport's greatest climbs, *Mountain High*, the focus on high-rise finales meant that, 'Now the big hitters could doze for the majority of a stage and count on the final obstacle to eliminate the weak…increasingly, riders forgot there were other ways to race in the mountains.'

Viewed more critically, though, Goddet's agitation against the Tour becoming 'a championship of the mountains' came eight decades too late. While the Tour achieved instant popular acclaim on its launch in 1903, thereby saving organising newspaper *L'Auto-Vélo* from extinction, the paper's editor and original Tour director Henri Desgrange realised that if his event were to become a legitimate race around the whole of the French nation, he would have to send it into the mountains.

He started tentatively down this path, including the Vosges massif for the first time in 1905. But it was already a question of when rather than if the Alps and Pyrenees could feature. Beset by fears of riders being attacked by wild animals or suffering complete physical collapse, Desgrange didn't dispatch the Tour into the mountainous border country with Spain until 1910, and even then found a convenient excuse for being back in the sanctuary of his Paris office when the riders tackled the 2,100-metre Tourmalet pass.

Fielding dispatches from his reporters back in the Pyrenees, Desgrange rapidly realised the potential the mountains presented for delivering drama and heroics. This would, of course, result in increased circulation and profits. The following year, Desgrange was present to see the riders tackle the immensity of the 2,645-metre Galibier, his famously over-the-top eulogy of this pass – 'Oh Sappey! Oh Laffrey! Oh Col Bayard! Oh Tourmalet!…beside the Galibier you are nothing but pale babies...' – highlighting his clear belief that it was the mountains that would make the race. The epic nature of their setting and the action they guaranteed sealed their position as the Tour's fulcrum. Celebrated French cycling journalist Albert Baker d'Isy later commented that, 'Before the mountains came along, no one talked very much about the Tour,' his exaggeration purposely stressing their importance.

The only surprise about the Tour's love affair with the mountains was that so many years passed before that first high-altitude finale at Alpe d'Huez. To a large extent this was purely for practical reasons. Stage finishes required a crowd to ensure atmosphere and good communications to enable the media to dispatch details of events that had taken place on the road as quickly as possible. Mountain passes could guarantee neither. Until the 1950s most ski resorts couldn't either. Some didn't even exist.

The Tour's first two high-rise finishes at Alpe d'Huez and Sestrières in 1952 pointed the way towards a change of perspective, despite the fears that Goddet and many others had that this innovation would dampen the action on mountain stages until the critical final climb, that they would put an end to the day-long heroic raids that had been the staple of the sport's climbing specialists. But having let the genie out of the bottle, Goddet couldn't get it back in. He tried to by including just another half a dozen road stage finishes at high altitude up to the 1970s, but two fundamental factors undermined his attempt to prevent the mountains dominating his race.

The first was evident on that 1952 stage which Coppi won on the Alpe. It was the first occasion that television images of the race had been shot from a motorbike. Each evening, the footage was transported back to Paris for broadcast on the fledgling TV network the following day. At the time, there were only 5,000 or so television sets across the whole of France. Fifteen years later, when French TV began broadcasting in colour, there were seven and a half million sets in the country. Once events from the 1968 Mexico Olympics had been broadcast to these viewers as they happened, live transmissions from the Tour were sure to follow.

As television began to set the sporting agenda from the end of the 1960s, it was no coincidence that the number of summit finishes picked up dramatically. High-rise finales all but guaranteed two audience-boosting ingredients that other stages, and lots of other sports, could not: drama and spectacle. On the Puy de Dôme and the Tourmalet, at Pla d'Adet and Orcières–Merlette that drama came tidily packed into the last hour of racing, when the TV audience was at its largest.

The spectacle came from the mountains. For seventy years, fans depended on race reports, Pellos' cartoons in L'Équipe, specialist magazines and the occasional bit of shaky footage to portray the action. Finally, though, images broadcast live from motorbikes, static cameras and, above all, helicopters transformed the Tour into an event that surpassed the realm of sport. They revealed the majesty of the French landscape and the racers' place within it. Television magnified their deeds. Despite Goddet's ongoing attempts to rein in the importance of the mountains, to spread the action across the whole Tour route, the television audience got more and more of the mountain action it craved, that it tuned in for.

The second factor that argued for high-rise finishes was the growing size of the Tour. From the early 1970s, both the number of riders and the number of followers increased substantially. What had been a large village decamping from place to place each night gradually evolved into a small town. Accommodating this mobile settlement was straightforward in French cities, but it was much more complicated for small towns – unless, that is, they were empty. In mid-summer months, ski resorts in the Alps and Pyrenees had thousands of beds available and no one in them. Consequently, the development of a cosy relationship between the Tour and the resorts was inevitable.

In this environment, Alpe d'Huez's initially unplanned return to the Tour itinerary was very much a case of the resort being in the right place at the right time. When the Tour's co-director Félix Lévitan called Alpe d'Huez hotelier Georges Rajon in October 1975, neither man could have realised what the Tour and the resort were going to do for each other. A first inkling may have come on that July day when Joop Zoetemelk won the stage up to the resort and the balance of the race was left on a knife edge. Those watching the live broadcast that began that day just as the riders were heading out of Bourg d'Oisans witnessed something special and quite unique.

It wasn't so much the duel on the road that captivated, although the battle between Zoetemelk, Lucien Van Impe, Bernard Thévenet and Freddy Maertens was gripping, but the view of the mountain on which it was taking place. Together, they combined to create something very extraordinary indeed. The 1992 Alpe d'Huez winner Andy Hampsten, who does the climb regularly leading rides with his bike holiday company, encapsulates the remarkable nature of the Alpe perfectly when he describes the climb as ugly and even rather dull. What captivates, says Hampsten, is the mountain's amphitheatrical aspect.

Initially piqued by Millar's and Hampstens's critiques and set on taking them apart, I have ended up agreeing with their assessments. For the most part gouged out of the mountainside, the climb up to Alpe d'Huez doesn't compare to any number of more breathtaking ascents in the vicinity. It defies nature rather than bending to it or fitting in with it. The views are magnificent in places, but take away the Tour and all of its history and you end up with what Hampsten describes as 'a very good road to get to a ski resort'.

Add the Tour and all that comes with it to the Alpe, though, and the result is an arena that is unparalleled across the cycling world. For spectators standing on almost any part of it, there are long-ranging views down the mountain and towards the resort nestled beneath the Grandes Rousses massif. The density of the crowds on the day the Tour visits increases the mountain's sense of specialness, especially at bend seven, where racers know they are going to get an ear-splitting and uniquely colourful reception from the oranged-up Dutch fans, who have become just as much a part of the occasion as the riders. Yes, there is an ugly side to this mayhem, as Mart Smeets points out with unconcealed disgust, but the majority of fans on the mountain do want to remember the occasion rather than spend it in drunken oblivion.

'It's got such a special reputation that you have a real sense of pride when you go up it,' says Linus Gerdemann, who wore the yellow jersey in the 2008 Tour and was one of Andy Schleck's support riders when he led the race going up Alpe d'Huez three years later. 'When you're young and you start cycling, Alpe d'Huez is always the place you dream of racing. It's like wanting to play in a cup final at Wembley. The noise is absolutely incredible as well. There is nowhere else like it in cycling with that kind of atmosphere.'

Alpe d'Huez's reputation as the Wembley or Maracanã of cycling is just as apparent to the millions watching the stage on TV. For many of these armchair spectators, the Tour is as much about the beauty of France as it is about cycling and, within this context of France as a landscape, few of its locations are quite as spectacular as the Alpe. This is especially true when the climb is seen in the pictures broadcast from helicopters buzzing like bees over an enormous, action-packed hive. These images provide such a different perspective that anyone seeing them would think Andy Hampsten's description of the climb being 'ugly' as unhinged.

The twenty-one hairpins, highlighted by a black-and-white line of fans and camper vans, weave unsteadily up to the resort, bouncing the riders from one corner to the next. Seen from this vantage point, the fourteen-kilometre route to the resort is like the road from a child's drawing, zigzagging steeply up apparently sheer rock faces. It is a wondrous sight, 'like a compressed version of the whole twenty-one-day race,' says Tour historian Serge Laget, or 'like all the Alps encapsulated in one mountain,' according to L'Équipe's Gérard Ejnès. It is a frenzy of action where the spectators create the atmosphere and are very much part of the race.

Other climbs and passes have history and nature on their side but, despite their beauty, the epic deeds for which they have been the stage and the emotions they arouse, none can match the majesty or the magnetism of the Alpe. Tim Moore, whose book French Revolutions recounted his ride around the route of the 2004 Tour, which included the Tour's only time trial thus far to take place on the climb, wrote that the Alpe has become 'the Glastonbury festival for cycling fans', and the analogy is apposite. Like that festival's bill, it doesn't matter all that much to fans who the headliners are. They will turn out no matter what and they will enjoy the experience, whoever is topping the bill.

This sanctification of Alpe d'Huez as, according to Daniel Friebe, 'a place of convergence and gathering for millions of devotees, who come from all of the countries of the world to celebrate this great cycling mass, just as others go in search of spirituality at Lourdes or Santiago de Compostela', has had a significant impact on the Tour de France and bike racing as a whole. For the Tour, the inclusion of the climb is a guarantee of massive crowds both at the roadside and in front of the TV.

Consequently, the balance in the love affair between race and mountain, where the Tour was the dominant partner, has now shifted to the degree that each entity needs the other to the same extent. The Tour may be no less testing without Alpe d'Huez on the route, but its absence diminishes the race, deprives it of an essential ingredient. Christian Prudhomme and his organising team can include other climbs to other resorts, but they do so in the knowledge that the wider audience won't get as excited by visits to La Toussuire, Risoul or Chamrousse, which are like Wembley finals shifted to second-division grounds.

Alpe d'Huez's director of tourism, Fabrice Hurth, insists the Tour and the Alpe have both benefited from their long-standing love affair, that their stories have both developed together. But Hurth also suggests that, 'The climb has become a concept. It has its own personality, almost like a rider perhaps.' It is this aspect of the Alpe that has been more significant for professional cycling.

Although doping has long been an issue for the sport, its impact has been particularly severe since the Festina Affair of 1998 and during the ructions of the later Lance Armstrong era, when it eventually became clear that a large proportion of the peloton was resorting to the use of performance-enhancing drugs. As doping affairs, scandals and confessions have piled up, and the credibility of racers has plummeted, fans have begun to focus much less on personalities and performances that could end up being tainted and much more on the stages and arenas where they perform.

I could see this clearly as editor of one of the leading professional road magazines during this period. Personalities didn't sell in the way that they once had, but features and profiles of the terrain, and particularly the mountains, on which they performed did boost sales. Confirming Nathaniel Hawthorne's description of them as 'the Earth's undecaying monuments', mountains can also provide thrills without taint. They are wild, but totally reliable. Their qualities and deficiencies are open to critical rather than cynical debate.

As this shift towards route over riders has taken place, it has been complemented by an upsurge in the popularity of road bikes and riding since the turn of the century. There's no single reason why cycling has become 'the new golf', with its MAMILs and, increasingly, other bike fanatics who regard riding, touring and racing as the perfect way to fulfil physical and social objectives. Lance Armstrong's incredible story and victories undoubtedly played a role in bringing the sport into the popular mainstream. In the UK, success at the Olympics and, more recently, on the road, where Sir Bradley Wiggins, Mark Cavendish and Team Sky have been particularly prominent, has also been very noteworthy. Just as significant, though, is the human quest for a challenge, which the mountains offer in abundance.

This growing desire for adventure is most obviously highlighted by the increasing number of sportives and those taking part in them, with Alpe d'Huez an obvious focus. When the Étape du Tour de France, the doyen of sportives, was established in 1993, it attracted just 1,700 participants. In 2011, more than 10,000 riders took part in the most recent Étape to finish on the Alpe. Each July thousands more take part in the outstandingly tough but equally stunning Marmotte sportive which finishes on the climb, while thousands of Dutch cyclists commit themselves to six torturous ascents of the mountain in the Alpe d'HuZes. Like myself, many of these riders will have been reminded as they climbed it that taking part in sport is almost always better than watching it, especially in such a legendary arena.

But these thousands are just a small part of the tens of thousands who tackle the Alpe each year. Their presence reveals how much Alpe d'Huez has advanced beyond

Georges Rajon's original goal of popularising it as a ski destination. 'We're better known in summer thanks to the Tour de France than we are in winter thanks to the skiing,' Fabrice Hurth confirms. 'Alpe d'Huez is known all over the world thanks to its summer connection to cycling, and it's only known in Europe due to the skiing.'

Over the four decades since Van Impe and Zoetemelk's duel on its slopes, the fourteen-kilometre ascent from Bourg d'Oisans has become the people's climb. Its only rival is Mont Ventoux, but the Provençal mountain's treeless, wind-whipped summit is rarely a place to dwell for more than a few minutes. The Alpe may not be as striking or anywhere near as tough as the Ventoux, but it has all the qualities required to guarantee high drama and a huge audience in this televisual age. Cycling writer Christian Montaignac rightfully describes it as 'the cathedral of climbs...a place of pilgrimage for cycling fans, the Versailles in their little kingdom'.

Like Wembley, St Andrews and Centre Court, it is a prime strip of sporting real estate, its iconic status supported by history, its unique atmosphere and its emblematic twenty-one hairpin bends. Unlike those other arenas, however, it is unmistakably open to anyone. Just as winning on the Alpe has become the Holy Grail for any racer, in this most democratic of sports, riding up it has taken on the same status for every rider. It is undoubtedly cycling's greatest climb.

Appendix

Alpe d'Huez's vital statistics

Length: 13.8km
Average gradient: 8.1%
Steepest gradient: 13%
Altitude at base: 744m
Altitude at top: 1860m
Altitude gained: 1116m

Tour de France stages that have finished at Alpe d'Huez

1952
Sunday 4 July
Stage 10: Lausanne-Alpe d'Huez

1 Fausto Coppi (Ita) 266 km in 8-51-40
2 Jean Robic (Fra) at 1-20
3 Stan Ockers (Bel) at 3-22
4 Antonio Gelabert (Fra)
5 Jean Dotto (Fra) at 3-27
6 Andrea Carrea (Ita) at 3-29
7 Pierre Molinéris (Fra) at 4-00
8 Jan Nolten (Ned) at 4-02
9 Fiorenzo Magni (Ita) at 4-13
10 Alex Close (Bel) at 4-15

Categorised climbs: Alpe d'Huez (cat. 1)

Yellow jersey at start: Andrea Carrea (Ita)

Yellow jersey at finish: Fausto Coppi (Ita)

Yellow jersey in Paris: Fausto Coppi (Ita)

1976
Sunday 4 July
Stage 9: Divonne les Bains-Alpe d'Huez

1 Joop Zoetemelk (Ned) 258km in 8-31-49
2 Lucien Van Impe (Bel) at 3 secs
3 Francisco Galdos (Spa) at 58 secs
4 André Roméro (Fra) at 1-38
5 Fausto Bertoglio (Ita) at 1-45
6 Gianbattista Baronchelli (Ita)
7 José Martins (Spa) at 1-50
8 Bernard Thévenet (Fra)
9 Raymond Poulidor (Fra)
10 Walter Riccomi (Ita) at 2-00

Categorised climbs: Luitel (cat. 1), Alpe d'Huez (cat. 1)

Yellow jersey at start: Freddy Maertens (Bel)

Yellow jersey at finish: Lucien Van Impe (Bel)

Yellow jersey in Paris: Lucien Van Impe (Bel)

1977
Tuesday 19 July
Stage 17: Chamonix-Alpe d'Huez

1 Hennie Kuiper (Ned) 184.5km in 6-00-20

2 Bernard Thévenet (Fra) at 41 secs

3 Lucien Van Impe (Bel) at 2-06

4 Francisco Galdos (Spa) at 2-59

5 Joop Zoetemelk (Ned) at 4-40

6 Raymond Martin (Fra) at 8-15

7 Sebastian Pozo (Spa) at 8-39

8 Joaquim Agostinho (Por) at 8-44

9 Michel Laurent (Fra) at 9-29

10 Pedro Torres (Spa) at 10-49

Categorised climbs: Madeleine (cat. 1), Glandon (cat. 1), Alpe d'Huez (cat. 1)

Yellow jersey at start: Bernard Thévenet (Fra)

Yellow jersey at finish: Bernard Thévenet (Fra)

Yellow jersey in Paris: Bernard Thévenet (Fra)

1978
Sunday 16 July
Stage 16: St Etienne-Alpe d'Huez

1 Hennie Kuiper (Ned) 240.5km in 7-23-45

2 Bernard Hinault (Fra) at 8 secs

3 Joop Zoetemelk (Ned) at 41 secs

4 Joaquim Agostinho (Por) at 1-34

5 Henk Lubberding (Ned) at 2-14

6 Lucien Van Impe (Bel) at 2-23

7 Francisco Galdos (Spa)

8 Sven-Ake Nilsson (Swe) at 3-25

9 Paul Wellens (Bel) at 3-43

10 Raymond Martin (Fra) at 4-48

Note- Stage winner Michel Pollentier (Bel) was disqualified for trying to cheat the dope control.

Categorised climbs: République (cat. 3), Luitel (cat. 1), Alpe d'Huez (cat. 1)

Yellow jersey at start: Jos Bruyère (Bel)

Yellow jersey at finish: Joop Zoetemelk (Ned)

Yellow jersey in Paris: Bernard Hinault (Fra)

1979
Sunday 15 July
Stage 17: Les Menuires-Alpe d'Huez

1 Joaquim Agostinho (Por) 166.5km in 6-12-55

2 Robert Alban (Fra) at 1-57

3 Paul Wellens (Bel) at 2-45

4 Michel Laurent (Fra) at 2-48

5 Jean-René Bernaudeau (Fra) at 3-17

6 Sven-Ake Nilsson (Swe) at 3-19

7 Giovanni Battaglin (Ita)

8 Bernard Hinault (Fra)

9 Joop Zoetemelk (Ned)

10 Raymond Martin (Fra) at 3-34

Categorised climbs: Madeleine (cat. 1), Télégraphe (cat. 2), Galibier (HC), Alpe d'Huez (HC)

Yellow jersey at start: Bernard Hinault (Fra)

Yellow jersey at finish: Bernard Hinault (Fra)

Yellow jersey in Paris: Bernard Hinault (Fra)

Monday 16 July
Stage 18: Alpe d'Huez-Alpe d'Huez

1 Joop Zoetemelk (Ned) 118.5km in 4-23-28

2 Lucien Van Impe (Bel) at 40 secs

3 Bernard Hinault (Fra) at 47 secs

4 Joaquim Agostinho (Por) at 1-05

5 Giovanni Battaglin (Ita) at 2-21

6 Mariano Martinez (Fra)

7 Paul Wellens (Bel) at 2-23

8 Hennie Kuiper (Ned) at 2-48

9 Jean-René Bernaudeau (Fra) at 3-29

10 Christian Levavasseur (Fra)

Categorised climbs: La Morte (cat. 2), Alpe d'Huez (HC)

Yellow jersey at start: Bernard Hinault (Fra)

Yellow jersey at finish: Bernard Hinault (Fra)

Yellow jersey in Paris: Bernard Hinault (Fra)

1981
Tuesday 14 July
Stage 17: Morzine-Alpe d'Huez

1 Peter Winnen (Ned) 230.5km in 7-36-18

2 Bernard Hinault (Fra) at 8 secs

3 Lucien Van Impe (Bel) at 9 secs

4 Robert Alban (Fra) at 12 secs

5 Johan De Muynck (Bel) at 1-38

6 Joop Zoetemelk (Ned) at 2-01

7 Claude Criquielion (Bel) at 3-23

8 Paul Wellens (Bel) at 3-33

9 Alfons De Wolf (Bel) at 4-14

10 Jean-René Bernaudeau (Fra) at 4-16

Categorised climbs: Madeleine (cat. 1), Glandon (HC), Alpe d'Huez (HC)

Yellow jersey at start: Bernard Hinault (Fra)

Yellow jersey at finish: Bernard Hinault (Fra)

Yellow jersey in Paris: Bernard
   Hinault (Fra)

1982
Tuesday 20 July
Stage 16: Orcières Merlette-Alpe
   d'Huez

1 Beat Breu (Swi) 123km in 3-24-22

2 Robert Alban (Fra) at 16 secs

3 Alberto Fernández (Spa) at 1-18

4 Raymond Martin (Fra) at 1-22

5 Bernard Hinault (Fra) at 1-26

6 Joop Zoetemelk (Ned)

7 Peter Winnen (Ned) at 2-12

8 Bernard Vallet (Fra)

9 Johan Van De Velde (Ned) at
   2-51

10 Paul Wellens (Bel) at 2-54

Categorised climbs: Ornon (cat. 2),
   Alpe d'Huez (HC)
Yellow jersey at start: Bernard
   Hinault (Fra)
Yellow jersey at finish: Bernard
   Hinault (Fra)
Yellow jersey in Paris: Bernard
   Hinault (Fra)

1983
Monday 18 July
Stage 18: La Tour de Pin-Alpe
   d'Huez

1 Peter Winnen (Ned) 223km in
   7-21-32

2 Jean-René Bernaudeau (Fra)

3 Edgar Corredor (Col) at 57 secs

4 Robert Alban (Fra) at 1-22

5 Laurent Fignon (Fra) at 2-07

6 Lucien Van Impe (Bel) at 2-09

7 Pedro Delgado (Spa) at 2-10

8 Raymond Martin (Fra) at 2-42

9 Patrocinio Jiménez (Col) at 3-05

10 Gerard Veldscholten (Ned) at
   3-07

Categorised climbs: Cucheron (cat.
   1), Granier (cat. 2), La Table
   (cat. 2),
Grand Cucheron (cat. 2), Glandon
   (cat. 1), Alpe d'Huez (HC)
Yellow jersey at start: Pascal Simon
   (Fra)
Yellow jersey at finish: Laurent
   Fignon (Fra)
Yellow jersey in Paris: Laurent
   Fignon (Fra)

1984
Monday 16 July
Stage 17: Grenoble-Alpe d'Huez

1 Luis Herrera (Col) 151km in
   4-39-24

2 Laurent Fignon (Fra) at 49 secs

3 Angel Arroyo (Spa) at 2-27

4 Robert Millar (GB) at 3-05

5 Rafael Acevedo (Col) at 3-09

6 Greg LeMond (USA) at 3-30

7 Bernard Hinault (Fra) at 3-44

8 Pascal Simon (Fra) at 3-58

9 Pablo Wilches (Col) at 4-10

10 Pedro Munoz (Spa) at 4-12

Categorised climbs: St Pierre de Chevreuse (cat. 1), Coq (cat. 1), Laffrey (cat. 1), Alpe d'Huez (HC)

Yellow jersey at start: Vincent Barteau (Fra)

Yellow jersey at finish: Laurent Fignon (Fra)

Yellow jersey in Paris: Laurent Fignon (Fra)

1986
Monday 21 July
Stage 18: Briançon-Alpe d'Huez

1 Bernard Hinault (Fra) 162.5km in 5-03-03

2 Greg LeMond (USA)

3 Urs Zimmermann (Sui) at 5-15

4 Reynel Montoya (Col) at 6-06

5 Yvon Madiot (Fra) at 6-20

6 Andy Hampsten (USA) at 6-22

7 Ronan Pensec (Fra) at 6-26

8 Samuel Cabrera (Col) at 6-34

9 Pascal Simon (Fra) at 6-45

10 Alvaro Pino (Spa) at 6-48

Categorised climbs: Galibier (HC), Croix de Fer (cat. 1), Alpe d'Huez (HC)

Yellow jersey at start: Greg LeMond (USA)

Yellow jersey at finish: Greg LeMond (USA)

Yellow jersey in Paris: Greg LeMond (USA)

1987
Tuesday 21 July
Stage 20: Villard de Lans-Alpe d'Huez

1 Federico Echave (Spa) 201km in 5-52-11

2 Anselmo Fuerte (Spa) at 1-32

3 Christophe Lavainne (Fra) at 2-12

4 Martin Ramirez (Col) at 3-00

5 Luis Herrera (Col) at 3-19

6 Laurent Fignon (Fra) at 3-25

7 Pedro Delgado (Spa) at 3-44

8 Guido Van Calster (Bel)

9 Claude Criquielion (Bel) at 4-23

10 Gerhard Zadrobilek (Aut) at 4-43

Categorised climbs: Cucheron (cat. 2), Coq (cat. 1), Laffrey (cat. 1), Alpe d'Huez (HC)

Yellow jersey at start: Stephen Roche (Irl)

Yellow jersey at finish: Pedro Delgado (Spa)

Yellow jersey in Paris: Stephen Roche (Irl)

1988
Thursday 14 July
Stage 12: Morzine-Alpe d'Huez

1 Steven Rooks (Ned) 227km in 6-55-44

2 Gert-Jan Theunisse (Ned) at 17 secs

3 Pedro Delgado (Spa)

4 Fabio Parra (Col) at 23 secs

5 Luis Herrera (Col) at 1-06

6 Thierry Claveyrolat (Fra) at 2-31

7 Steve Bauer (Can) at 2-34

8 Eric Boyer (Fra) at 3-08

9 Peter Winnen (Ned)

10 Andy Hampsten (USA) at 4-21

Categorised climbs: Pont d'Arbon (cat. 2), Madeleine (cat. 1), Glandon (HC), Alpe d'Huez (HC)

Yellow jersey at start: Steve Bauer (Can)

Yellow jersey at finish: Pedro Delgado (Spa)

Yellow jersey in Paris: Pedro Delgado (Spa)

1989
Wednesday 19 July
Stage 17: Briançon-Alpe d'Huez

1 Gert-Jan Theunisse (Ned) 165km in 5-10-39

2 Pedro Delgado (Spa) at 1-09

3 Laurent Fignon (Fra)

4 Abelardo Rondón (Col) at 2-08

5 Greg LeMond (USA) at 2-28

6 Marino Lejarreta (Spa) at 2-41

7 Steven Rooks (Ned) at 3-04

8 Gianni Bugno (Ita)

9 Robert Millar (GB) at 3-08

10 Pascal Simon (Fra) at 3-48

Categorised climbs: Galibier (HC), Croix de Fer (HC), Alpe d'Huez (HC)

Yellow jersey at start: Greg LeMond (USA)

Yellow jersey at finish: Laurent Fignon (Fra)

Yellow jersey in Paris: Greg LeMond (USA)

1990
Wednesday 11 July
Stage 11: St Gervais-Alpe d'Huez

1 Gianni Bugno (Ita) 182.5km in 5-37-51

2 Greg LeMond (USA)

3 Eric Breukink (Ned) at 1 sec

4 Thierry Claveyrolat (Fra) at 4 secs

5 Fabio Parra (Col) at 6 secs

6 Abelardo Rondón (Col) at 40 secs

7 Andy Hampsten (USA)

8 Pedro Delgado (Spa)

9 Claude Criquielion (Bel) at 47 secs

10 Ronan Pensec (Fra) at 48 secs

Categorised climbs: Madeleine (HC), Glandon (cat. 1), Alpe d'Huez (HC)

Yellow jersey at start: Ronan Pensec (Fra)

Yellow jersey at finish: Ronan Pensec (Fra)

Yellow jersey in Paris: Greg LeMond (USA)

1991
Tuesday 23 July
Stage 17: Gap-Alpe d'Huez

1 Gianni Bugno (Ita) 125km in 3-25-48
2 Miguel Indurain (Spa) at 1 sec
3 Luc Leblanc (Fra) at 2 secs
4 Jean-François Bernard (Fra) at 35 secs
5 Steven Rooks (Ned) at 43 secs
6 Claudio Chiappucci (Ita)
7 Thierry Claveyrolat (Fra)
8 Pedro Delgado (Spa) at 45 secs
9 Laurent Fignon (Fra) at 1-12
10 Alvaro Mejia (Col) at 1-13

Categorised climbs: Bayard (cat.2), Ornon (cat. 2), Alpe d'Huez (HC)

Yellow jersey at start: Miguel Indurain (Spa)

Yellow jersey at finish: Miguel Indurain (Spa)

Yellow jersey in Paris: Miguel Indurain (Spa)

1992
Sunday 19 July
Stage 14: Sestrières-Alpe d'Huez

1 Andy Hampsten (USA) 186.5km in 5-41-58
2 Franco Vona (Ita) at 1-17
3 Eric Boyer (Fra) at 2-08
4 Jan Nevens (Bel) at 2-46
5 Claudio Chiappucci (Ita) at 3-15
6 Miguel Indurain (Spa)

7 Jon Unzaga (Spa) at 3-28
8 Richard Virenque (Fra) at 4-04
9 Gert-Jan Theunisse (Ned) at 4-13
10 Erik Breukink (Ned) at 4-42

Categorised climbs: Montgenèvre (cat. 2), Galibier (HC), Croix de Fer (HC), Alpe d'Huez (HC)

Yellow jersey at start: Miguel Indurain (Spa)

Yellow jersey at finish: Miguel Indurain (Spa)

Yellow jersey in Paris: Miguel Indurain (Spa)

1994
Tuesday 19 July
Stage 16: Valréas-Alpe d'Huez

1 Roberto Conti (Ita) 224.5km in 6-06-45
2 Hernan Buenahora (Col) at 2-02
3 Udo Bölts (Ger) at 3-49
4 Alberto Elli (Ita)
5 Giancarlo Perini (Ita) at 4-03
6 Jörg Müller (Swi) at 4-39
7 Bruno Cenghialta (Ita) at 5-05
8 Marco Pantani (Ita) at 5-41
9 Roberto Torres (Spa) at 5-55
10 Angel Camargo (Col) at 7-15

Categorised climbs: Menée (cat. 2), Ornon (cat. 2), Alpe d'Huez (HC)

Yellow jersey at start: Miguel Indurain (Spa)

Yellow jersey at finish: Miguel
Indurain (Spa)

Yellow jersey in Paris: Miguel
Indurain (Spa)

1995
Wednesday 12 July
Stage 10: Aime-Alpe d'Huez

1 Marco Pantani (Ita) 162.5km in
5-13-14

2 Miguel Indurain (Spa) at 1-24

3 Alex Zülle (Swi)

4 Bjarne Riis (Den) at 1-26

5 Laurent Madouas (Fra) at 1-54

6 Fernando Escartín (Spa) at 2-01

7 Laurent Jalabert (Fra) at 2-26

8 Richard Virenque (Fra) at 2-50

9 Ivan Gotti (Ita)

10 Claudio Chiappucci (Ita) at 3-02

Categorised climbs: Madeleine
(HC), Glandon (HC), Alpe
d'Huez (HC)

Yellow jersey at start: Miguel
Indurain (Spa)

Yellow jersey at finish: Miguel
Indurain (Spa)

Yellow jersey in Paris: Miguel
Indurain (Spa)

1997
Saturday 19 July
Stage 13: St Etienne-Alpe d'Huez

1 Marco Pantani (Ita) 203.5km in
5-02-42

2 Jan Ullrich (Ger) at 47 secs

3 Richard Virenque (Fra) at 1-27

4 Francesco Casagrande (Ita) at
2-27

5 Bjarne Riis (Den) at 2-28

6 Beat Zberg (Swi) at 2-59

7 Udo Bölts (Ger)

8 Roberto Conti (Ita)

9 Laurent Madouas (Fra)

10 Laurent Jalabert (Fra) at 3-22

Categorised climbs: Grand Bois
(cat. 3), Alpe d'Huez (HC)

Yellow jersey at start: Jan Ullrich
(Ger)

Yellow jersey at finish: Jan Ullrich
(Ger)

Yellow jersey in Paris: Jan Ullrich
(Ger)

1999
Wednesday 14 July
Stage 10: Sestrières-Alpe d'Huez

1 Giuseppe Guerini (Ita) 220.5km
in 6-42-31

2 Pavel Tonkov (Rus) at 21 secs

3 Fernando Escartín (Spa) at 25
secs

4 Alex Zülle (Swi)

5 Lance Armstrong (USA)

6 Richard Virenque (Fra)

7 Laurent Dufaux (Swi)

8 Kurt Van de Wouwer (Bel)

9 Manuel Beltrán (Spa) at 32 secs

10 Carlos Contreras (Col) at 49
secs

Categorised climbs: Mont Cenis (HC), Croix de Fer (HC), Alpe d'Huez (HC)

Yellow jersey at start: Lance Armstrong (USA)

Yellow jersey at finish: Lance Armstrong (USA)

Yellow jersey in Paris: Lance Armstrong (USA)

Note: Lance Armstrong was stripped of his Tour stage wins and victories in 2013 after an admission of doping

2001
Tuesday 17 July
Stage 10: Aix les Bains-Alpe d'Huez

1 Lance Armstrong (USA) 209km in 6-23-47

2 Jan Ullrich (Ger) at 1-59

3 Joseba Beloki (Spa) at 2-09

4 Christophe Moreau (Fra) at 2-30

5 Oscar Sevilla (Spa) at 2-54

6 Francisco Mancebo (Spa) at 4-01

7 Laurent Roux (Fra) at 4-03

8 Igor González de Galdeano (Spa)

9 Roberto Laiseka (Spa)

10 Leonardo Piepoli (Ita) at 4-07

Categorised climbs: Frêne (cat. 3), Madeleine (HC), Glandon (HC), Alpe d'Huez (HC)

Yellow jersey at start: Stuart O'Grady (Aus)

Yellow jersey at finish: François Simon (Fra)

Yellow jersey in Paris: Lance Armstrong (USA)

Note: Lance Armstrong was stripped of his Tour stage wins and victories in 2013 after an admission of doping

2003
Sunday 12 July
Stage 8: Sallanches-Alpe d'Huez

1 Iban Mayo (Spa) 219km in 5-57-30

2 Alexandre Vinokourov (Kaz) at 1-45

3 Lance Armstrong (USA) at 2-12

4 Francisco Mancebo (Spa)

5 Haimar Zubeldia (Spa)

6 Joseba Beloki (Spa)

7 Tyler Hamilton (Usa)

8 Ivan Basso (Ita)

9 Roberto Laiseka (Spa)

10 Pietro Caucchioli (Ita) at 3-36

Categorised climbs: Mégève (cat. 3), Rafforts (cat. 3), Télégraphe (cat. 2), Galibier (HC), Alpe d'Huez (HC)

Yellow jersey at start: Richard Virenque (Fra)

Yellow jersey at finish: Lance Armstrong (USA)

Yellow jersey in Paris: Lance Armstrong (USA)

Note: Lance Armstrong was
stripped of his Tour stage wins
and victories in 2013 after an
admission of doping

2004
Wednesday 21 July
Stage 16: Bourg d-Oisans-Alpe
d'Huez time trial

1 Lance Armstrong (USA) 15.5km
in 39-41

2 Jan Ullrich (Ger) at 1-01

3 Andreas Klöden (Ger) at 1-41

4 José Azevedo (Por) at 1-45

5 Santos González (Spa) at 2-11

6 Giuseppe Guerini (Ita)

7 Vladimir Karpets (Rus) at 2-15

8 Ivan Basso (Ita) at 2-23

9 David Moncoutié (Fra)

10 Carlos Sastre (Spa) at 2-27

Categorised climbs: Alpe d'Huez
(HC)
Yellow jersey at start: Lance
Armstrong (USA)
Yellow jersey at finish: Lance
Armstrong (USA)
Yellow jersey in Paris: Lance
Armstrong (USA)

Note: Lance Armstrong was
stripped of his Tour stage wins
and victories in 2013 after an
admission of doping

2006
Tuesday 18 July
Stage 15: Gap-Alpe d'Huez

1 Frank Schleck (Lux) 187km in
4-52-22

2 Damiano Cunego (Ita) at
11 secs

3 Stefano Garzelli (Ita) at 1-10

4 Floyd Landis (USA)

5 Andreas Klöden (Ger)

6 Rubén Lobato (Spa) at 1-14

7 Sylvain Chavanel (Fra) at 1-18

8 Eddy Mazzoleni (Ita) at 1-28

9 Carlos Sastre (Spa) at 1-35

10 Levi Leipheimer (USA) at 1-49

Categorised climbs: Izoard (HC),
Lauteret (cat. 2), Alpe d'Huez
(HC)
Yellow jersey at start: Oscar Pereiro
(Spa)
Yellow jersey at finish: Floyd Landis
(USA)
Yellow jersey in Paris: Oscar Pereiro
(Spa)

Note: Floyd Landis was stripped
of his Tour victory after testing
positive

2008
Wednesday 23 July
Stage 17- Embrun-Alpe d'Huez

1 Carlos Sastre (Spa) 210km in
6-07-58

2 Samuel Sánchez (Spa) at 2-03

3 Andy Schleck (Lux)

4 Alejandro Valverde (Spa) at 2-13

5 Frank Schleck (Lux)

6 Vladimir Efimkin (Rus) at 2-15

7 Cadel Evans (Aus)

8 Denis Menchov (Rus)

9 Christian Vande Velde (USA)

10 Bernhard Köhl (Aut)

Categorised climbs: Sainte Marguerite (cat. 3), Galibier (HC), Croix de Fer (HC), Alpe d'Huez (HC)

Yellow jersey at start: Frank Schleck (Lux)

Yellow jersey at finish: Carlos Sastre (Spa)

Yellow jersey in Paris: Carlos Sastre (Spa)

2011
Friday 22 July
Stage 19: Modane-Alpe d'Huez

1 Pierre Rolland (Fra) 190.5km in 3-13-25

2 Samuel Sánchez (Spa) at 14 secs

3 Alberto Contador (Spa) at 23 secs

4 Peter Velits (Svk) at 57 secs

5 Cadel Evans (Aus)

6 Thomas De Gendt (Bel)

7 Damiano Cunego (Ita)

8 Frank Schleck (Lux)

9 Andy Schleck (Lux)

10 Ryder Hesjedal (Can) at 1- 15

Categorised climbs: Télégraphe (cat. 1), Galibier (HC), Alpe d'Huez (HC)

Yellow jersey at start: Thomas Voeckler (Fra)

Yellow jersey at finish: Andy Schleck (Lux)

Yellow jersey in Paris: Cadel Evans (Aus)

2013
Thursday 18 July
Stage 18: Gap-Alpe d'Huez

1 Christophe Riblon (Fra) 172.5km in 4-51-32

2 Tejay van Garderen (USA) at 59 secs

3 Moreno Moser (Ita) at 1- 27

4 Nairo Quintana (Col) at 2-12

5 Joaquim Rodríguez (Spa) at 2-15

6 Richie Porte (Aus) at 3-18

7 Chris Froome (GB)

8 Alejandro Valverde (Spa) at 3-22

9 Mikel Nieve (Spa) at 4-15

10 Jakob Fuglsang (Den)

Categorised climbs: Manse (cat. 2), Motty (cat. 3), Ornon (cat. 2), Alpe d'Huez (cat. 1), Sarenne (cat. 2), Alpe d'Huez (HC)

Yellow jersey at start: Chris Froome (GB)

Yellow jersey at finish: Chris Froome (GB)

Yellow jersey in Paris: Chris Froome (GB)

2015
Saturday 25 July
Stage 20: Modane Valfréjus-Alpe
  d'Huez

1 Thibaut Pinot (Fra) 110.5km in
  3-17-21

2 Nairo Quintana (Col) at 18 secs

3 Ryder Hesjedal (Can) at 41 secs

4 Alejandro Valverde (Spa) at 1-38

5 Chris Froome (GB)

6 Pierre Rolland (Fra) at 1-41

7 Richie Porte (Aus) at 2-11

8 Winner Anacona (Col) at 2-32

9 Wouter Poels (Ned) at 2-50

10 Rubén Plaza (Spa)

Categorised climbs: Col de la Croix
  de Fer (HC), Alpe d'Huez (HC)

Yellow jersey at start: Chris Froome
  (GB)

Yellow jersey at finish: Chris
  Froome (GB)

Yellow jersey in Paris: Chris
  Froome (GB)

22 of 29 riders who were in yellow
  at Alpe d'Huez won the Tour
  in Paris

Fausto Coppi, Lance Armstrong
  (twice) and Carlos Sastre are the
  only riders to win on the Alpe
  and go on to win in Paris

Coppi and Sastre are the only
  riders to win and take the yellow
  jersey on the Alpe and go on to
  win in Paris

Bends and riders commemorated on them

Several of the signposts have three numbers below the image of a marmot
and the name Alpe d'Huez. The first is 1450, the altitude of the village of
Huez, the second is 1860, the altitude of Alpe d'Huez, and the third is 3300,
the altitude of the start of the resort's highest run. Each individual signs shows
the altitude and that point and commemorates a stage winner or winners at
Alpe d'Huez, starting from bend 21 towards the foot of the climb...

21: 806m, Fausto Coppi (Ita) and
  Lance Armstrong (USA)

20 (Virage Le Gène Vignon):
  880m, Joop Zoetemelk (Ned)
  and Ibán Mayo (Spa)

19: 900m, Hennie Kuiper (Ned)
  and Lance Armstrong (USA)

18: 922m, Hennie Kuiper (Ned)
  and Fränk Schleck (Lux)

17 (Virage de la Coute: 965m,
  Joaquim Agostinho (Por) and
  Carlos Sastre (Spa)

16 (Virage de la Meule): 980m,
  Joop Zoetemelk (Ned) and
  Pierre Rolland (Fra)

15: 1025m, Peter Winnen
  (Ned) and Christophe Riblon
  (Fra)

14: 1055m, Bret Breu (Swi) and Thibaut Pinot (Fra)

13: 1120m, Peter Winnen (Ned)

12: 1161m, Luis Herrera (Col)

11: 1195m, Bernard Hinault (Fra)

10: 1245m, Federico Echave (Spa)

9: 1295m, Steven Rooks (Ned)

8: 1345m, Gert-Jan Theunisse (Ned)

7: 1390m, Gianni Bugno (Ita)

6: 1480m, Gianni Bugno (Ita)

5: 1512m, Andrew Hampsten (USA)

4: 1553m, Roberto Conti (Ita)

3: 1626m, Marco Pantani (Ita)

2: 1669m, Marco Pantani (Ita)

1: 1713m, Guiseppe Guerini (Ita)

FASTEST TIMES FOR 13.8KM ASCENT OF ALPE D'HUEZ

1 Marco Pantani (Ita) 36-50 in 1995

2 Marco Pantani (Ita) 36-55 in 1997

3 Marco Pantani (Ita) 37-15 in 1994

4 Lance Armstrong (USA) 37-36 in 2004

5 Jan Ullrich (Ger) 37-42 in 1997

6 Lance Armstrong (USA) 38-05 in 2001

7 Miguel Indurain (Spa) 38-14 in 1995

8 Alex Zülle (Swi) 38-14 in 1995

9 Bjarne Riis (Den) 38-16 in 1995

10 Richard Virenque (Fra) 38-22 in 1997

11 Floyd Landis (USA) 38-36 in 2006

12 Andreas Klöden (Ger) 38-36 in 2006

13 Jan Ullrich (Ger) 38-40 in 2004

14 Laurent Madouas (Fra) 38-44 in 1995

15 Richard Virenque (Fra) 38-55 in 1994

16 Carlos Sastre (Spa) 39-01 in 2006

17 Ibán Mayo (Spa) 39-09 in 2003

18 Andreas Klöden (Ger) 39-12 in 2004

19 José Azevedo (Por) 39-14 in 2004

20 Levi Leipheimer (USA) 39-15 in 2006

21 Francesco Casagrande (Ita) 39-22 in 1997

22 Nairo Quintana (Col) 39-23 in 2015

23 Bjarne Riis (Den) 39-23 in 1997

24 Miguel Indurain (Spa) 39-30 in 1994

25 Luc Leblanc (Fra) 39-30 in 1994

26 Carlos Sastre (Spa) 39-32 in 2008

27 Vladimir Poulnikov (Ukr) 39-37 in 1994

28 Giuseppe Guerini (Ita) 39-40 in 2004

29 Santos González (Spa) 39-41 in 2004

30 Vladimir Karpets (Rus) 39-41 in 2004

31 Fernando Escartín (Spa) 39-45 in 1995

32 Denis Menchov (Rus) 39-47 in 2006

33 Michael Rasmussen (Den) 39-47 in 2006

34 Pietro Caucchioli (Ita) 39-47 in 2006

35 Nairo Quintana (Col) 39-50 in 2013

36 Claudio Chiappucci (Ita) 39-52 in 1995

37 Paolo Lanfranchi (Ita) 39-52 in 1995

38 Joaquim Rodríguez (Spa) 39-53 in 2013

39 Beat Zberg (Swi) 39-54 in 1997

40 Udo Bölts (Ger) 39-54 in 1997

41 Roberto Conti (Ita) 39-54 in 1997

42 Laurent Madouas (Fra) 39-54 in 1997

43 David Moncoutié (Fra) 39-56 in 2004

44 Carlos Sastre (Spa) 39-57 in 2004

45 Ivan Basso (Ita) 39-58 in 2004

46 Stéphane Goubert (Fra) 39-58 in 2004

47 Tony Rominger (Swi) 39-58 in 1995

48 Pavel Tonkov (Rus) 40-01 in 1995

49 Piotr Ugrumov (Lat) 40-10 in 1994

50 Alex Zülle (Swi) 40-01 in 1994

Other notable marks

55 Oscar Pereiro (Spa) 40-15 in 2006

57 Cadel Evans (Aus) 40-15 in 2006

62 Roberto Conti (Ita) 40-19 in 1994

64 Gianni Bugno (Ita) 40-25 in 1991

78 Chris Froome (GB) 40-43 in 2015

84 Frank Schleck (Lux) 40-46 in 2006

90 Chris Froome (GB) 40-56 in 2013

105 Giuseppe Guerini (Ita) 41-10 in 1999

112 Thibaut Pinot (Fra) 41-20 in 2015

129 Samuel Sánchez (Spa) 41-24 in 2011

131 Alberto Contador (Spa) 41-33 in 2011

140 Lance Armstrong (USA) 41-35 in 1999

153 Greg LeMond (USA) 41-42 in 1991

158 Andy Hampsten (USA) 41-45 in 1991

160 Cadel Evans (Aus) 41-47 in 2008

167 Luis Herrera (Col) 41-50 in 1987

169 Laurent Fignon (Fra) 41-56 in 1987

179 Pierre Rolland (Fra) 42-02 in 2011

199 Pedro Delgado (Spa) 42-15 in 1987

Note: Stage winners in bold

Source: @ammattipyoraily

Glossary

à l'ancienne – doing it the old way.

à bloc – riding flat out, now often described as 'full gas'.

à l'eau minérale – derived from five-time Tour winner Jacques Anquetil's famous observation that it had become impossible to win the race by drinking mineral water alone.

baroudeurs – riders who like nothing more than a stage-long escapade, sometimes solo but usually in the company of a fellow band of 'adventurers'.

cadors – heavyweights or big-hitter. Used to denote cycling's dominant figures.

cyclisme à deux vitesses – literally 'cycling at two speeds', it was coined by French rider in 1990s to describe competing against riders allegedly using the full armoury of doping products.

cyclo-cross – a discipline run on short courses that typically feature a mix of surfaced and unsurfaced roads and tracks, steep hills and obstacles, which force the rider to dismount and carry their bike.

domestique – a rider whose primary role is to support the other members of their team. Literally 'servant'.

directeur sportif – a team's sporting director, often seen issuing instructions from the team car.

drafting – riding in the slipstream of another cyclist, thus taking advantage of the reduced wind resistance and being able to maintain the same speed for less effort.

EPO (Erythropoietin) – a banned product that increases the red blood cell count and therefore its oxygen-bearing capacity, which can enhance performance.

espoirs – age classification for riders between nineteen and twenty-three years old. Literally 'hopes'.

general classification – the standings based on time elapsed that ranks riders during a stage race (often abbreviated to GC).

gregario – the equivalent in Italian teams of domestique.

grimpeur – a rider who is particularly strong at climbing.

hunger knock – the physical weakness brought on by not eating enough.

jour sans – best translated as 'an off day', though more literally 'a day without'.

King of the Mountains – the name given to the leader of a secondary classification within the Tour in which cyclists receive points for points at categorised summits. The leader of the classification wears a red polka-dot jersey.

lanterne rouge – the competitor in last place, literally 'red light', as seen on the back of a train.

MAMIL – a middle-aged man in lycra.

palmarès – a rider or a race's roll of honour.

Parcours – a race's route or significant characteristics.

peloton – the main group of riders, who bunch together for efficiency until the last stages of a race.

rouleur – a rider known for their power on the flat and rolling terrain.

soigneur – a team member whose role is to look after the riders' wellbeing by preparing food and drink or performing massages.

souplesse – suppleness, used to describe smoothness of pedalling.

UCI (Union Cycliste Internationale) – the sport's supreme governing body.

Wheelsucker – a rider who sits on the wheels of others and doesn't contribute to the pace-making.

Bibliography

I turned first to the back catalogue of *Procycling*, a magazine with which I have had a long and happy association. Among other publications and newspapers I drew on for my research and would highly recommend are *L'Équipe*, *La Stampa* and *Le Soir*. The pages of Cyclingnews.com and Memoire-du-Cyclisme.eu were also a vital and very reliable source of detail.

For further insight into the history of Alpe d'Huez and the personalities associated with it, I would also recommend the following books and publications:

Bassons, Christophe, *A Clean Break* (Bloomsbury, London, 2014)

Chany, Pierre, *La Fabuleuse Histoire du Tour de France* (Éditions de la Martinière, Paris, 1995)

Fignon, Laurent, *We Were Young and Carefree* (Yellow Jersey Press, London, 2010)

Fillion, Patrick, *L'Alpe-d'Huez: Les Virages de la Gloire* (L'Équipe, Paris, 2013)

Friebe, Daniel and Goding, Pete, *Mountain High* (Quercus, London 2012)

Goddet, Jacques, *L'Équipée Belle* (Robert Laffont/Stock, Paris, 1991)

Guimard, Cyrille, *Dans Les Secrets du Tour de France* (J'ai Lu, Paris, 2012)

Hinault, Bernard and Brouchon, Jean-Paul, *Hinault* (Éditions Jacob-Duvernet, 2005)

Leblanc, Jean-Marie, *Le Tour de Ma Vie* (Solar, France, 2007)

Nicholson, Geoffrey, *The Great Bike Race* (Hodder & Stoughton, London, 1977)

Roche, Stephen, *Born to Ride* (Yellow Jersey Press, London, 2012)

Scheepmaker, Nico, *Theo Koomen: Een Leven in Woord en Beeld* (RPL, Netherlands, 1986)

Thévenet, Bernard and Brouchon, Jean-Paul, *Thévenet* (Éditions Jacob-Duvernet, 2006)

Vespini, Jean-Paul, *Le Grand Roman de l'Alpe-d'Huez* (Romillat, Paris, 1995)

Vespini, Jean-Paul, *The Tour is Won on the Alpe* (Velo Press, Boulder, 2008)

Zoetemelk, Joop, *La Prochaine Étape* (Solar, Paris, 1980)

Acknowledgements

Much like the 1976 stage between Divonne les Bains and Alpe d'Huez, writing this book has been a long journey that has required a huge effort and couldn't have been completed without a great deal of support along the way. I owe particular thanks to Iain MacGregor, who saw the potential for a book on Alpe d'Huez when we were discussing a very different project for Aurum, and then offered me the opportunity to take it on. I am especially grateful to Iain for continuing to provide much-appreciated advice after he had moved on to a new job.

As Iain pulled aside, Lucy Warburton and Josh Ireland emerged at Aurum and guided me through the final stages of the book. Josh offered a deft and insightful touch during the editing process, keeping me and the book on track. Thanks also to Andrew Compton at Aurum for his expertise on the marketing side.

This project would never have come to fruition without the assistance of my literary agent, David Luxton. Many thanks for continuing to 'open the road' for me, David. I think that's at least two Elland Road meat pies I owe you now.

I would also like to express my gratitude to fellow journalists who provided advice, contacts and Alpe-related anecdotes: including Daniel Benson, Alasdair Fotheringham, Jeremy Whittle, Chema Rodríguez, Simon Wilkinson, Mart Smeets and James Poole. I owe a particular debt to Daniel Friebe for his insight and suggestions, which led to the discovery of several unexpected nuggets, and also to Leon de Kort, whose anecdotes and contacts were especially useful for the chapters covering the Dutch links to Alpe d'Huez.

My thanks also go to the many current and former riders and members of the Tour de France organisation who offered me their time and insight into this special mountain including: Jean-Étienne Amaury, Fabian Cancellara, Chris Froome, Linus Gerdemann, Thierry Gouvenou, Andy Hampsten, Bernard Hinault, Servais Knaven, Freddy Maertens, David Millar, Wout Poels, Christian Prudhomme, Christophe Riblon, Stephen Roche, Carlos Sastre, Fränk Schleck, Gert-Jan Theunisse, Bernard Thévenet, Lucien Van Impe (together with his wife Rita and daughter Suzy), Tom Veelers, Peter Winnen, Merrijn Zeeman and Joop Zoetemelk.

For the assistance they offered during my time at Alpe d'Huez I would also like to say thank you to Fabrice Hurth, the resort's director of tourism, and Sylvie and

Yves Forestier at the Hôtel L'Ancolie in Huez, who were not only perfect hosts but also answered my many questions with great courtesy and knowledge. I highly recommend their hotel with its unforgettable view across the Romanche valley. My thanks also to the staff at Cycles et Sports in Bourg d'Oisans for providing me with a BMC bike that was much better equipped than me for the ride up to Alpe d'Huez.

My research for the book took me to Paris, where the staff at the Bibliothèque Nationale de France guided me expertly through the archives of *L'Équipe*. I should mention too the staff at La Galcante, who unearthed some much-treasured issues of that same newspaper. I'd recommend any bike fan to visit the shop, which bisects the Rue de Rivoli and is close to the Louvre.

Finally, my love and gratitude goes to my wife, Elaine, and children, Lewis and Eleanor, for providing unwavering support and encouragement. A little treat awaits, although there's a 13.8-kilometre climb to reach it…

Index